Voting in Indian Country

VOTING IN INDIAN COUNTRY

The View from the Trenches

Jean Reith Schroedel

PENN

UNIVERSITY OF PENNSYLVANIA PRESS

PHILADELPHIA

HANEY FOUNDATION SERIES
A volume in the Haney Foundation Series,
established in 1961 with the generous
support of Dr. John Louis Haney

Published by
University of Pennsylvania Press
Philadelphia, Pennsylvania 19104-4112
www.upenn.edu/pennpress

Printed in the United States of America on acid-free paper
1 3 5 7 9 10 8 6 4 2

Library of Congress Cataloging-in-Publication Data

Names: Schroedel, Jean Reith, author.
Title: Voting in Indian country : the view from the trenches / Jean Reith Schroedel.
Other titles: Haney Foundation series.
Description: 1st edition. | Philadelphia : University of Pennsylvania Press, [2020] | Series: Haney Foundation series | Includes bibliographical references and index.
Identifiers: LCCN 2020001885 | ISBN 9780812252514 (hardcover)
Subjects: LCSH: United States. Voting Rights Act of 1965. | Indians of North America—Suffrage—United States. | Indians of North America—Government relations. | Indians of North America—Legal status, laws, etc. | Indians of North America—Civil rights. | Race discrimination—Political aspects—United States.
Classification: LCC E91 .S27 2020 | DDC 323.1197—dc23
LC record available at https://lccn.loc.gov/2020001885

For OJ, Barb, and Bret. Thanks for the journey

CONTENTS

PREFACE

Writing a book is a journey that occurs in stages. The origins of a particular project go back long before the actual eureka moment when the hapless person realizes, "Oh my God, I have to write this book." When asked about this project, I typically identify it as beginning in the period around the 2010 midterm elections, when it became clear that Obama's victory in 2008 had not ushered in a new postracial era. States were adopting new voting laws and procedures—restricting hours at polling places, closing polling locations, limiting registration, and culling people from the lists of eligible voters. Some states also passed laws that excluded people who didn't have the "proper," state-mandated ID when they went to vote. All of these made it much more difficult for many people to vote. There was concern that these laws could disenfranchise large numbers of African Americans and, to a lesser extent, the elderly, students, and the poor. While not naïve enough to think voting rights abuses had been completely eradicated, I was confident that civil rights attorneys and activists would not allow the country's progress toward racial equality to be reversed. As Martin Luther King Jr. noted, "The arc of the moral universe is long, but it bends towards justice." Also, as a white woman living in California, I was not personally affected, and although I am a political scientist, my research interests never had included voting laws and electoral procedures. Moreover, I was beginning to think seriously about retirement and had no desire to take on a new research area, much less a book project.

Life, however, has a way of hitting us upside the head when we least expect it. In my case, it started with a visit from a former student, Deron Marquez. Marquez, who is a member of the San Manuel Band of Mission Indians, started recounting stories of truly egregious vote denial, dilution, and suppression directed against Native Americans, incidents that sounded as though they had come out of the Deep South of the 1950s as opposed to Obama's America. While Deron never explicitly stated that he expected me to do something, I certainly felt nudged to do so. I decided to do a little digging, perhaps write a short thought piece about why Native Americans were affected by these new laws. Writing that little article turned out to be a lot more difficult than anticipated. Untangling the many factors affecting the civic status of American Indians and Alaska Natives was not easy and required perusing treaties from as far back as the colonial era, as well as Supreme Court precedents established in the 1820s and 1830s. Also, following the 1924 passage of the Indian Citizenship Act, states adopted a whole range of legal strategies designed to make it extremely difficult, if not impossible, for Native Americans to vote. While some of the legal strategies were similar to those utilized to disenfranchise African Americans in the South, others were uniquely tied to the continuing existence of Native Nations. Understanding all of this required drawing upon history, law, public administration, and sociology, as well as political science—and that first article took more than four years to write.

Just as I was completing the article, I got a telephone call that completely upended my comfortable academic life. Bret Healy, a consultant with the grassroots voting rights group Four Directions, asked me to run some data for a Native American voting rights case in Montana. Healy had gotten my name from someone, who had gotten it from someone else, and that person had heard about me from Deron Marquez. Three days after agreeing to run data, I discovered this meant I was the expert witness in the *Wandering Medicine v. McCulloch* case and I had one month to pull together an expert witness report. I had never seen an expert witness report, much less written one. It was nothing short of insane. The only possible way to complete the report was to shamelessly exploit family, friends, and colleagues who were willing to help. Claremont Graduate University (CGU) faculty Tom Horan and Brian Hilton used Geographic Information System (GIS) mapping to calculate the distances that whites and Native Americans had to travel to access voting. My husband, Paul Peretz, and former student Moana Vercoe helped analyze census, registration, and turnout data, while I handled most of the writing.

There was no way that I could be an "expert" about communities I had never seen, so I traveled to Montana, where I visited reservations and border towns. Mostly I spent time just hanging out, trying to get a feel for what life was like in these communities. Among political scientists, this is called "soaking and poking" research, a way to get a sense of place and context through spending time in a particular area, watching and conversing with people. I talked with local people in cafés, some that were designated as "Indian friendly" and some that Native people avoided. I spent many hours with Native people traveling the dirt roads that cut across their reservations. Mostly I listened to people's stories. Nearly every Native person framed current stories in the context of what had happened to their parents, grandparents, great-grandparents, and going back even further. One man explained that his people, the Sioux, viewed events from seven generations back as though they had just occurred and that the shape of time was spiral rather than linear. While I don't fully understand this, what I can attest is that I came away with a deep sense that the past, including scars of the Indian Wars, are very much still present.

After returning home, I began telling people what I had learned. What I started hearing back was that I should write a book. I refused, noting there were several very fine books about Native American voting rights, but the seed was planted. Shortly after the Montana case was settled, the Native American Voting Rights Coalition (NAVRC) was created. Although not involved in creating NAVRC, I have worked with them as an academic consultant over the past four years. I also have been part of teams doing survey research that figured in voting rights litigation in South Dakota and Nevada. And along the way, I heard more stories and had encounters that made me very aware of the reality of my "white privilege."

I became convinced that what happens in Indian Country is crucial to determining whether "the arc of the moral universe" in the United States does indeed bend "towards justice." If there is no justice for those descended from the nation's original inhabitants, how can one claim there is justice for anyone else? Albeit in a limited way, this book is my attempt to contribute to moving that arc, not through a legal treatise but by weaving together history and law along with the stories of the people engaged in voting rights struggles in Indian Country. My goal is to provide the reader with a nuts and bolts understanding of the legal issues involved in Native American voting rights cases, the ways that they resemble and differ from voting rights cases involving African Americans, and their relationship to broader social justice movements for Native civic inclusion and self-determination.

Again and again, Native people framed voting rights within this broader context of historical struggles for social justice—their right to control the Native lands and resources promised to them in perpetuity through treaties, as well as gaining the basic civil rights promised to all American citizens. Stories, as Ganz (2009) notes, "speak to the language of emotion, the language of the heart, they teach us not only how we 'ought to' act, but can inspire us with the 'courage to' act." Sometimes it is the small stories that are most memorable. One of my favorites involves a young man from the Gros Ventre Nation in Montana. He stated that the behavior of local government officials changed after they won a voting rights suit. For the first time he was treated with respect when registering his car at the DMV. This man linked his personal story of "the arc of the moral universe" bending "towards justice."

By this juncture, you—the reader—will have recognized that I am hardly a dispassionate observer and may question my objectivity. That is a valid concern, and my response is the same one I gave to Bret Healy when he starting telling me what I should find as an expert witness in the *Wandering Medicine* case. I told him that I would write a report that honestly reflected what I found, full stop, and if he was not comfortable with that, he needed to find someone else. My commitment to accurately recounting what I have found has not changed. What follows is different, however, in that I do not limit myself to traditional political science approaches (e.g., case law, survey research, and quantitative analysis) but instead add in historical materials, including first-person accounts and oral histories. While these accounts bring the issues to life in a way that is impossible to achieve using other methods, I recognize that different individuals' memories of the events may vary. In some places I have been able to triangulate using multiple sources, but that is not always possible. What is true, however, is that across the different settings, the accounts are very similar, lending credence to the stories of widespread discrimination. But readers should feel free to draw their own conclusions.

PART I

THE QUESTION OF CITIZENSHIP

CHAPTER 1

The Framing of American Indian Citizenship

Two Stories of Political Engagement

Even though pundits devote enormous amounts of attention to changing demographics, pontificating about whether the fabric binding the nation together will hold as the population becomes increasingly diverse, these discussions rarely mention the descendants of the original inhabitants of the North American continent.[1] Perhaps this erasure of Native people's existence is a way to "whitewash" the past and allow the rest of the country to enjoy Thanksgiving meals without thinking about promises made and broken by earlier generations of American leaders.[2] The relatively small numbers of Native Americans and the geographic isolation of reservation lands contribute to this collective amnesia. Only rarely do issues affecting American Indians force their way into the nation's consciousness, as occurred more than four decades ago in the "Red Power" era when activists engaged in highly visible protests, including the seizure of Alcatraz Island, the Trail of Broken Treaties, and the 1973 standoff at Wounded Knee.

Standing Rock and the Dakota Access Pipeline

The current historical moment is another time when, thanks to heavy media coverage of the Standing Rock protests, it is impossible to ignore American Indians. The Dakota Access Pipeline's route was shifted away from North Dakota's capital, Bismarck, after public complaints that an oil spill could contaminate the city's water supply and rerouted to pass near the borders of the Standing Rock Reservation.[3] The Standing Rock Sioux immediately raised objections but were ignored, so they initiated acts of civil disobedience to halt construction.[4] Even though the protests started in April 2016, most early coverage was limited to web posts on Facebook and stories in Native press outlets. By early November, at least 1.3 million Facebook users had "checked in" to show support on the Stand with Standing Rock page (Tchekmedyian and Etehad 2016). Alternative media were capturing very powerful visual images—young men on horseback, women placing their bodies in front of bulldozers, and spiritual leaders blessing the acts of the protesters, as well as disturbing pictures of security guards with clubs and snarling dogs with bloody muzzles—so going to that chilly corner of North Dakota became de rigueur for the mainstream media. Reporters from the *New York Times*, *Washington Post*, and even *Vogue* descended on the Oceti Sakowin encampment (Monet 2016). Enhanced coverage meant people from across the country, as well as around the world, began talking about Standing Rock. The pictures are reminiscent of those taken a generation earlier of law enforcement officers wielding batons and snarling dogs assaulting peaceful civil rights marchers.

While press coverage of 1960s civil rights stories with the visuals from places such as the Edmund Pettus Bridge, near Selma, where police clubbed praying activists, galvanized the nation and led to the passage of the Voting Rights Act (VRA), the Trump administration was unfazed by the public protests. President Trump, who owned stock in the main company doing pipeline work, had received a campaign contribution of more than $100,000 from the chair and chief executive officer of the company and subsequently got a $250,000 donation for his inauguration (Leonard 2019).[5] Standing Rock, however, may go down as a catalyst for a new era of Red Power activism. The number of American Indians acting as water protectors at Standing Rock was many times greater than the largest protests during the Red Power era.[6] Thousands of people from more than three hundred different Native Nations, including some traditional enemies of Standing Rock's Lakota and Dakota Sioux, came in solidarity.[7]

Voting on the Pyramid Lake Reservation

Just as the media was descending on Standing Rock, another important, albeit unreported, story of Native political activism was occurring 1,400 miles distant in Nixon, Nevada. Nixon, located roughly fifty miles north of

Reno, is the headquarters of Pyramid Lake Paiute.[8] During the 2016 election, Flora Greene, a ninety-nine-year-old Paiute elder, was able to vote at a polling place on the reservation for the first time ever. Greene, who is respected for her knowledge of traditional handicrafts and her willingness to pass on skills, such as how one softens deerskin through soaking and scraping so it can be used for baby baskets and moccasins, was modest when asked about the significance of her voting.[9] However, it is worth recalling that when she was born, neither women nor American Indians had the right to vote. Greene was three years old when women got the franchise through the passage of the Nineteenth Amendment and seven years old when the American Indian Citizenship Act (ICA) that gave citizenship to all Native Americans born within the borders of the country was adopted. While women's right to vote was ensured by the Nineteenth Amendment, voting rights for American Indians did not automatically follow passage of the ICA; instead, the descendants of the continent's original inhabitants have been engaged in a nearly one-hundred-year struggle to gain equal access to the ballot box.

The 2016 election was the first time the 2,253 members of the Pyramid Lake Paiute had a polling place in their community. In the past, they had to either vote by mail or travel nearly one hundred miles round trip to Reno to register, use early voting procedures, or vote on Election Day.[10] Greene viewed being able to vote as part of her effort to pass on Paiute traditions: "These days kids don't really learn about Paiute or any of the things, the traditions, the way I learned them. Having a voice is so important. That's what Native people need" (Prakash 2016).[11]

One might have thought the lack of access to voting on the Pyramid Lake Reservation was simply due to an oversight by election officials—something that could be easily solved when officials learned of the need—but that was not the case. The Pyramid Lake Paiute, along with members of the Walker River Paiute, had to sue their counties (Mineral and Washoe) and Nevada to gain the same access to voting that most Americans take for granted (*Sanchez v. Cegavske* 2016). The defendants described the request for reservation voting sites as "convenience" voting and argued that Section 2 of the Voting Rights Act only applied to outright denial of voting. Judge Miranda Du disagreed, and in 2016 Flora Greene was able to vote in her community, albeit under the watchful eye of monitors from the Civil Rights Division of the Department of Justice (Department of Justice 2016; Richardson 2016a).

Nevada, however, refused a request from the Inter-Tribal Council of Nevada (ITCN) for polling places on other reservations prior to the 2016 elections. The state ignored the plight of people living on the Duck Valley Shoshone Paiute Reservation in the extreme northern part of the state. According to elders, there used to be a polling station at the local school, but it was closed to save money and now they have to travel more than 270 miles to cast an in-person vote. That is the longest distance that any person must travel to reach one of the state's 437 polling places. The Duck Valley Shoshone Paiute wrote to Secretary of State Barbara Cegavske requesting a site, but she refused (Montero 2016).

Voting rights litigation is expensive. The Pyramid Lake and Walker River Paiute were fortunate in being able to find experienced voting rights attorneys who took their case on a pro bono basis.[12] They also were fortunate that the Department of Justice (DOJ) issued a "statement of interest," which is a way of signaling their position but without committing resources to fighting on behalf of the plaintiffs. The DOJ only brings a small number of actual voting rights cases because the Civil Rights Division's portfolio encompasses the entire panoply of civil rights issues and its willingness to advocate on behalf of people whose civil rights have been violated varies across administrations. People living on the Pyramid Lake and Walker River reservations benefited from assistance provided by Four Directions, a grassroots Native voting rights organization (Four Directions 2016).

Threads Linking the Two Stories

Nearly a half century ago, Native scholar and activist Vine Deloria Jr. (1969: 54) wrote words that could just as easily have been penned today: "People [white people] often feel guilty about their ancestors killing all those Indians years ago. But they shouldn't feel guilty about the distant past. Just the last two decades have seen a more devious but hardly less successful war waged against Indian communities." Both the Standing Rock and Pyramid Lake stories provide insights into current "devious" means used to deny justice to Native people.

While American Indians and Alaska Natives are no longer statutorily disenfranchised, they still face barriers that prevent many from voting. Although the Pyramid Lake and Walker River Paiutes were successful, the Nevada secretary of state refused to extend similar relief to the other reservations. In the course of my research for this project, one Nevada election official bragged to me about how easy it is to register and vote, stating that registration and voting sites probably could be found at every mini-mall in the state, without ever acknowledging that this was not true for American Indians.

Along with voting, citizens can petition the government when they believe their issues are not being addressed. Before beginning mass protests the Standing Rock Sioux registered their concerns to multiple government agencies but were ignored. Although they failed to stop construction of the Dakota Access Pipeline, the Standing Rock protests forced American Indian issues onto the national public agenda.[13] Without social media, the issues raised by the Standing Rock Sioux, as well as the use of tear gas, water cannons, and attack dogs to intimidate protesters, whether by private security firms, police officers, or the North Dakota National Guard, would have gone unnoticed.[14] In contrast, the ITCN's request for polling places within their communities generated no media notice and was refused. Only with outside pro bono legal assistance were the people on the Pyramid Lake and Walker River reservations able to succeed; without those resources, the residents of the Duck Valley Reservation were denied equal access in 2016.

The Nevada story, however, did not end with the state's denial of equal voting access to other reservations. The legislature, which switched from Republican to Democratic control following the election, subsequently passed legislation allowing for the establishment of satellite voting sites on reservations. Also just after the election, three of the individuals (Ralph Burns, Jimmie James, and Johnnie Williams Jr.) who had sued the state in *Sanchez v. Cegavske* were given the state's American Indian Community Leader of the Year award (Richardson 2016b).

Developing a Framework for Understanding American Indian Citizenship

While the protests at Standing Rock generated enormous publicity, the equally important story of the generations-long and continuing struggle of the descendants of the continent's original inhabitants to gain equal access to the ballot box is largely untold—and telling that larger story of courage and tenacity is the purpose of this book. Also like the Standing Rock protests, the voting rights struggle of the Paiutes cannot be separated from history; instead the past and present form a continuum, where the voting rights struggle is woven into a broader story of Native activism aimed at achieving social justice. Part of that history is the story of the U.S. government making promises and then violating them, but it is also about the continuing existence of Native Nations that predate the arrival of Europeans—which distinguishes American Indians from any other population within the United States. But there are other factors, such as the relatively small numbers of Native people and their geographic isolation, that often allow violations of their civil rights to be ignored. Finally, the experiences of the Standing Rock protesters and the ITCN illustrate the importance of outside support and how difficult it is to gain those resources.

Tripartite Citizenship

Many people are woefully ignorant about the citizenship status of American Indians. President Ronald Reagan revealed this kind of ignorance when asked a question about American Indians: "Let me tell you just a little something about the American Indian in our land. We have provided them millions of acres of land and they, from the beginning, announced that they wanted to maintain their way of life. We've done everything we can to meet their demands as to how they want to live. Maybe we made a mistake. Maybe we should not have humored them in that wanting to stay in that kind of primitive lifestyle. Maybe we should have said, no, come join us; be citizens along with the rest of us" (Landry 2016). While there are many troubling parts of this statement, the fact that the president suggested that Native Americans are not actually citizens is most concerning.[15]

While the 1924 Indian Citizenship Act unilaterally gave national citizenship to all Native Americans, their civic status is radically different from that of both Euro-Americans and other racial and ethnic minorities. The fundamental difference—one that undergirds all other factors—is the "preexisting status of indigenous communities as separate and sovereign peoples with histories that long predate the American republic" (Wilkins and Stark 2011: xxxix). As descendants of the continent's original inhabitants, their roots do not lie outside of the United States but with the 7–10 million people who belonged to the 500 to 600 nations that inhabited the continent north of the Rio Grande at the time of first European settlement. As such, many maintain citizenship status within those indigenous nations, resulting in their holding tripartite citizenship: U.S. citizenship, state citizenship, and Native Nation citizenship.[16] Individuals who belong to federally recognized

Native Nations also have very specific rights based on that citizenship status that are recognized by U.S. law and enshrined in treaties and other legal compacts entered into with the U.S. government. Having access to the ballot box is a necessary element in protecting treaty rights, as well as Natives' fundamental rights as U.S. citizens.

But the question of Native American citizenship is more complicated. Although Wilkins and Stark (2011: 33) emphatically point out that "indigenous peoples are nations, not minorities," less than half of the 5.2 million people who self-identify on U.S. Census forms as American Indian/Alaska Native are enrolled members in the 574 federally recognized Native Nations.[17] While some are members of non–federally recognized Nations, many are mixed-race individuals with tenuous connections to Native Nations but who may experience racial discrimination due to non-white physical appearance. As Champagne (2015) has noted, some individuals with indigenous ancestries identify as racial and ethnic minorities rather than with Native Nations. This is only one of several interrelated reasons why many people are confused about the civic status of Native Americans.

History and the "Stickiness" of Social Processes

A useful starting point is to consider encounters between European settlers and indigenous peoples as being at least partially a version of Samuel Huntington's (1993, 1996) "clash of civilizations"—a conflict between peoples with starkly different cultural, religious, and economic values.[18] Many indigenous nations had long histories of peaceful interactions and trade with one another (Stubben 2006: 4–9), but this was less possible with Europeans, who largely considered them to be "heathens" or "barbarians"—either to be civilized and turned into Christians or wiped out. Native people's understanding of their relationship to the land did not include the concept of individual ownership, which made it easy for Europeans and their descendants to argue that indigenous peoples were "occupants" of land but not actual owners, thus facilitating the wholesale expropriation of large swaths of land (Deloria 2004: 144). Although there were broad differences in the worldviews of the two groups, as is consistent with the "clash of civilizations" thesis, one cannot ignore the economic basis of many conflicts. Colonists and their descendants wanted access to the Native lands and resources. Even Native Nations that adopted European ways of life faced having their land expropriated, as occurred with the so-called Five Civilized Tribes of the Southeast.

The civic status of indigenous people in the United States is still being shaped by economic and social processes rooted in actions of people long dead. Pierson (2004: 8) described this phenomenon as a "stickiness" that inhibits change in social relations even after the root causes are long past. While most people recognize that economic and social relations in the South are still affected by the legacy of slavery, there is little understanding of how Euro-American westward expansion and the displacement of indigenous peoples still shape relations among the descendants of both groups in much of the country. Moreover, there continue to be conflicts over land and mineral resources as well as cultural and social practices.[19]

Louise Erdrich (2016) describes history as a "living force," where current events are inextricably linked to past actions. This sense of history as a "living force" is evident in courtrooms where arguments about treaty rights—for example, promises made by the U.S. government to the Sioux with respect to what territory was to be held by them in perpetuity and that subsequently were broken in the theft of the Black Hills and the appropriation of lands for the Dakota Access Pipeline—are ongoing. On a smaller scale, history as a "living force" is evident in day-to-day interactions of ordinary people. Consider, for example, what it feels like for both parties when a Northern Cheyenne in Rosebud County, Montana, goes to the county clerk's office in the county seat of Forsyth[20] to register to vote or cast an early ballot and discovers that the person in charge of elections is Geraldine Custer.[21]

Structure of the Material

The chapters that follow are divided into three parts, each of which is organized around a specific general topic, but there are themes that appear and reappear throughout the book. The contemporary voting rights issues covered in this book can be viewed as part of a struggle for civic inclusion and self-determination, all of which is rooted in historical experiences. The arguments in each part are supported by a broad range of secondary and primary source materials, including but not limited to historical documents, legal cases, newspapers and blogs, survey research, and in-depth interviews. But they also are given life through the stories of Native people, both living and dead.

Part I, "The Question of Citizenship," which includes the present chapter, provides a historical backdrop and introduces the conflicts over economic resources and political power that have shaped debates over the citizenship status of Native Americans. Chapter 2, "Ambiguous Civic Status," covers major debates and judicial rulings from the colonial era through the early 1960s and shows their connection to ongoing struggles over treaty rights. Although the 1924 Indian Citizenship Act resolved the question of citizenship, it did not explicitly identify what rights and privileges were associated with citizenship. States developed a range of legal strategies to ensure that citizenship did not entail the right to vote. This made it possible for state governments, as well as the national government, to continue to adopt policies that resulted in the further loss of lands and resources ostensibly protected by treaties—actions that ignited decades of Native activism. Some of this activism was similar to Black civil rights struggles but often reflected broader Native Nationalist claims for indigenous sovereignty.

Part II, "The Promise of the Ballot Box," covers the period from the 1965 passage of the Voting Rights Act (VRA) through the present. Chapter 3, "The Voting Rights Act Reaches Indian Country," covers early attempts to utilize the VRA to stop egregious forms of vote denial but places that history within the context of broader Native struggles for social justice. "First-generation" voting rights abuses (e.g., those that explicitly disenfranchise American Indians) continued much longer in Indian Country than did those affecting other communities and likely would have continued even longer without the Red Power protests that forced the nation to pay attention to Native issues. Chapter 4, "The Shift to Vote Dilution, Suppression, and Abridgment," examines the ways that Native activists have tried to combat "second-generation" voting rights abuses that fall short of outright denial but make electoral participation far more difficult and dilute Natives' political power. Chapter 5, "A Case Study of Jackson County, South Dakota," is an in-depth look at how the "stickiness" of history continues to influence and shape much of the county's politics and contributes to an electoral system that makes it difficult for Oglala Lakota to have a meaningful voice in governance.

Part III, "Grassroots Perspectives," looks at the ways that the past and present come together in the lives of the mostly unrecognized people who have been engaged in Native struggles for social justice, including but not limited to voting rights.[22] The use of oral histories and storytelling serves as a counterbalance to the heavy focus on case law and statistics in the earlier chapters. Narratives can render abstract struggles more real by providing texture, nuance, and relatability but need to be used in conjunction with other sources (Farmer 2005; Slovic et al. 2013), as is done here.

Chapter 6, "Lawyers and Native Voting Rights," focuses on four lawyers—two white and two Native—who have chosen to devote chunks of their legal careers to litigating Native voting rights cases as opposed to pursuing more lucrative options. What motivates them? While both the white and Native attorneys view their commitment to voting rights litigation as being rooted in their understanding of history, the specific historical events that triggered their activism are quite different. Chapter 7, "Lifetimes of Activism," focuses on the experiences of two individuals who have spent decades engaged in social justice struggles for Native people. For them, the decision to fight for voting rights is clearly an outgrowth of this broader struggle—one that goes back in their families for generations. The people whose stories are recounted in Chapter 8, "Grassroots Voting Rights Activism," did not come from families with traditions of political engagement and leadership. Instead, these two Rosebud Sioux became activists when local government entities ignored needs on the reservation, and then they went on to became a national force for Native voting rights. Chapter 9, "Stepping Forward," provides insights into why individuals take on the challenges of being plaintiffs in these cases and how justice is or is not achieved. Finally Chapter 10, "Why It Matters," opens with stories from the 2018 election that remind us that the struggle for voting rights is not simply waged in courtrooms but requires continual mobilization, and then it considers whether we have entered into a new Red Power era with greater representation in the corridors of power and at the grassroots level.

CHAPTER 2

Ambiguous Civic Status

A Clash of Civilizations

Even before the establishment of successful colonies, Europeans had engaged in trade with Native Nations along the Atlantic coast, but they had very little knowledge about the continent's indigenous nations. Each Nation had its own form of government, language, culture, and economic structure (Dunbar-Ortiz 2014: 15–31; McMaster and Trafzer 2004; O'Brien 1989). These differences contributed to a "clash of civilizations" and misunderstandings that have continued for four centuries.[1] At least three of these differences have affected relations between Euro-Americans and Natives in ways that continue to have reverberations today. On a philosophical level, a major difference is whether one believes that events across time transpire in a linear or circular fashion. For Euro-Americans time is a linear progression of events taking place in a sequential fashion, but Native thought conceptualizes time as a "great circle" where past events greatly impact present-day actions (McMaster and Trafzer 2004: 116). This is why many Native Americans see history as a "living force."

A second major difference involves views of humans' relationship to the land. While most indigenous peoples recognized some forms of private property, that concept generally did not extend to land.[2] They had no sense of land as a commodity to be bought and sold in the way Euro-Americans took for granted (McMaster and Trafzer 2004: 116), so there was no shared understanding of treaty language involving the transfer of territory. If there is no sense of land as a commodity owned by individuals, how does one person's signing a treaty bind other Native people?[3] In addition, the treaties were written in European languages, which none of the Native signatories could read.[4]

Third, religious differences became a bigger factor after the arrival of Puritans. While many early colonists believed they had a duty to "civilize" and convert Natives to Christianity, Puritans were not interested in friendship or coexistence. They saw themselves as God's chosen people with a divine mandate to create their "City on the Hill" in the New World. Puritans believed that Satan was an "active agent on Earth" and equated Native ceremonies with Devil worship (McMaster and Trafzer 2004: 122).[5]

Whether viewed as peoples who might become civilized or as savages, there was a consensus among Euro-Americans about the inferiority of Native peoples. The use of the term "tribe" to describe indigenous nations helped build the perception that Natives did not belong to "real" nations. Yet European nations and colonial governments entered into treaties with Native Nations—an action that carries an implicit recognition of sovereignty among contracting parties.[6] During the colonial era, the English signed 180 treaties with indigenous nations, but most seventeenth-century treaties were signed by state governors or heads of specific colonies. For example, Virginia entered into forty-seven treaties with different Native Nations (DeJong 2015: 88–129).[7] Following the American Revolution and continuing until Congress halted the practice in 1871, U.S. commissioners negotiated hundreds of treaties with Native Nations, nearly 400 of which were ratified by the Senate.[8] According to Gover (2014: xi), treaties "rest at the heart of Native American history as well as contemporary tribal life and identity."

The Early American Republic

The Revolutionary War rendered invalid treaties signed by European powers, since the colonial signatories no longer controlled territory. The validity of earlier treaties with state governments also became questionable, since the Constitution reserved treaty-making power for the federal government (DeJong 2015), but state treaty-making continued (Deloria and DeMallie 1999: 1084–1086).[9] The new U.S. government set a precedent in its abrogation of the 1778 treaty, signed by the Continental Congress, with the Delaware Nation (Deloria 2004: 145–146; Wilkins and Stark 2011: 39–40).[10] This was only the first instance in which the federal government scrapped a treaty it no longer wished to honor.[11]

The Civic Status of Indigenous Peoples

When creating their new government, the Founding Fathers had to consider the civic status of indigenous peoples living within the boundaries of the nation, as well as those in the periphery. This issue, like the government's experiences with treaty-making, generated ambiguous and often contradictory responses. Thomas Jefferson (in a less quoted part of the Declaration of Independence) criticized King George: "He has excited domestic Insurrections amongst us, and has endeavored to bring on the Inhabitants of our Frontiers, the merciless Indian Savages, whose Known Rule of Warfare, is an undistinguished Destruction, of all Ages, Sexes and Conditions." Alexander Hamilton's language in *Federalist Papers 24* is similar, describing indigenous peoples as "savage tribes" and "natural enemies."

James Madison, however, in *Federalist Papers 42* suggests American Indians may become part of the body politic. After criticizing governmental actions during the Articles of Confederation period for being "obscure and contradictory" in their interactions with Native Nations, Madison writes, "What description of Indians are to be deemed members of a State is not yet settled, and has been a question of frequent perplexity and contention in federal councils." The Continental Congress also passed the Northwest Ordinance, which committed the new government to act in "good faith" in their dealings with Native Nations, although the ordinance's primary goal was to open up the Ohio Valley to settlers.[12]

The Constitution of 1789 failed to resolve whether Native peoples were "natural enemies" or potential members of the body politic. Article 1, Section 2 excludes "Indians not taxed" from being counted in apportioning representatives for the House, while Article 1, Section 8 on Congress's power to regulate trade lumps "Indian tribes" with "foreign Nations."[13] During the 1790s, the government entered into treaties with the Iroquois, Lenape, Shawnee, Wyandot, Ottawa, and Cherokee, which implies recognition of Native sovereignty and established the principle of a nation-to-nation relationship, even though those agreements were later violated by the U.S. government (McMaster and Trafzer 2004: 123–124).

Civilizing Versus Expulsion

From the earliest period, some U.S. leaders advocated policies that would allow "civilized" indigenous individuals to become citizens, but those plans often conflicted with policies to move Native populations ever further westward so that their lands could be expropriated. Settlers on the periphery generally favored expulsion while elites in the Capitol were more likely to consider assimilation as a long-term strategy. The Washington administration had an assimilation program under Secretary of War Henry Knox, who favored extinguishing Native lands held in common and allotting plots to individual Native families, who would be encouraged to become farmers and integrate into the broader society.[14] At several points, members of the Cherokee, Chickasaw, and Choctaw Nations were offered U.S. citizenship in exchange for giving up Native citizenship and lands (Deloria 2004: 146). These plans included making a large portion of Native lands available for white settlers, a politically strategic move to dampen settler hostility.

As settlers moved into southeastern territory occupied by the so-called Five Civilized Tribes (Cherokee, Muscogee, Seminole, Chickasaw, and Choctaw), tensions escalated. The 1828 discovery of gold in northern Georgia, combined with steps taken by these Nations to create Euro-American style governments, led to demands for their expulsion (Cherokee Nation 2017b). The Cherokee adopted a constitution that claimed territory in Georgia, Tennessee, North Carolina, and Alabama. Georgia responded by passing laws that nullified all laws of the Cherokee Nation, confiscated their property, and banned Cherokee from testifying in court (Mankiller 2004: 254).

With Andrew Jackson's election, land-hungry white southerners gained a powerful ally in the White House. Jackson demanded that Native peoples move into unsettled territories in the West or place themselves under the jurisdiction of state governments. Despite opposition from Whig senators Henry Clay and Daniel Webster, Congress in 1830 passed the Indian Removal Act, which resulted in tens of thousands of people, including Black slaves held by Native owners, being forcibly moved west of the Mississippi to Indian Territory (now Oklahoma).[15] Nearly a quarter of the Cherokee population died during the removal, which was carried out throughout the year—even during freezing weather in the winter and the heat of the summer (Mankiller 2004: 255).[16]

Early Supreme Court Decisions

In the midst of this heated political climate, the Supreme Court for the first time considered the relationship between U.S. government entities and

Native Nations/people. Under Chief Justice Marshall, the Supreme Court issued three landmark rulings—known as the Marshall Trilogy—dealing with Native Nations and the civic status of indigenous people. In *Johnson v. McIntosh* (1823), Marshall, drawing upon the "discovery doctrine," held that indigenous people were "merely as occupants" and lacked "absolute title" to their ancestral lands.[17] This doctrine held that when European nations "discovered" the Americas, those nations gained sovereign title to the land, which was passed on to the United States as the successor nation. The Court stated that the United States had the "exclusive right to extinguish the Indian title of occupancy, either by purchase or by conquest."[18] This ruling provided a legal rationale for Georgia to claim that British colonial title to lands occupied by the Cherokee had been passed to them and that the Cherokee had no claim to the lands and were subject to the previously mentioned 1828 state laws. Mississippi and Alabama passed similar laws that dispossessed the Choctaw, Chickasaw, and Muscogee (Creek), and Congress followed up with the Indian Removal Act (Robertson 2014: 73).

Then in *Cherokee Nation v. Georgia* (1831), Marshall described Native Nations as "domestic dependent nations," whose relationships with the United States were akin to that of a "ward to his guardian," which implied a "tutelary" obligation to Native Nations.[19] Since Native Nations existed within the boundaries of the United States and its territories, they were "dependent" and not fully capable of exercising sovereignty, but the ruling did not specify how much internal autonomy was retained by "domestic dependent" nations. In *Worcester v. Georgia* (1832), Marshall, again writing for the Court, stated that the United States considers "Indian nations as distinct political communities, having territorial boundaries, within which their authority is exclusive, and having a right to all the lands within those boundaries, which is not only acknowledged, but guaranteed by the United States."[20] The ruling also reiterated that the federal government, not state governments, was the sole entity with authority to determine relations with Native Nations.

The Marshall Court rulings left a whole range of questions unresolved.[21] What rights did Native Nations and peoples retain? *Cherokee Nation v. Georgia* implied there was a "tutelary" relationship with the dependent party (wards) moving toward majority over time, but *Worcester v. Georgia* suggested Native Nations were separate entities, with their own territories. Yet in light of *Johnson v. McIntosh* it is not clear what protections they had with respect to those territories. The Court was clear on one point: the primacy of the federal government rather than state governments in interactions with indigenous nations. This was a very unpopular stance in regions far distant from the nation's capital.[22]

Civic Status Debates of the Mid-Nineteenth Century

In the mid-nineteenth century, eastern elites continued to be divided over the citizenship status of Native people. Was their status akin to that of foreign nationals, and if so, could they become naturalized in the same manner as immigrants from Europe?[23] These questions became more pressing after the Mexican-American War when the United States gained title to half of Mexico's territory. Treaties ending the war provided pathways for Mexican nationals to become U.S. citizens but did not explicitly extend the option to Native people living in what had formerly been Mexico.[24] In 1856, U.S. attorney general Caleb Cushing unequivocally rejected this possibility (Horsman 1981: 253). However, the Court's endorsement of a "tutelary" relationship in *Cherokee Nation v. Georgia* (1831) was picked up by Chief Justice Taney in the infamous *Dred Scott v. Sandford* (1857) decision. In his opinion, the Chief Justice described members of the "Indian race" as being "in a state of pupilage," before going on to suggest that like other foreigners they could become naturalized citizens. Taney stated, "If an individual should leave his nation or tribe, and take up his abode among the white population, he would be entitled to all the rights and privileges which belong to an emigrant from any other foreign people."

Questions related to the civic status of American Indians were largely pushed to the periphery during the 1850s and early 1860s as the conflict over slavery heated up. The 1854 passage of the Kansas-Nebraska Act, which allowed western territories to vote on whether to allow or ban slavery, led to bloody guerilla skirmishes between pro-slavery forces and free-soil settlers. The political conflicts over slavery were of great importance in Indian Territory, since Black slavery was a well-established practice among wealthy Cherokee, Choctaw, Chickasaw, Muscogee, and Seminole (Krauthamer 2013; Naylor 2008).

The free-soilers were a key voting bloc for the Republican Party in the 1860 presidential election. Republicans solidified their free-soil base by enacting the 1862 Homestead Act, which made 500,000 square miles of land west of the Mississippi available to homesteaders. Given that the land already had inhabitants, it provided an additional reason for the Cherokee, Muscogee, Seminole, Choctaw, and Chickasaw Nations to sign treaties with the Confederate States. Nearly 7,000 of their men fought for the South. But another group of roughly 10,000 men, a mixed force of Natives, whites, and freedmen living in Indian Territory, aligned themselves with the Union and waged guerilla warfare in Oklahoma and Kansas (Dunbar-Ortiz 2014: 134–141).[25]

Early Postbellum Responses to the "Indian Problem"

Several events in the mid- to late 1860s provide insights into the often contradictory views of Euro-Americans about the "Indian problem." The 1864 Sand Creek Massacre illustrates these different impulses. On November 29, 1864, militias from Colorado and New Mexico attacked a Cheyenne and Arapaho settlement about forty miles from Fort Lyon, whose authorities had promised them "perfect safety" if they camped there. At least two hundred people, mostly women and children, were killed, their bodies mutilated. Several militia members refused to participate in the slaughter and reported what had occurred. Congress subsequently issued a report labeling Sand Creek "a foul and dastardly massacre" involving "murder, in cold blood" (Horwitz 2014).[26]

When news of the massacre became public, eastern reformers demanded that the Grant administration solve the "Indian problem." Grant adopted a policy whereby Native Nations were to be treated as "wards" of the federal government, which would provide them with the skills and tools needed for assimilation. The treaties signed during the mid- to late 1860s committed the U.S. government to providing the resources—farming tools, agricultural and mechanical shops, vocational education, medical services, and so on—that would allow Native individuals to take on the habits of their Euro-American neighbors (DeJong 2015: 31).

The civic status of American Indians was raised during postwar congressional debates about the status of freedmen. The 1866 Civil Rights Act, designed to ensure the citizenship of freed slaves, included the following language: "all persons born in the United States and not subject to any foreign power, excluding Indians not taxed, are hereby declared to be citizens of the United States." Since reservation lands were not subject to state and local taxation, the phrase "Indians not taxed" effectively meant the promise of citizenship would not apply to indigenous peoples. Republicans then incorporated most of the Act's language into what became Section 1 of the Fourteenth Amendment.[27] The phrase "excluding Indians not taxed," however, was dropped. Westerners thought this might be an attempt to sneak in citizenship rights for American Indians, but the sponsors convinced them that the amendment would not apply to "Indian savages" (Martin 2002). The Senate Judiciary Committee even issued a report stating that the Fourteenth Amendment did not apply to Native Americans who maintained Native Nation identities (Wilkins and Stark 2011: 42).[28]

The End of Treaty-Making

Although the U.S. government has a long history of upholding treaty obligations with foreign countries, its record of honoring commitments enshrined in treaties with Native Nations is poor (Deloria 1969: 81). Treaty-making affirms sovereignty on the part of both signatories. Even when a weaker nation is pressured into signing a treaty with a more powerful nation, it still affirms the inherent sovereignty of the weaker party (DeJong 2015: 65). During the postbellum era, westerners wanted treaty-making to come to an end so they could have access to reservation lands. Eastern reformers opposed treating American Indians as belonging to nations with even limited sovereign rights on the grounds that it was a barrier to assimilation (DeJong 2015: 31–33).[29]

Treaty language that promised to provide benefits (such as the "arts of civilization") was viewed by Native signatories as a commitment to provide Western education to their children but not as an agreement to supplant their own ways with those of Euro-Americans. Indian agents viewed this language as giving them the power to enforce rules prohibiting Indians from venturing off reservations and to ban spiritual practices, such as the Sun Dance. As Harjo (2014: 4) notes, "The civilization regulations criminalized everything that was traditional or customary in Indian life, even banning ponies. Pigs, however, were allowed, the idea being that without ponies, Indians could not ride away, but with pigs they would take up farming."

In 1871 Congress added a rider to the Indian Appropriation Act prohibiting treaty-making (DeJong 2015: 31).[30] Interestingly, the impetus for the end of treaty-making had little to do with disagreements about the status of Native Nations but instead was the result of a conflict between the two branches of Congress. The Constitution gives the power to approve treaties to the Senate, but all appropriations legislation is to be initiated in the House of Representatives. Because the treaties commit the U.S. government to providing funds for treaty-promised benefits, leaders in the House of Representatives came to believe their constitutionally defined prerogatives were being usurped when the Senate approved treaties (Clinton 2014: 26–27). The U.S. government then switched to signing nontreaty agreements with Native Nations; more than 250 of these were reached between 1870 and 1911 (DeJong 2015: 195–218). The Supreme Court has allowed the federal government great latitude in modifying and even abrogating treaties.[31] In short, these actions continue to exemplify the ambiguous, contradictory, and confusing position of the U.S. government vis-à-vis American Indians but one that generally has been more favorable than those taken by state governments.

Late Postbellum Trends

The possibility of assimilation and citizenship, along the lines as put forth by Justice Taney in *Dred Scott v. Sandford* (1857), was undercut by the Supreme Court in *Elk v. Wilkins* (1884). John Elk, who lived among whites, tried to register and vote in Omaha, Nebraska. Even though he was fully assimilated, the registrar stopped Elk from voting. The Court ruled that Elk was not a citizen and therefore could not vote. The Justices suggested the civic status of American Indians was akin to that of U.S.-born children of foreign ambassadors residing within the nation's territorial boundaries.

The impact of *Elk v. Wilkins* was mitigated by a series of laws (the 1887 General Allotment Act, its 1901 amendments, and the 1906 Burke Act) that provided paths to citizenship for American Indians who agreed to have their reservations broken up into individual plots with the remaining land made available for purchase by non-Natives.[32] It was supported by easterners, who viewed themselves as pro-Indian, but also was backed by land-hungry westerners.[33] The thought was that checker-boarding (i.e., interspersing Native and white farms) would foster assimilation by encouraging Native Americans to adopt the farming practices of their white neighbors.[34] These acts provided a path to citizenship, albeit at a huge cost in terms of the loss of treaty lands. In some cases, 80–90 percent of lands belonging to Native Nations were declared "surplus" and sold off to whites.

The Indian Citizenship Act

By the early 1920s, nearly two-thirds of Native Americans had gained citizenship, whether through the acts discussed in the previous section or as a result of military service during World War I.[35] In 1924 Congress passed the Indian Citizenship Act (ICA), which unilaterally granted citizenship to all American Indians and Alaska Natives. Much of the support for the Act came from Progressive Era reformers, who felt that Native Americans' high level of military service in World War I demonstrated their fitness for citizenship. The reformers also hoped that citizenship would give them a means to attack the widespread corruption in the Bureau of Indian Affairs (Schroedel and Hart 2015: 8).[36] This "gift" of citizenship was not universally embraced because it implied a legitimation of the U.S. government's usurpation of Native lands (Bruyneel 2004).

The ICA left unresolved the question of what rights and privileges accompanied the "gift" of citizenship. While the Act did not include specific provisions delineating the rights of citizenship, the minutes of the House Indian Affairs Committee show the intent was for Native Americans to be able to participate in politics on an equal basis with other citizens. Federal government entities issued statements indicating the ICA conferred full voting rights to American Indians, who met the same qualifications as other citizens. But many, if not most, whites in states with large Native populations were opposed to enfranchisement. Bureau of Indian Affairs commissioner Charles Burke recognized there might be concerted opposition to Native voting in the West and expressed as much in a letter sent out to local Indian superintendents (Schroedel and Hart 2015: 8).

Although Section 1 of the Fourteenth Amendment states that "No State shall make or enforce any law which shall abridge the privileges or immunities of citizens of the United States," this does not necessarily include the right to vote. The administration of elections is left to state governments, as proscribed in Article 1, Section 4, which assigns to state governments the responsibility to regulate "The Times, Places and Manner of holding Elections for Senators and Representatives" and is then silent on all other elections, thereby leaving those completely under the authority of state governments. At the time of the ICA's passage, seven states had constitutional provisions prohibiting Native Americans from voting (Cohen 1942: 157–158).

Western State Disenfranchisement

Western states used different strategies to disenfranchise American Indians. Some mimicked Jim Crow laws in the South, while others were crafted to be applicable only to Native Americans. Six western states adopted literacy tests (McCool, Olson, and Robinson 2007: 18–19). The state constitutions of Idaho, Washington, and New Mexico prohibited "Indians not taxed" from voting—language that mimicked the wording of the 1787 U.S. Constitution with respect to the counting of persons when determining representation in the House and for direct taxes and drew upon the precedent established by the *Opsahl v. Johnson* (1917) Minnesota State Supreme Court decision. In that case the judges held that because Red Lake Chippewa living on the reservation did not pay taxes (sales and property taxes on reservation purchases and lands), they had not "yielded obedience and submission" to the laws of the state and thus should not have a voice in how the state was run or be in a position to impose burdens on taxpaying citizens.

Five states (Idaho, Maine, Mississippi, New Mexico, and Washington) still had laws with the "Indians not taxed" language in 1940 (Wolfley 1991: 185). New Mexico, Utah, and Arizona argued that Native Americans living on reservations were not actually residents of those states and were ineligible to vote in state and local elections. South Dakota, North Dakota, and Minnesota had statutes requiring "self-termination" by Native Americans who wanted to vote (McCool, Olson, and Robinson 2007: 11–12). Arizona argued that clauses in their state constitution that precluded the mentally incompetent from voting applied to all Native Americans. A similar clause had previously been ruled unconstitutional in a North Dakota case (*Swift v. Leach* 1920), but that did not deter Arizona.[37]

Prior to World War II, there were a couple of legal challenges to discriminatory laws that prevented Native Americans from voting. Two Pima (Peter Porter and Rudolph Johnson) living on the Gila River Reservation in Arizona tried to vote in the 1928 presidential election, but the local election official refused to put them on the voting rolls. The Arizona State Supreme Court rejected the state's argument that the Gila River Reservation was not part of Arizona but accepted the argument that Native Americans were "under guardianship" and therefore incompetent to vote (*Porter v. Hall* 1928).

Four years later, Cheyenne River Sioux in South Dakota tried to register and vote in school board elections. County auditors drew upon a ruling from the state attorney general to preclude them from the rolls. The attorney general had used convoluted and ostensibly nonracial criteria in his ruling: "Indians are entitled to vote in South Dakota under the same conditions as white people, and if they reside within a voting precinct on the Indian reservation and not upon the land. . . . under the exclusive jurisdiction of the federal government, they are entitled to vote" (Report of the Attorney General, State of South Dakota 1932: 360). Given that trust lands are under the "exclusive jurisdiction of the federal government," this decision disenfranchised nearly all reservation Indians.

Federal Government Policy Shifts

Government reports and congressional investigations in the 1920s and 1930s concluded that governmental policies and corruption within the Bureau of Indian Affairs had led to disastrous conditions among the Native American populations.[38] Officials decided the best way to address problems was through rebuilding some self-rule among Native Nations.[39] Native culture and institutions would be used as "transitional devices for the gradual assimilation of Indians into American society" (Wilkins and Stark 2011: 129). Congress passed the Indian Reorganization Act (1934), which restored some measure of self-government to Native Nations, ended the allotment policy, provided credit for economic development initiatives, and created mechanisms for rebuilding reservation land bases.[40] Then in 1946 Congress passed the Indian Claims Commission Act, which allowed Native Americans to file claims against the federal government for monetary compensation for lands taken in violation of treaties.[41]

Post–World War II Activism

An estimated 25,000 American Indian men served in the armed forces during World War II (Wilkins and Stark 2011: 217). On some reservations, the proportion of men from 18 to 50 years of age who served reached as high as 70 percent (Ferguson-Bohnee 2015: 1109). Just as was true of African American veterans, Native veterans felt their military service entitled them to full citizenship, including the right to vote. Military service also facilitated ties across the different Native Nations. This recognition of shared interests led to creation of the National Congress of American Indians

(NCAI). From its founding in 1944 until the early 1960s, NCAI was the only national Native-led organization involved in lobbying Congress and government bureaucracies on behalf of Native issues, including voting rights (Smith and Warrior 1996: 43).

Many liberals found it very troubling that minorities had defended democracy against the Axis nations but then returned home to face discrimination. The role of the Navajo code talkers in the victory at Iwo Jima, as well as Ira Hayes's participation in the raising of the flag following that victory, generated positive press for returning American Indian veterans.[42] In 1947, President Truman created the Committee on Civil Rights, which was tasked with determining ways to strengthen and improve the civil rights of minorities. While the committee mostly focused on African Americans, its 1947 report also recommended that American Indians in Arizona and New Mexico be given the right to vote (President's Committee on Civil Rights 1947).

Legal Challenges to State Laws

On November 8, 1947, two Yavapai veterans, Frank Harrison and Harry Austin from the Fort McDowell Indian Reservation, tried to register to vote in Maricopa County but were turned away. They decided to sue for the right to vote.[43] The Arizona Supreme Court ruled that the Nationality Act and the Selective Service Act had "emancipated the Indians from guardianship" and opened up voting for Native Americans who passed the state's literacy test (*Harrison v. Laveen* 1948).[44] But only a very small portion of Native Americans in Arizona could pass the literacy test, since 80–90 percent were functionally illiterate (Ferguson-Bohnee 2015: 1112).

In 1948 with support from NCAI, Miguel Trujillo, a former Marine sergeant, tried to register to vote in Valencia County, New Mexico, but was rejected because the state had an "Indians not taxed" provision in its constitution. The Isleta Pueblo man filed a legal challenge, pointing out that he paid income taxes, sales taxes, and a motor vehicle tax, although he did not pay property taxes on reservation land. The court agreed and issued a permanent injunction barring the government from enforcing the "Indians not taxed" provision (*Trujillo v. Gurley* 1948).[45]

The legality of Utah's self-termination and residency requirement was raised in the *Allen v. Merrell* (1956) case. The attorney general in Utah had issued an opinion stating that "Indians who live on the reservations are not entitled to vote in Utah" (Opinion of the Attorney General of Utah 1956). After a Northern Ute living on the Uintah and Ouray Reservation challenged the law, the Utah Supreme Court ruled that the provision stating that "Any person living upon an Indian or military reservation shall not be deemed a resident of Utah" was an appropriate use of state power. Their argument had three parts: (1) reservation Indians are members of Native Nations that have "sovereignty independent of state government"; (2) the federal government has "a high degree of responsibility" for reservation Indians, who are not yet ready for termination; and (3) reservation Indians are "much less concerned with paying taxes" and lack an interest in non-Native governments. The Utah Supreme Court decided it would be wrong to allow non-taxpaying Indians to exert "substantial control of county government," which is responsible for expending funds provided by taxpaying citizens (*Allen v. Merrell* 1956). They stated the denial was based on residency, not on race. The U.S. Supreme Court disagreed and vacated the decision, forcing Utah to change its laws.

A few years later, the New Mexico Supreme Court also rejected the residency argument in a case involving a challenge to results in the 1960 election, where the losing candidate for lieutenant governor argued that he lost because his opponent had received votes from reservation Navajo, who therefore were not residents of New Mexico (*Montoya v. Bolack* 1962).

The Termination and Relocation Years

Very few Native Americans voted in the 1950s and early 1960s. This was due in part to the fact that states and localities had erected substantial barriers to electoral participation. It also was a function of a belief among many American Indians that such participation signaled acquiescence to the status quo. While arguably a principled stand, this meant elected officials who supported policies detrimental to Native communities need not fear a political backlash. In the 1950s politicians began passing laws that directly attacked sovereignty and treaty rights. Republicans argued that the patriotism demonstrated by American Indians in World War II showed that they should no longer be considered "wards" of the federal government and they needed to be emancipated (in other words, the dissolution of Native Nations and the abrogation of rights/benefits due to members of federally recognized Native Nations). Congress passed laws known as "termination policies" aimed at assimilation and the complete dissolution of Native Nations (Iverson 1985; Wilkinson and Briggs 1977). These laws allowed the federal government to save money by eliminating services and benefits to Native Nations and to break up reservation lands and make them available to outsiders—a move that was popular with non-Native voters in western states.

Much of the congressional support for these termination policies came from members of Congress who represented states and districts with large Native reservations. The initial impetus for termination came from Senator Hugh Butler (R-NE), who sponsored legislation in 1947 that undermined federal protections and legal jurisdiction involving the Iroquois in New York. He also was a major force behind the 1953 passage of Public Law 280 and House Concurrent Resolution 108, which terminated the trust status of federally recognized Native Nations.[46] But these laws also were a unique reflection of that particular historical moment and the anticommunist hysteria associated with McCarthyism and the Red Scare era. Senator George Malone (R-NV) expressed this sentiment when he argued, "While we are spending billions of dollars fighting Communism . . . we are at the same time . . . perpetuating the systems of Indian reservations and tribal governments, which are natural Socialist environments" (reprinted in Blansett 2018: 51–52).

Termination policies resulted in more than 1.3 million acres of reservation lands being opened up to non-Native buyers (Wilkins and Stark 2011: 130–131). More than 100 Native Nations, bands, and *rancherias* lost their status as "recognized" American Indian communities.[47] Services provided through entities such as the Indian Health Services were no longer available to the more than 11,000 people from terminated Nations (Wilkins and Stark 2011: 10). By the mid-1960s, support began to grow for the "restoration" of federal recognition, but Congress waited until 1988 to repudiate the termination policies (Wilkins and Stark 2011: 11).

The federal government also adopted an aggressive urbanization/assimilation plan, aimed at moving Native Americans into urban areas where they would be living among non-Native peoples. In 1948, the Bureau of Indian Affairs launched a pilot relocation program involving Hopi and Navajo. Eight years later, Congress passed Public Law 959, which expanded the program. People willing to relocate were given a one-way bus ticket to Chicago, Cleveland, Dallas, Denver, Los Angeles, or San Francisco, all of which had relocation centers. The centers were to provide housing, jobs, financial assistance, and vocational education, but many people did not receive these services (Blansett 2018: 81–82). The Eisenhower administration moved more than 12,500 Native peoples to urban "relocation centers" (Wilkins and Stark 2011: 131).[48]

Native American Activism

Although most early postwar activism was legal in nature, this began to change in the 1950s as the U.S. government initiated major development projects that required the acquisition of reservation lands. The first project was the St. Lawrence Seaway, which was started in 1954 and created a 2,400-mile waterway that linked the Atlantic Ocean to the Great Lakes and generated cheap hydroelectric power for the region. The project undermined the ecosystem of Mohawk peoples living on both the Canadian and U.S. sides of the border and triggered public protests as well as legal challenges (Blansett 2018: 52–54).[49] By the time the seaway was completed in 1959, a total of 1,392 acres of riverfront land had been taken and over 15,500 Native people displaced. Major corporations, including Alcoa, Reynolds Metals, and General Motors, opened factories and provided jobs for some displaced people, but the companies also illegally dumped hazardous waste into the river and heavy metals into the air. It is now a Superfund site, where no one can live due to the environmental degradation (Blansett 2018: 55).

The resistance to the St. Lawrence Seaway project was followed in 1959 by the Tuscarora protests against New York's plan to take land to build a reservoir. While these two events are generally viewed as launching a new era of Native activism, the seizure of treaty protected lands and resources was taking place in other parts of the country. The Pick-Sloan Plan, designed to promote development and control flooding in the Missouri River Valley, enabled the Army Corps of Engineers to build five extremely large earthen dams from 1946 to 1966 on the Missouri River in South Dakota and North Dakota, including the Oahe Dam that has figured recently in the Standing Rock protests (Otstot n.d.).[50] All the fertile bottom lands of the Crow Creek, Lower Brule, Cheyenne River, Standing Rock, and Fort Berthold Sioux were taken for the dams, as well as lands from the Yankton, Rosebud, and Santee reservations. In total 353,313 acres and at least twelve reservation towns were flooded by the project (Schneiders 1997).[51]

One of the most important early affirmations of indigenous rights was the Declaration of Indian Purpose, which was written in 1961 by a group of youthful activists, academics, and individuals from the National Congress of American Indians during a meeting in Chicago. The Declaration called for an end of termination policies and home rule for Native Nations. An important Native activist youth organization—the National Indian Youth Council—that sprang up on college campuses and embraced Native Nationalism also formed in 1961 (Blansett 2018: 72).[52] The National Indian Youth Council coined the phrase "Red Power,"[53] a term later popularized by the American Indian Movement (AIM) that gained widespread notice during the seventy-one-day-long Wounded Knee occupation in 1971.[54] One of the most successful Red Power strategies of the 1960s and early 1970s was the fish-in. Native Americans and their supporters attempted to exercise treaty-granted fishing rights, triggering backlash from state governments and whites. These resulted in court rulings that affirmed the continuing viability of treaty provisions giving much of the salmon in the Northwest to Native people (Chrisman 2006; Galligan and Reyvaan 1981; Satz 1996; Wilkins and Stark 2011: 189–209).[55]

Summary

Without an awareness of historical context, it is impossible to understand the issue of contemporary voting rights in Indian Country. History can be understood as constituting a "stickiness"—the phrase used by academics to explain why contemporary social processes are shaped by patterns of behavior rooted in the past and may no longer be appropriate—or as a "living force" that inextricably links past, present, and future in a circular web.[56] In both views, the key takeaway is that history exerts a powerful influence on people's lives.

The treaties entered into by the United States and Native Nations provide a concrete example of the confusing and contradictory civic status of American Indians. Treaties are legal contracts that commit the signatories to carry out duties and obligations and to respect the rights of the other party. They are a reminder of a history of "the promises, promises broken," to use Deloria's succinct phrasing (2004), but also a recognition of indigenous sovereignty. However, the nature of that sovereignty, given that one of the parties is a "domestic dependent nation," is still in dispute. What does it mean to be engaged in both civil rights struggles, akin to those waged by other minority populations, and struggles for Native Nation autonomy?

Much of the inconsistent nature of national-level policies is due to splits among leaders over the intrinsic worth of the indigenous inhabitants of North America: Were they "wards" who over time could be incorporated into the body politic or were they "savages" incapable of civilization? While national policies tended to at least ostensibly commit the federal government to having a "tutelary" responsibility vis-à-vis American Indians, this did not preclude many of the actual policies from having disastrous effects. Whether through annihilation or expulsion, the goal of state governments generally was to gain access to Native resources, particularly land. Following the passage of the Indian Citizenship Act, politicians in western states engaged in a variety of legal strategies to prevent American Indians from being able to vote. This lack of a political voice made it possible for government entities, both at the state and national levels, to ignore the commitments made in treaties in ways that inflicted serious cultural, economic, social, and political harm on Native people across the country—and that triggered a growing Native Nationalism and the Red Power movement in the 1960s and 1970s.

PART II

THE PROMISE OF THE BALLOT BOX

CHAPTER 3

The Voting Rights Act Reaches Indian Country

The Racial Framing of Voting Rights

The promise of the 1965 Voting Rights Act (VRA) was slow to be applied to Native Americans. The most obvious reason for this is that racial issues typically are framed in terms of a black/white paradigm (Hattam 2007: 13), but there are other contributing factors: the relatively small number of American Indians, the geographic isolation of Indian Country, and the minimal resources available for voting rights litigation. Moreover, the Act's passage occurred before the Red Power movement forced the country to pay attention to Native issues.

Although there is a tendency to view *Brown v. Board of Education of Topeka* (1954) as the Supreme Court's most significant civil rights ruling in the past seventy-five years, the often forgotten decision in *Smith v. Allwright* (1944) banning the white primary in Texas was equally important and laid the groundwork for the Voting Rights Act. According to Davidson (1992: 13), the ruling unleashed a fierce backlash with "the ever-present threat of violence and economic reprisal in the Deep South." While *Smith* made it possible for civil rights activists to succeed in registering African Americans in Border States, resistance in the Deep South was fierce. Civil rights groups in the early 1960s launched campaigns, such as Mississippi Freedom Summer, aimed at raising national awareness of southern brutality against civil rights workers. Two events in 1964—the murders of three civil rights organizers (Michael Schwerner, James Chaney, and Andrew Goodman) followed by police use of billy clubs against praying civil rights marchers on "Bloody Sunday" in Selma—shocked the nation and led to the passage of the Voting Rights Act.[1]

The symbolism associated with the signing of the VRA signaled that its intent was to address the country's failure to fulfill its commitment to full citizenship for African Americans as embodied in the Fourteenth and Fifteenth Amendments. President Lyndon Johnson signed the Act exactly 104 years to the day after Lincoln signed legislation freeing slaves held in the Confederacy, and did so in exactly the same room as used by Lincoln (Davidson 1992: 17). There is no indication that the VRA's proponents considered that it might be used to address the systematic disenfranchisement of American Indians. In the *Congressional Record*, there are nearly a thousand pages devoted to debates and reports about the VRA, but there are only two very brief mentions of Native Americans (Schroedel and Hart 2015: 10).

Major Provisions of the 1965 Voting Rights Act

The VRA is a complex piece of legislation that includes permanent provisions and nonpermanent provisions that require reauthorization. The most important permanent provision is Section 2, which included the following language when passed: "No voting qualification or prerequisite to voting or standard, practice or procedure shall be imposed or applied by any State or political subdivision to deny or abridge the right of any citizen of the United States to vote on account of race or color."[2] The wording in Section 2 was quite similar to that in the Fifteenth Amendment, albeit with one significant departure. The Fifteenth Amendment does not include language explicitly making it clear that other political subdivisions also are prohibited from vote denial and abridgment, although it is implied, since political subdivisions are created by states.

Section 2's reach is very broad and encompasses any governmental unit that holds elections, so it is equally applicable to states, counties, cities, and school districts, as well as less known units, such as water and sewer districts, that might hold elections. Section 2's broad language makes it particularly subject to differing judicial interpretations. In addition, Section 2 is not geographically limited.[3]

The nonpermanent provisions expire if not renewed by Congress.[4] When the Act was passed initially, Section 4, which banned literacy tests, was a nonpermanent provision and only applied to a limited geographic area, primarily in the Deep South. However, Congress made the provision permanent and removed the geographic limitation in 1975. Section 5 was designed to proactively stop political jurisdictions with egregious histories of voting rights discrimination from adopting new discriminatory procedures and laws. The expectation was that the "covered states"—all of which were in the South—would within a few years undergo a change in their "long-established political atmosphere and tradition of discrimination in voting because of color" and Section 5 would no longer be needed (House Judiciary Committee, HR Rep. 439, reprinted McDonald 2010: 33).[5] Section 5 was set to expire in five years, but it was reauthorized numerous times, most recently in 2006.

Section 4(b) laid out that Section 5 "covered jurisdictions" were required to pre-clear changes in their voting laws and procedures with the Department of Justice or the Circuit Court for the District of Columbia.[6] Within a year, the law had ushered in dramatic changes in the South; all political jurisdictions in Alabama, Georgia, Louisiana, Mississippi, South Carolina, and Virginia, as well as thirty-nine counties in North Carolina, were designated as "covered jurisdictions" (Department of Justice 2013). Alaska and two Arizona counties initially were included, but they "bailed out" by convincing the Circuit Court for the District of Columbia that they had not used literacy tests in a discriminatory manner within the previous five years (Davidson 1992: 18–19).[7] They persuaded the judge that their literacy testing had been done in an evenhanded manner and was not designed to discriminate against Native Americans even though the tests resulted in their widespread disenfranchisement (*Apache County v. United States* 1966).[8] During the early years, there was confusion over whether Native Americans and Alaska Natives were to be considered a protected class on the basis of "race or color" and therefore covered by the VRA (McDonald 2010: 36).

Other important nonpermanent provisions are Sections 6–9, which allow courts and the Department of Justice to send observers and examiners to monitor elections in jurisdictions with a history of discrimination. The examiners and observers provide information to the DOJ about whether political jurisdictions designated for "special coverage" are allowing qualified people to vote and accurately recording votes. They can testify about what they have observed if there is litigation, and their presence may deter election officials from engaging in prohibited behaviors.

The 1970 Renewal of the Voting Rights Act

The systematic disenfranchisement of Native Americans was not a prominent issue during debates over the 1970 reauthorization of nonpermanent provisions. Congress focused on the Act's implementation and impact on

African American voting in southern states. They discovered widespread noncompliance in Section 5 "covered" jurisdictions, leading them to reauthorize Section 5 for an additional five years.[9] The most important change Congress made was banning literacy tests throughout the country. Congress also changed the benchmark year for measuring electoral participation to the 1968 presidential election. This slightly expanded the formula for "special coverage" to include some Arizona counties and districts in Alaska with American Indian and Alaska Native populations. This resolved the question of whether American Indian and Alaska Native populations were a protected class on the basis of "race or color."

Heightened Awareness of Native Issues

Over the next several years, public awareness of Native issues increased dramatically, at least in part as a result of events that occurred during the Red Power period when a series of very public acts of protest and civil disobedience took place from the late 1960s through 1978. The most publicized actions were the 1969 occupation of Alcatraz Island, the Trail of Broken Treaties and BIA takeover in 1972, the 1973 standoff at Wounded Knee, and the Longest Walk in 1978 (Wilkins and Stark 2011: 206), which brought Native issues to the public consciousness for a short period.[10] During the early 1970s, there also were a handful of egregious voting rights cases—two in Arizona and another in South Dakota—that were sufficiently unjust and harmful that they garnered substantial attention from federally funded Legal Services attorneys, the Department of Justice, and the United States Commission on Civil Rights.[11]

The Navajos' Fight in Apache County, Arizona

The two Arizona cases, *Shirley v. Superior Court for Apache County* (1973) and *Goodluck v. Apache County* (1975), provide a window into Native vote denial and dilution strategies prevalent during the early 1970s. Apache County, located in the northeastern corner of the state, encompasses a landmass of more than 11,200 square miles. The county initially was designated a covered jurisdiction under Section 4(b), but it had been removed from coverage after it convinced the court that its use of literacy tests was not discriminatory in intent.

The entire upper half of the county is within the boundaries of the Navajo Reservation, and American Indians (primarily Navajo but also Apache and Hopi) comprised a majority of the population in the early 1970s. However, none had ever been elected to the three-person Board of Supervisors. In 1972 shortly after the ban on literacy tests in the state went into effect, Tom Shirley, a Navajo living on the reservation, decided to run for supervisor in District 3, which covered the northern part of the county. Shirley had served in numerous positions within Navajo Nation and on the school board. Even though most of the 26,700 people living in District 3 were Navajo, literacy tests previously had prevented Navajo from voting for and electing one of their own (Yurth 2009).[12]

Shirley got 3,169 votes versus 1,105 votes for his white opponent, Thomas Minyard. A couple of days before Shirley was slated to be sworn in, the Board of Supervisors sent a letter to Shirley stating they would not issue the required certificate stating Shirley was the duly elected supervisor from District 3. His defeated opponent had gotten a preliminary injunction ordering the board to not accept the election results. Minyard argued that Shirley, as a resident of the Navajo Reservation, did not own property that could be taxed by the state and therefore could not run for political office—a version of the "Indians not taxed" argument that courts previously had disallowed. Shirley contacted Navajo Nation chairman Peter MacDonald, who lined up legal and public support.[13] His legal team was able to get the case moved out of Apache County to the adjacent Coconino County, where the judge ruled against the county (Yurth 2009). The county appealed to the Arizona Supreme Court but lost, and Shirley had to be seated (*Shirley v. Superior Court for Apache County* 1973).[14]

The white political elite still was able to maintain the "stranglehold" on power within the county because the two other districts elected white supervisors. The Board of Supervisors, which had the legal authority to establish district boundaries, had drawn the lines in such a way that nearly all of the Navajo were packed into District 3. In keeping with Arizona's long-held practice of not accepting Native Americans living on reservations as actually being citizens, the board had not included them in population counts for the three districts. As is shown in Table 1, the supervisor districts had an enormous population disparity, with the heavily Native District 3 having 6.9 times more people than District 2 and 15.7 more people than District 1. The state and county justified this by arguing that the Indian Citizenship Act of 1924 was unconstitutional, so they did not need to count

Table 1. Apache County Supervisory Districts

District	*Total Population*	*Native American Population*
1	1,700	70
2	3,900	300
3	26,700	23,600

Native Americans when calculating district populations. Obviously this resulted in the voting clout of Native Americans (mostly Navajo but also some Hopi and Apache) being massively diluted.[15]

In 1973 Leslie Goodluck, editor of the *Navajo Times*, became the lead plaintiff in a suit charging that the Apache County Board's drawing of district lines constituted a denial of equal protection in violation of Arizona laws and the Fourteenth Amendment and a denial of the right to vote on account of race in violation of the Fifteenth Amendment and the VRA. The Navajo plaintiffs were able to secure lawyers from Legal Services and the Department of Justice. The attorneys representing the Board of Supervisors and the state of Arizona cited the 1884 *Elk v. Wilkins* Supreme Court ruling that held American Indians could not be citizens, further drawing upon the fact that most of the people residing in District 3 live on the Navajo Reservation and therefore fall under the "Indians not taxed" exclusion. In addition, the fact that they were on a reservation meant that they were not "subject to the jurisdiction" of the U.S. government. The district court disagreed and reiterated that Native Americans have the same rights as any other citizen (*Goodluck v. Apache County* 1975).

The Board of Supervisors was forced to redraw districts so that they conformed to the requirements of the *Baker v. Carr* (1962) and *Avery v. Midland County* (1968) rulings, which require districts to have substantially equal populations. *Goodluck v. Apache County* radically changed the balance of political power within the county. When Navajo realized their votes could have an impact, their registration rate increased dramatically—nearly 20 points between 1972 and 1974. In 1974, three Navajo were elected for the first time to the state legislature (United States Commission on Civil Rights 1975: 58). The 1976 elections resulted in two Navajo gaining seats on the three-person Board of Supervisors. Tom Shirley, however, did not run for reelection in 1976. His widow, Nellie Shirley, described her husband as a "trailblazer" but noted that his legal battle and subsequent fights within the board had taken a significant toll on him (Ruelas 2014).[16]

Vote Denial in South Dakota's "Unorganized Counties"

South Dakota has a particularly troubled history with respect to Native American voting. For example, in 1963, just prior to the passage of the VRA, Yankton Sioux in Charles Mix County tried to vote on a proposal to establish a water district in their part of the county, but the county auditor, citing the state's attorney general, refused to allow them to vote. The attorney general's report stated the Yankton Sioux lived on a reservation, and therefore their names were not on the county tax rolls and they did not have full control over their affairs since they were under federal jurisdiction (Report of the Attorney General, State of South Dakota 1963: 115).[17]

South Dakota law distinguishes between "organized" and "unorganized counties"; the former have a full range of officials who administer local government affairs while the latter have none of these officials. Instead of electing their own county commissioners, sheriff, judges, and other officials, the unorganized counties are "attached" to other counties, whose officials carry out all the business normally handled by county officials. This meant the residents of the unorganized counties had very little control over much of the running of their counties. While the distinction made sense when the state was admitted to the union, in that it allowed for some limited government services to be provided in sparsely settled areas, that rationale was no longer applicable.

By the late 1960s, only three South Dakota counties were designated as "unorganized," and those just happened to be counties (Todd, Washabaugh, and Shannon) that included the Rosebud Sioux and Pine Ridge reservations.[18] In 1974 with help from Legal Services lawyers, Native Americans challenged the VRA's provisions that resulted in their disenfranchisement. The lead plaintiff, Jake Little Thunder, had served on the Oglala Sioux Tribal Council and was a World War II veteran (American Horse 2016). The plaintiffs argued that their near total exclusion from voting constituted a violation of the Equal Protection Clause of the Fourteenth Amendment. Defense attorneys argued the exclusion from voting was reasonable because Indians living on reservations do not have the same degree of interest in county government as people living off-reservation in organized counties. The district court agreed with the state's position, but the

Eighth Circuit Court reversed the decision, stating, "Such unequal application of fundamental rights we find repugnant to the basic concept of representative government" (*Little Thunder v. South Dakota* 1975).

The 1975 U.S. Commission on Civil Rights Report

In its 1975 report *The Voting Rights Act: Ten Years After*, the U.S. Commission on Civil Rights stated that the voting barriers faced by Native Americans are "not dissimilar from those encountered by Southern blacks" (United States Civil Rights Commission 1975: 16).[19] Although most of the report chronicles the VRA's impact on African Americans in the South, it included testimony and information about Arizona voting rights abuses against Navajo. Along with Apache County's refusal to accept Tom Shirley's election and the gross malapportionment of districts, the report identified other vote denial and dilution strategies. They discovered a severe shortage of polling places on the Navajo Reservation in Apache County and Coconino County after the counties chose to save money by eliminating polling places on the reservation. In the 1972 general election, there were only ten reservation polling places in Apache County. People who wanted to vote had to wait in bad weather for several hours to do so. Many were physically unable to wait, while others had to leave without voting because they had to return to work. In the Chinle polling place, some people waited until 12:30 a.m. to vote (United States Commission on Civil Rights 1975: 110).

The report also highlighted difficulties experienced by Native Americans whose first language is not English. Although most states had eliminated laws mandating elections be conducted in English, Arizona did little to accommodate voters with limited English. This was a huge problem for Navajo. Apache County did not provide translators for Navajo voters with limited or no English (United States Commission on Civil Rights 1975: 121). Conditions were only slightly better in Coconino County. The county provided an interpreter at the Tuba City polling place, but the need was so great that people had to wait three hours in order to vote with assistance (United States Commission on Civil Rights 1975: 117).[20]

The 1975 Renewal of the Voting Rights Act

The blatant discrimination uncovered in cases such as *Shirley v. Superior Court for Apache County* (1973), *Goodluck v. Apache County* (1975), and

Little Thunder v. South Dakota (1975) garnered attention within Congress when the VRA's nonpermanent provisions came up for renewal. The outright denial of the right to vote, as occurred in the "unorganized" South Dakota counties, and the continuing attempts to disenfranchise Navajo in Arizona were factors in the decision to extend Section 5's geographic reach. Sections of the Commission on Civil Rights' report detailing widespread voting rights abuses against Native Americans were included in the House of Representatives hearings on the proposed VRA amendments (McCool, Olson, and Robinson 2007: 26).

While the main push for minority language assistance came from Puerto Ricans in the Northeast and Mexican Americans in Texas, deliberations in the House and Senate included discussions about American Indian populations.[21] The decision to protect groups of "language minorities" defined as Asian Americans, American Indians, Alaska Natives, and persons of Spanish heritage was a compromise between those who wanted to only cover Spanish-speaking populations and those who favored protection for any "race or color group whose mother tongue is other than English" (Hunter 1976: 262).

Representative Robert Drinan (D-MA) cited the DOJ's involvement in thirty-three Native American voting discrimination cases since 1970 (McDonald 2010: 37). Republicans in states with large Native populations were strong opponents of the minority language provisions. Senator Pete Domenici (R-NM) tried to get his state excluded from coverage but failed. Senator Barry Goldwater (R-AZ) actively opposed the provisions, as did nearly the entire Alaska congressional delegation. Although the Alaska delegation failed to get their state excluded, they were able to get a provision adopted requiring only oral translations of English when the minority language was "historically unwritten." Given that American Indian and Alaska Native languages had no written forms, aside from some using hieroglyphics prior to their contact with Euro-Americans, this provision allowed some states to refuse to provide written materials in languages other than English.[22] Most votes to eliminate or weaken minority language provisions came from Republicans in these states, along with white Democrats and Republicans from the South.

Section 4(f), adopted in 1975, required political jurisdictions that had provided election materials only in English despite having more than 5 percent of voting-age citizens whose sole language was one of those identified in the VRA and less than half of their voting-age citizens registered to conduct bilingual registration and elections. Section 208, also adopted in 1975, which allows limited English proficiency (LEP) voters to bring someone to assist them in voting, also is relevant.[23] These changes affected Texas, Arizona, and Alaska, as well as some jurisdictions in California, Colorado, Florida, Michigan, New Mexico, New York, North Carolina, Oklahoma, and South Dakota (McCool, Olson, and Robinson 2007: 27).[24]

Congress revised Title 4 to allow judges to authorize the payment of attorney fees when the prevailing party is trying to safeguard minority access to voting. The aim was to make it easier for private parties to pursue voting rights litigation (Hunter 1976: 261). This is significant because the DOJ can pursue only a small number of voting rights cases. In describing the DOJ in the years following the passage of the VRA, McDonald, Pease, and Guest (2007: 205) note, "Indian Country was largely bypassed by the extensive voting rights litigation campaign that was waged elsewhere, particularly in the South."

The DOJ's mandate is determined by who controls the executive branch. The legal client of the DOJ is the U.S. government, not people whose rights may have been violated. The Civil Rights Division within the DOJ has been called the "fulcrum of government's civil rights efforts," but its priorities change when partisan control of the presidency changes. When an administration is pro–civil rights, that stance is reflected within the DOJ, but the reverse is also true. During the Johnson administration, Attorney General Nicholas Katzenbach, Solicitor General Archibald Cox, and lawyers from the Civil Rights Division drafted much of the language in the Voting Rights Act (Graham 1992: 93–96). There were some disputes between civil rights attorneys in the Civil Rights Division and Nixon appointees, but conflicts increased dramatically with each subsequent Republican administration (Rich 2007).[25]

Responses to the Changes in the Voting Rights Act

While case and statutory laws delineating civil rights are essential, for rights actually to be more than words requires access to substantial legal and financial resources that can be mobilized when infringements occur. Often this depends upon private resources. Although the DOJ is important, government-plaintiff voting rights cases are only a very small portion of cases—less than 5 percent of all voting rights cases involving racial minorities (McCool, Olson, and Robinson 2007: 39).

Cases typically are brought by private parties, most often the ACLU, but their resources are stretched thin and tend to be concentrated in southern states.[26] Starting in the mid-1980s, some of the legal burden for Native voting rights litigation began to be picked up by groups such as the National Indian Youth Council, the Indian Law Resource Center, and the Native American Rights Fund, and occasionally by private pro bono attorneys, all of which have competing demands and limited resources.[27] The remainder of this chapter is devoted to providing an introduction to the types of voting rights abuses these entities sought to end in the quarter century after the 1975 amendments were adopted.

Opposition to Voting Rights in South Dakota

In no state was the response to Native voting rights more vitriolic than in South Dakota, after two counties (Todd and Shannon) became "covered" under Section 5. These counties, along with six others (Bennett, Charles Mix, Corson, Lyman, Mellette, and Washabaugh), also were covered via the minority language provisions. South Dakota state attorney general William Janklow, using language akin to that used by southern racists in the 1960s, demanded the immediate repeal of the VRA. Janklow advised state officials and local political jurisdictions to ignore pre-clearance provisions (Report of the Attorney General, State of South Dakota 1977: 175).

Between 1976 and 2002, officials in "covered" Todd and Shannon counties adopted hundreds of new registration and voting procedures without getting cleared by the DOJ or the Circuit Court for the District of Columbia. Although the DOJ sued over violations in 1978 and 1979, they largely ignored later violations—perhaps due to the DOJ's elimination of the Office of Indian Rights following Reagan's inauguration in 1981. At that point, all voting rights litigation was consolidated in the Office of Civil Rights (McCool, Olson, and Robinson 2007: 37).

Vote Denial and Dilution Strategies

Most early voting rights cases involved litigation against state and local registration and voting procedures that disenfranchised Native peoples within political jurisdictions. Initially officials tried to argue that American Indians living on reservations were not actually residents of the political jurisdictions that included their reservations and as such should not be allowed to vote or run for political office.[28] One Oklahoma school district argued Cherokee was historically an unwritten language so they did not need to provide election materials in Cherokee.[29] When such strategies failed, officials occasionally passed statutes that created subgovernment units that excluded Indian lands or even de-annexed Indian lands from existing governmental units.[30] Again, these efforts failed to withstand judicial scrutiny, but affected Native people had to bear the personal and financial costs of fighting these battles.

After courts ruled against statutes that explicitly disenfranchised Native Americans, political jurisdictions adopted more subtle vote denial strategies. Some localities placed limits on the numbers of registration cards given to individuals doing voter registration drives on reservations, while others rejected registration cards from reservations.[31] Failing to provide sufficient polling locations on reservations was another common strategy.[32] There were many cases of failure to adhere to the minority language requirements.[33] Other common dilution strategies included using multimember at-large election districts and redistricting plans that pack the minority population into a single district or splitting a cohesive minority population up into multiple districts (Cornell University Law School 2017).[34]

Civil rights abuses against Native Americans only sporadically garner elite attention, as occurred during the Red Power era. But even during those periods, the systematic denial of voting rights in Indian Country often is ignored. This is especially true if the DOJ is not vigorously protecting voting rights among Native Americans, either because the administration is not interested in voting rights per se or if their primary focus is on voting rights abuses outside of Indian Country.

Summary

While passage of the Voting Rights Act was one of the most significant legislative achievements of the twentieth century, the law initially had little impact on widespread abuses in Indian Country. Indeed, there were even arguments about whether American Indians/Alaska Natives were covered by the VRA. However, a combination of heightened awareness of Native issues due to media coverage of protests, beginning with the occupation of Alcatraz Island, and the egregious nature of the voting rights abuses in states such as Arizona and South Dakota made it difficult for political elites in Washington, D.C., to ignore the need for the VRA to be applied in Indian Country.

While some means of disenfranchising Native voters were the same as those used against African Americans, there were important differences, rooted in the history and unique civic status of Native peoples. No other population had to deal with arguments about whether they paid taxes or were subject to "guardianship" in order to vote. With respect to the VRA's minority language provisions, only American Indians/Alaska Natives had to overcome arguments about whether their languages were "historically unwritten" and therefore not covered by the Act.

CHAPTER 4

The Shift to Vote Dilution, Suppression, and Abridgment

The Legal Framing of Voting Rights

Although some of the most egregious ways of disenfranchising Native Americans and Alaska Natives can no longer pass judicial muster, this does not mean the problem has disappeared. Instead of overt denials of the right to vote, often labeled "first-generation" voting rights abuses, there has been a shift to "second-generation" abuses: laws and procedures that dilute the electoral clout of minority populations. Second-generation issues involve the manipulation of the electoral process to make it difficult for minority populations to meaningfully affect political outcomes. Determining whether election laws and procedures result in impermissible vote dilution, suppression, and/or abridgment is much more difficult than identifying vote denial laws and procedures. Not only are second-generation legal disputes harder for the average citizen to understand, courts have found it hard to develop legal tests that can be applied in these cases. This section traces the progression of judicial reasoning on vote dilution and suppression. This background will help clarify the legal system's approach to second-generation voting rights issues and how those general approaches are modified to take into account the unique characteristics of the Native electorate.

Three early vote dilution cases, involving African American populations in the South, have shaped judicial thinking. These cases show how the Supreme Court struggled with how to respond to laws and procedures that adversely affected minority electoral participation but fell short of outright vote denial. The cases also illustrate the differences in arguing cases in

Section 5 covered jurisdictions versus those litigated using Section 2. Finally, these cases show the interplay between the DOJ, Congress, and the Court in shaping voting rights.

Allen v. State Board of Elections

Allen v. State Board of Elections (1969) is a Section 5 pre-clearance case involving a DOJ challenge to a Mississippi law adopted immediately after the passage of the VRA. The law included provisions that diminished the voting clout of newly registered Black voters. One provision required that all county boards of supervisors and boards of education be elected through at-large elections, which generally dilutes the clout of minority populations. This case broke new legal ground because the DOJ previously had only litigated Section 5 cases involving voter registration.

DOJ attorneys argued the VRA gave them broad authority over election procedures in Section 5 covered states and the Supreme Court agreed. The decision established two important legal precedents. First, the ruling made it clear that the DOJ's pre-clearance authority under Section 5 extended to all changes in election laws and procedures that might impact minority representation. Second, this was the first indication that the Court considered minority vote dilution as a group-based action, not simply a phenomenon that affected individual voters (Davidson 1994: 32–33).[1]

City of Mobile v. Bolden

The next significant case made winning Section 2 vote dilution cases much harder. Despite the 6–3 vote, the Court was deeply divided in *City of Mobile v. Bolden* (1980). In the plurality opinion, Justice Potter Stewart concluded that Section 2—the relevant VRA language—was largely a restatement of the Fifteenth Amendment and only prohibited formal obstacles to registration and voting, not laws and procedures that resulted in minority vote dilution. Moreover, the Court held that electoral districts, which are drawn without discriminatory intent, do not violate the Fourteenth Amendment.[2] The at-large voting system in Mobile had been adopted by Progressive Era reformers in 1911, and proving they had been motivated by racial animus would require months of archival research—something that could not generally be undertaken.[3] Proving discriminatory intent is a very high standard, which would have made Section 2 cases nearly impossible to win. This meant the VRA really only had teeth in jurisdictions covered under Section 5 pre-clearance.[4]

Congress Responds by Amending Section 2

In the early 1980s, civil rights advocates lobbied Congress to change Section 2's language. The VRA's nonpermanent provisions were up for renewal in 1982, but President Reagan had appointed conservatives William French Smith and William Bradford Reynolds, respectively, as attorney general and assistant attorney general for civil rights (Davidson 1994: 34–35) and the Senate recently had switched from Democratic to Republican control. Changes to the language in Section 2 were not a major source of contention during Democratic-controlled House debates and the administration remained silent about its stance (Boyd and Markman 1983: 1347–1379).

The tenor was dramatically different in the Senate, where Majority Leader Howard Baker's (R-TN) desire to avoid a bitter debate was derailed. Senator Strom Thurmond (R-SC) and Senator Orrin Hatch (R-UT), both of whom had well-established histories of opposition to civil rights, were chairing, respectively, the Judiciary Committee and its Subcommittee on the Constitution. But there was Republican support in the committee for revised Section 2 language, cosponsored by Senators Robert Kennedy (D-MA) and Charles Mathias (R-MD). Conservatives, however, thought the proposed language might be interpreted by courts as requiring electoral quotas. Senator Robert Dole (R-KS), who had remained undecided throughout the debates, then crafted language that most Republicans, as well as the administration, could support (Boyd and Markman 1983: 1414–1418). The new language prohibited voting procedures that resulted in minorities having "less opportunity than other members of the electorate to participate in the political process and to elect representatives of their choice."[5] The final vote in the House was 385–24 and the Senate margin was 85–8. The no votes came from conservatives worried about quotas (King and Smith 2008: 695–696).

The revised Section 2 language shifted the legal debate from whether political jurisdictions intentionally discriminated to whether the results were discriminatory, regardless of intent.[6] Section 2 now also required courts to consider the "totality of circumstances" that affect minority participation. While the revised language did not specify what a "results" test would require, the Senate Judiciary Committee issued a report laying out "totality of circumstances" factors that courts should consider in Section 2 cases. After listing nine factors (subsequently referred to as the "Senate Factors"), the report stated the list was not to be considered exhaustive and that courts should not require that all or even a majority of the factors be present in order to determine that an electoral system produced discriminatory results.[7]

Thornburg v. Gingles

Thornburg v. Gingles (1986), which challenged North Carolina's 1982 redrawing of seven state legislative districts (one single-member district and six multimember districts), was the first case decided after the Section 2 language was revised. The Court agreed that the redistricting plan diluted the African American vote and established a three-pronged "results" test for proving Section 2 violations in vote dilution cases. Plaintiffs had to show the following:

1. The minority group is large and compact enough to be able to constitute a majority in a single-member district.
2. The minority group is politically cohesive.
3. The majority group votes as a bloc to defeat the minority group's preferred candidates.

The Court explicitly stated that plaintiffs need not prove discriminatory intent or causation and that a history of some minority candidates being elected to office is not enough to foreclose a Section 2 violation. *Thornburg v. Gingles* was extremely important in Indian Country, since most political jurisdictions with large Native populations were not covered by Section 5.[8]

Issues Raised in the 2006 Voting Rights Act Renewal

In the years leading up to the VRA's fiftieth anniversary and renewal of nonpermanent provisions in 2006, the question of whether the Act had outlived its usefulness was raised in different settings—among members of Congress and on the Commission on Civil Rights, as well as within the judiciary with conservatives arguing the VRA was no longer needed. Senator Orrin Hatch was a particularly vocal critic. Another prominent critic, Abigail Thernstrom, had been appointed to the U.S. Commission on Civil

Rights.[9] Republican Supreme Court appointees issued a series of 5–4 rulings, starting with *Shaw v. Reno* (1993), which placed limits on the extent to which race could be used in determining districts.[10]

Supporters of renewal invoked the symbolism of the 1960s civil rights era, naming the legislation The Fannie Lou Hamer, Rosa Parks and Coretta Scott King Voting Rights Reauthorization and Amendments Act of 2006. Opposition was much stronger in the House than in the Senate. Conservatives proposed four amendments that would have decreased the renewal period for nonpermanent provisions from twenty-five to ten years, made it easier for jurisdictions to bail out of Section 5 coverage, required the DOJ to demonstrate why Section 5 coverage was still needed in the South, and eliminated minority language provisions. None of the amendments passed, but almost 60 percent of Republican House members supported shortening the extension period and more than 80 percent favored eliminating minority language provisions (King and Smith 2008: 699). Dana Rohrabacher (R-CA) labeled minority language provisions as "multiculturalism at its worst" (Hernandez 2006). But in the end, the Act passed the House on a vote of 390–33 and the Senate on a 98–0 vote.

Despite the large vote in favor of renewal, there still was significant conservative opposition. Supreme Court Justice Antonin Scalia stated the vote reflected Congress's fear of political backlash rather than a continuing need to combat discriminatory electoral practices (Whitaker 2013). During oral arguments in *Shelby County v. Holder* (2013), Justice Scalia stated that the Act's renewal was a "perpetuation of racial entitlement"—a comment he repeated a couple of months later in speech (May 2013). The issues raised in *Shelby County v. Holder* were similar to those raised during the 2006 renewal. Many of the amicus curiae briefs were from conservative groups, former Justice Department employees from the George W. Bush administration, and southern states subject to pre-clearance under Section 5. Two states with substantial Native populations (Alaska and Arizona) filed briefs supporting the repeal of these provisions, as did the Mountain States Legal Foundation, but only the Alaska Federation of Natives and Navajo Nation wrote briefs in favor of the provisions (Schroedel and Hart 2015: 26).

Then on June 25, 2013—the 137th anniversary of Custer's defeat at Little Big Horn—the Supreme Court ruled that Section 4(b)'s formula for determining whether a jurisdiction is subject to pre-clearance under Section 5 was unconstitutional because it violated the "equal sovereignty" of states by treating them differently based on "40 year old facts" (*Shelby County v. Holder* 2013). The decision did not resolve the question of whether Section 5 was constitutional, but without a formula for determining pre-clearance, the section has no utility. While Congress could craft a new Section 4(b) formula, this will not occur unless Democrats gain control of the House and Senate. In concrete terms, *Shelby County v. Holder*'s ruling means most voting rights cases will have to rely on Section 2, which requires a higher standard of proof.

Framing Vote Dilution and Suppression Cases in Indian Country

Many different types of second-generation cases have been litigated over the past two decades in Indian Country, but it is useful to think of them as falling into two broad categories. The first category includes cases where the disputed practices closely resemble those raised in litigation involving other minority populations. These cases involve disputes over whether at-large electoral systems and electoral districts that are malapportioned and/or redistricted impermissibly dilute the Native vote. They can be labeled as generic vote dilution and suppression cases. The second category includes cases that affect Native populations in unique ways that do not apply to other minority populations. This category encompasses cases dealing with the VRA's minority language provisions, unique issues related to voter identification, and the impact of travel distance on voting on reservation populations. These can be labeled as Indian Country specific cases.

The underlying argument in all of the cases is that Native populations must have an equal opportunity to "participate in the political process and elect representatives of their choice." Unlike in first-generation vote denial cases, the legal arguments raised in the second-generation dilution and suppression cases often are less intuitively easy to understand. A further complication is that some recent Section 2 cases are attempts to break new legal ground by arguing "abridgment" rather than dilution and suppression. Rather than providing a compendium of all Native voting rights cases that have been argued since the passage of the VRA—something that can be found in other places—the aim of the next two sections is to introduce the reader to the various types of cases through the use of illustrative examples.[11]

Generic Vote Dilution and Suppression Cases

There are three types of voting rights litigation (involving at-large elections, malapportioned districts, and redistricting disputes) that can be classified as generic vote dilution and suppression cases. This categorization should not be taken as implying the cases are not significant but simply that the issues under dispute are common to voting rights litigation that affects other minority populations. It is worth considering, however, whether some egregious attempts at dilution and suppression would have occurred if the affected population had not been poor and geographically isolated American Indians. Consider, for example, what happened to some Crow Creek Sioux during the 2004 election. There are Crow Creek Sioux living in three counties (Buffalo, Hughes, and Hyde), but the experience of those living in the Hyde County community of West Bend (population 250–300) is noteworthy and not in a positive way. After the Crow Creek won a voting rights case, Hyde County election officials used a not entirely clean chicken coop as a polling place. This non-ADA compliant polling place was located just outside of reservation boundaries.[12]

At-Large Elections: *U.S. v. Blaine County*

At-large electoral systems, where all voters in a jurisdiction cast ballots for several at-large members, can result in minority populations having little if any political representation. Courts generally require a switch to single-member district electoral systems when they find vote dilution in at-large systems. Even though courts have found at-large electoral systems involving Native populations to be impermissible,[13] political jurisdictions often will not switch to single-member district systems until forced to do so through litigation.

The legal question in *U.S. v. Blaine County* (2004) was whether choosing county council members through at-large elections was a violation of Section 2. Blaine County, in north-central Montana, encompasses 4,239 square miles and includes nearly all of the Fort Belknap Reservation, home to the Gros Ventre and Assiniboine.[14] Shortly after passage of the Indian Citizenship Act in 1924, the county switched to an at-large system for electing county commissioners. Even though Native Americans comprised roughly 45 percent of the population, none had been elected to the county council prior to the DOJ filing a Section 2 case in 1999. Potential Native candidates, including those with long records of serving in reservation offices, had thought it would be a waste of time and energy to run (Archambault interview 2017).

To satisfy the three-pronged test established in *Thornburg v. Gingles* (1986), DOJ attorneys provided data showing the Fort Belknap population was sufficiently geographically compact that they could comprise a single county council district; the DOJ also found evidence of racially polarized voting. In addition, the DOJ presented evidence demonstrating depressed socioeconomic conditions in the county, as specified by the 1982 "Senate factors" (*U.S. v. Blaine County*, Complaint 1999). Blaine County, which was represented by pro bono attorneys from the Mountain States Legal Foundation (MSLF),[15] argued the Gros Ventre and Assiniboine did not comprise a single group and suggested there might be polarized voting along tribal lines but not along white/Indian lines.[16] They also argued that the VRA was unconstitutional (*U.S. v. Blaine County*, Defendants' Answer to Complaint 2000: 4).[17] The district court rejected the county's arguments, as did the appeals court, and the Supreme Court refused to review the lower court rulings (*Blaine County v. U.S.* 2005).

The county agreed to adopt a single-member district plan that included one district with a roughly 90 percent Native population, a second district that was 40 percent Native, and a third heavily white district. Delores Plumage became the first member of the Fort Belknap Indian Community elected to the county council.[18] Ben Speakthunder, the Fort Belknap chairman, described her election as a major victory but lamented, "It's too bad it had to be filed in court" (Staff at *Havre Daily News* 2003).

Malapportionment of Districts: Kirkie v. Buffalo County

As far back as the early 1960s courts considered whether legislative districts with unequal population sizes violated the Fourteenth Amendment's "equal protection of the laws."[19] Many states had not adjusted district boundaries for a half century or more, the result of which was that conservative white voters in rural areas had vastly more electoral clout than more liberal and racially diverse voters in urban areas. Civil rights attorneys began challenging the constitutionality of the malapportioned districts. Beginning in the 1980s, the Supreme Court issued a series of decisions that established the following legal requirements: (1) the apportionment of district populations was justiciable (i.e., within the purview of the courts, not simply a political question), and (2) what degree of population deviation was permissible. Generally a population deviation of 10 percent or more was considered prima facie evidence of discriminatory intent,[20] although the Court has allowed greater leeway in setting congressional districts than state legislative districts.[21]

With respect to malapportionment, it is hard to find a more extreme example than Buffalo County. It is one of the oldest counties in South Dakota, dating to the period before statehood, and has a troubled history of white-Sioux relations. The 488-square-mile county includes a substantial portion of the Crow Creek Reservation, which initially was created as a prison camp following the Great Sioux Uprising of 1862 (Hyman 2008).[22] The Crow Creek Sioux, like their counterparts at Standing Rock, had large chunks of the most fertile reservation lands taken by the Army Corps of Engineers to build dams on the Missouri River.[23]

In the early 2000s, the county gained fame for having the highest poverty rate in the country, and the boundaries of the three county council districts had not been adjusted for decades. Nearly all of the Crow Creek Sioux, who comprised 83 percent of the county's population, were lumped into District 3, while the small white population was split between Districts 1 and 2. Donita Loudner, representing District 3, had roughly 1,700 constituents, while the other two districts had approximately 117 and 240 constituents (Loudner interview 2017). The overall deviation among districts was 218 percent or nearly 22 times greater than the deviation allowed by the Supreme Court (McDonald 2010: 144).[24] In 2003, ACLU lawyers launched a suit challenging the enormous population differences across the three districts. The county council, recognizing that it would not prevail in court, signed a consent decree, agreeing to redraw district lines and have DOJ oversight via Section 5 coverage until 2013 (see *Kirkie v. Buffalo County* 2003).[25]

The redrawn lines resulted in the creation of two districts where a majority of the registered voters are Sioux and a single district where a majority of the registered voters are white. County auditor Elaine Wulff then sent letters informing voters whose districts had been changed that they were no longer registered to vote and would need to reregister at her office in the courthouse. Most of those affected were Native. The courthouse is located off-reservation in Gann Valley, roughly twenty-five miles from the main population center on the reservation. Only after a complaint was made to the secretary of state did the auditor put people back on the list of registered voters (Loudner interview 2017). The newly elected majority Sioux council then voted in favor of requesting Help America Vote Act (HAVA) funds to open an early voting/late registration site on the reservation at Fort Thompson, but the auditor refused. Instead people living in Fort Thompson (population 1,282) had to travel off-reservation to the county auditor's office in Gann Valley (population 13) to have access to those services. But in 2018, Yvette Isburg, a Crow Creek Sioux who has promised to ensure full registration and voting access for people living on the reservation, was elected county auditor (Healy interview 2018).[26]

Reapportionment: "Packing" Native Voters in South Dakota

There are different ways redistricting can dilute the power of minority voters,[27] but the most commons forms are "packing" and "cracking" the population. For example, in 2001, South Dakota adopted a redistricting plan that adjusted the boundaries of four state legislative districts. As a result, Native Americans from the Pine Ridge and Rosebud Sioux reservations were "packed" such that they composed 90 percent of the electorate in one district and 30 percent in another district, leaving the remaining two districts nearly all white. Since the reservations were part of Section 5 covered counties, ACLU lawyers argued the state had failed to comply with preclearance and the redistricting plan deprived the Native Americans of an equal opportunity to elect representatives of their choice. The state argued that Sioux from the different reservations were not a politically coherent community as required by *Gingles*. Neither the lower federal court nor the Eighth Circuit Court agreed, and South Dakota had to revise the boundaries of legislative districts (*Bone Shirt v. Hazeltine* 2006), resulting in two Sioux being elected from reconfigured districts with majority Native American voters.[28]

Reapportionment: "Cracking" Native Voters in Montana

Montana has experienced heated conflicts over redistricting. State attempts to "crack" the Native population and limit their numbers in the state legislature triggered legal battles that lasted eight years. The state constitution, as amended in 1972, stipulates the power to reapportion legislative districts is solely delegated to the District and Apportionment Commission, which is established just prior to the decennial census. The state legislature can comment on their plan but not modify it. The plan becomes law as soon as the commission files it with the secretary of state.

The 1982 plan included only one majority Native state legislative district (House District 9). The Fort Belknap Reservation was divided into two senate districts, Fort Peck Reservation into three senate districts, Rocky Boy Reservation into two house districts, Blackfeet Reservation into four house districts, and Flathead Reservation into eight house districts (McDonald 2010: 99–100). The plan massively diluted the Native vote, but by 1990 the white population in districts decreased with three previously majority white house districts and one senate district switching to heavily Native. The changing makeup of the districts, as well as the election of Ramona Howe (D-Lodge Grass) to the house in 1982 and Bill Yellowtail (D-District 21) to the senate in 1984, meant that Native Americans were poised to gain numbers in the state legislature.

The 1992 District and Apportionment Commission held twelve closed working sessions, each followed by a public hearing. During these meetings, commissioners made racially derogatory comments about Native Americans and discussed plans to keep their numbers down in the state legislature (McDonald 2010: 101–105). They adopted a redistricting plan that "cracked" the population from five different reservations (Fort Belknap, Fort Peck, Rocky Boy, Blackfeet, and Flathead) in ways that splintered them between majority white districts. The most blatant example was the splitting of the Flathead Reservation into eight separate legislative districts. The plan included only one more majority Native house district (*Brown v. Montana Districting and Reapportionment Commission* 2003).[29]

ACLU lawyers filed a Section 2 case, which was dismissed by the district court, but the Ninth Circuit found the plaintiffs had satisfied the *Gingles* (1986) test criteria (compactness of population, political cohesion, and racially polarized voting) and remanded the case (*Old Person v. Cooney* 2000). By this time, a new commission had been appointed to develop a plan reflecting changes from the 2000 census. Janine Windy Boy, the lead plaintiff from the *Windy Boy v. Big Horn County* (1986) case, was appointed to the commission, along with two new members who openly stated that the 1992 plan had diluted Native voting clout. The district court, on remand, dismissed the complaint on the grounds that the new commission could handle any problems and the Ninth Circuit Court agreed (*Earl Old Person v. Brown* 2002).

In early 2003 the commission proposed a plan with Native majorities in six house districts and three senate districts and had less than 10 percent population deviation. The state legislature responded by passing HB 309, a bill to invalidate the redistricting plan and change the state constitution to limit the power of the commission. Under HB 309, the secretary of state could not accept a plan with a greater than 1 percent population deviation, a requirement that would make it impossible for additional Native districts to be created. The governor signed HB 309, even though it violated legal requirements for amending the constitution. The secretary of state then refused to accept the redistricting plan on the grounds that it violated HB 309. The state court, however, found HB 309 unconstitutional and instructed the secretary of state to accept the plan (*Brown v. Montana Districting and Reapportionment Commission* 2003). After redistricting, in 2006 ten American Indians were elected to the 150-person state legislature (McDonald 2010: 115–116).[30] As of early 2019, there were eleven Natives serving in the state legislature (10 Democrats and 1 Republican), as well as an American Indian Caucus with roughly 25 members, who meet weekly to discuss issues and bills (Ragar 2019).

Unique Aspects of Native American Voting Rights Cases

As noted earlier, there are a number of second-generation voting rights issues that are unique to Native American populations. While Native populations are not the only group affected by the VRA's minority language provisions, strict voter identification laws and travel distances to registration and polling sites uniquely disadvantage American Indians and Alaska Natives.

The Voting Rights Act and Indigenous Languages

While the minority language provisions (Sections 203 and 4(f)) apply to "American Indians, Asian Americans, Alaska Natives and those of Spanish heritage," several elements differentiate speakers of languages indigenous to the United States from the other covered groups. Indigenous languages are at risk of dying out because they are not continually reinvigorated by the arrival of immigrants speaking those languages. None had fully written forms prior to the arrival of Europeans, which allows voting rights opponents to argue that the VRA's provisions do not apply to "historically unwritten" languages. Also many speakers live in geographically isolated communities, where violations often go unnoticed. The early VRA minority language cases involved communities in the lower forty-eight states, with violations against Navajo speakers being the most common.[31]

Alaska arguably has the worst record of minority language violations, even though no one filed lawsuits until recently. Many older people in rural Native villages have limited English-language skills. Alaska did not provide education beyond the primary school until forced to do so by litigation (*Hootch v. Alaska State-Operated School System* 1975).[32] Indigenous languages, such as Central Yu'pik, Inupiaq, Siberian Yu'pik, Suypiaq, Gwich'in, Tlingit, and Tutchone, are the primary languages spoken in many villages (*Amicus Curiae Brief of the Alaska Federation of Natives, Alaska Native Voters and Tribes in Shelby County v. Holder* 2013, 17). Older villagers often are confused by the wording on ballots and end up voting for the opposite of what they wanted (Solomon interview 2017). Poll workers often do not themselves understand the wording on ballots or are unable to explain it in the indigenous languages (Phillip interview 2017).[33]

The 2010 *Nick v. Bethel* case was the first Alaskan Section 203 case. The Bethel Census Area, which encompasses roughly 45,000 square miles in the extreme western portion of the state, has a population of nearly 18,000. Thousands of residents only speak Yu'pik, but officials failed to provide written assistance in Yu'pik and gave little oral assistance to those needing help to vote. Also in violation of Section 208, election officials refused to allow Yu'pik speakers to bring someone with them into the voting booth.[34] Lawyers from the Native American Rights Fund (NARF) filed a case in 2007 and obtained a preliminary injunction forcing the state to provide Yu'pik language assistance for the 2008 election. Two years later, as part of a settlement, Alaska committed to providing translation and interpretive assistance for Bethel's Yu'pik speakers with limited English.

The Wade Hampton and Dillingham Census Areas, which adjoin the Bethel Census Area, also have many people who are Yu'pik and Gwich'in speakers, but following the 2010 ruling in *Nick v. Bethel*, the state chose to continue not providing them with competent language assistance. Election officials ignored gross errors in Gwich'in election materials. When Mike Toyukak, from the small village of Manokotak, noticed elders not voting because they did not understand the election materials, he sought help from

NARF. The state was found in violation of Section 203 and had to establish a comprehensive language assistance program (*Toyukak v. Treadwell* 2014).[35]

Voter Identification Laws

According to the National Conference of State Legislatures, as of early 2019 thirty-five states had laws requiring voters to show identification before being allowed to vote (National Conference of State Legislatures 2019). Although much has been written about how voter identification laws disenfranchise African Americans, Latinos, young people, the poor, and the elderly (Brennan Center for Justice 2012), these laws also suppress Native American voting in three ways.

First, some officials refuse to accept tribal IDs as valid identification. For example, in 2004, Minnesota secretary of state Mary Kiffmeyer instructed local election officials to not accept tribal identification, which resulted in roughly two hundred voters being unable to cast ballots.[36] Even though she subsequently lost in court,[37] Kiffmeyer continued her efforts to limit voting to those with specific forms of identification. She was elected to the state legislature, where she sponsored two strict voter ID bills that the Democratic governor vetoed. Then Kiffmeyer pushed a voter ID referendum to amend the state constitution. The referendum's language was identical to wording in a Tennessee law that has been interpreted as excluding tribal identification (Pember 2012). The referendum was voted down (Melillo 2012).

Second, there are logistical, geographical, and financial barriers that make it harder for many American Indians to obtain acceptable forms of identification (National Congress of American Indians 2012). Most reservations are in remote areas, far from government offices that issue identification documents. Many Native people lack birth certificates because they were born at home. In parts of Alaska, airlines do not even require picture identification because of the difficulties in obtaining it (Mauer 2012). Some states allow people without government-issued identification to use alternatives, such as utility bills showing a home address. However, many people living on reservations do not have street addresses and can get mail delivered only at post offices, so it is very difficult for them to convince registrars and poll watchers that they live within the district (Ferguson-Bohnee interview 2017).[38]

Third, people who come to the polls without the required identification may vote provisionally but must return within a short time frame with identification. However, people who live a long distance from the polling place may find it difficult to return, even if they have obtained the required documentation (Ferguson-Bohnee interview 2017).

North Dakota's Voter Identification Law

Shortly after the 2012 elections, North Dakota passed a law requiring voters to show approved identification with the person's name, date of birth, and residential address. While the law listed tribal ID as approved identification, most of these IDs could not actually be used because they listed post office box addresses. Without the required identification, even long-term voters would be prohibited from voting. Before the 2014 elections, Dorothy Herman, a retired schoolteacher living on the Turtle Mountain Reservation near the Canadian border, realized that she needed new government identification. Ms. Herman had voted for more than forty years, but her state-issued ID had expired and her tribal identification lacked a residential address. She went to the state office during the time when it was listed as being open, but it was not. Ms. Herman returned later, but officials said her expired identification was insufficient proof of her identity. Then Ms. Herman saw a state advertisement indicating that tribal identification could be used for voting. On Election Day, Ms. Herman went to vote, but she was turned away because the tribal ID had no residential address (Woodard 2016).

Ms. Herman and six other members of the Turtle Mountain Band of Chippewa Nation sued. NARF lawyers argued changes in the voter identification law between 2013 and 2015 "disproportionately burden and disenfranchise Native Americans." Although the state had required voter identification since 2003, the revised law allowed no exceptions. Secretary of State Al Jaeger argued that people can easily obtain identification cards at DMV offices, so the law was not a burden (*Brakebill v. Jaeger* 2016). Conservative bloggers agreed, one of whom suggested that plaintiffs "quit playing the victim card. Quit being an attention whore. Get off your ass and go get your free ID" (westfargomusings 2016).

Although many North Dakotans find it easy to get the state-issued identification, none of the state's 28 DMV offices are on reservations. One might argue that the lack of offices at places such as Turtle Mountain Reservation makes sense. The reservation's largest town, Belcourt, has only 2,078 people. However, 11 of the DMV offices are in towns with even fewer people. The closest office to Belcourt is in Rolla—population 1,325—which is 6.2 miles distant, but it is only open 10:20–12:00 and 1:00–2:35 on the second and fourth Tuesdays of the month. The next closest place is 33 miles away in Bottineau, and it also has very limited hours. Devil's Lake is the nearest location with longer hours, but that requires a 166-mile round trip (North Dakota Department of Transportation 2017).[39]

In summer 2016, District Court Judge Daniel Hovland blocked the law's enforcement because it lacked a fail-safe mechanism for qualified voters without identification to vote. He stated, "It is undisputed that the more severe conditions in which Native Americans live translates to disproportionate burdens when it comes to complying with the new voter ID laws" (*Brakebill v. Jaeger* 2016). As Ms. Herman's experience shows, getting the required state identification is not easy.

In April 2017, North Dakota passed a new law (HB 1369) that was only slightly different from the one just struck down. The rationale for passing HB 1369, as well as the earlier tightening of voter identification laws, was to eliminate voter fraud. However, Judge Hovland in *Brakebill v. Jaeger* had stated, "There is a total lack of any evidence to show voter fraud has ever been a problem in North Dakota," and the secretary of state in a 2006 letter stated he had not encountered any voting fraud in the previous fourteen years (Native American Rights Fund 2017). HB 1369 did not include the fail-safe mechanism required by Judge Hovland (Native American Rights Fund 2017).

Judge Hovland issued an injunction to stop the new law's enforcement, expanded the list of acceptable tribal-issued identification documents, and allowed the use of post office boxes instead of residential street addresses as proof of residency (Campbell and Landreth 2018). But then in September 2018 after the state's early voting period had begun, the Eighth Circuit Court of Appeals, on a 2–1 vote, rescinded the injunction and ruled that the law could be implemented (*Brakebill v. Jaeger* 2018). NARF attorneys filed an emergency appeal to the Supreme Court requesting the new law not be implemented, given that the election period already had begun and thousands of people lacked the required form of identification. However, on October 9—three weeks prior to Election Day—the Supreme Court denied the request (Native American Rights Fund 2018).[40]

Travel Distance

Even very short travel distances have a measurable effect on registration and voting. Increases in distances of less than a quarter of a mile significantly decrease voter turnout (Brady and McNulty 2011). Recent voting rights cases in Montana, South Dakota, and Nevada have drawn attention to the disparate impact of travel distances on Native voters' access to registration and voting. Geographic Information System (GIS) data, referenced in these cases, showed that Native voters face travel distances of up to two hundred miles to access registration and voting sites, while non-Native voters face only minimal travel distances (*Brooks v. Gant* 2012; *Wandering Medicine v. McCulloch* 2014; *Poor Bear v. County of Jackson* 2015; *Sanchez v. Cegavske* 2016).

Although scholars (e.g., Dyck and Gimpel 2005) have found increases in voting by mail among voters who live a long way from polling places, their data did not include reservation populations. Most reservations do not have home mail delivery, so people only have access to mail at post offices, many of which have very limited hours, and this often requires traveling great distances. Also many Native Americans do not trust that their votes will be counted if they vote by mail. Regardless of whether that is true, the perception adversely impacts the willingness to utilize mail in balloting.[41]

The Push for Satellite Registration and Early Voting on Reservations

In 2004, South Dakota passed a law allowing late registration and early in-person absentee voting at the county auditor's office. Not only did the new law provide people with a much longer period for voting, it allowed them to register and vote at the same time, hence making the entire process much more convenient. Shortly after the law's passage, activists from Four Directions realized the law created a new form of inequality in access to registration and voting.[42] While most white South Dakotans live in close proximity to the county auditor's office, Native Americans on reservations do not. What made the situation even more inequitable is that the "unorganized counties" (e.g., Shannon and Todd) did not even have county auditors; instead all of their government services were handled by adjacent counties.

Shannon County (now Oglala Lakota County) is contained entirely within the Pine Ridge Reservation and includes the western half of the reservation. After Native Americans complained, an early voting/late registration site was opened on the reservation but only for six days as opposed to the forty-six days available at the county auditor's office. To get access to registration and early voting for the remainder of the period allowed by state law, they had to travel to the county seat of Fall River, which handled government services for "unorganized" Shannon County. This entailed drive times ranging from 53 minutes to two hours and 45 minutes. This disparity in access was litigated in 2012. When it looked like the plaintiffs were going to succeed, the state and county decided to establish a site for the full early voting period in the 2012 elections and subsequently reached a settlement that covered through the 2018 elections (*Brooks v. Gant* 2012).[43]

Not surprisingly, people living in the eastern half of the Pine Ridge Reservation, in Jackson County, also wanted equal access. They asked for a site to be established in Wanblee, the main reservation population center, roughly twenty-seven miles from the county auditor's office in Kadoka. The county commissioners refused, sparking a lawsuit prior to the 2014 elections. Again, when it looked like the plaintiffs would prevail, the county agreed to a settlement establishing the satellite for three election cycles (*Poor Bear v. County of Jackson* 2015).[44]

Similar issues were raised in *Wandering Medicine v. McCulloch* (2014), where the Gros Ventre, Northern Cheyenne, Crow, and Assiniboine living on reservations in three Montana counties (Big Horn, Rosebud, and Blaine) requested satellites. The average disparity in travel distance ranged from 189 percent to 325 percent. After lengthy court battles, the parties entered into a settlement in 2014 (Schroedel and Saporito 2017).[45]

When cases are settled, plaintiffs are not automatically entitled to reimbursement of legal costs.[46] In the South Dakota and Montana cases discussed previously, the counties belonged to private insurance pools that cover the costs of litigation. This meant that lawyers for the defendants could run up costs without having to worry about being bankrupted. The plaintiffs, however, had to raise funds or get pro bono legal assistance (Schroedel et al. 2017: 11–12). Settlements also meant there was no legal precedent that could be cited in later cases.[47]

Abridgment in *Sanchez v. Cegavske* (2016)

As noted in Chapter 1, in 2016 Paiutes living on the Pyramid Lake and Walker River reservations succeeded in forcing Washoe County and

Mineral County, respectively, to establish early voting sites on the reservations. Nixon, the main population center on the Pyramid Lake Reservation, is 48 miles from the Washoe County seat in Reno. The county had established 21 early voting sites, but none on reservations. The nearest to Nixon was 32 miles away in Spanish Springs. The only early voting site in Mineral County was at the county seat in Hawthorne, 35 miles from Schurz on the Walker River Reservation. *Sanchez v. Cegavske* (2016) broke new legal ground when Judge Miranda Du ruled that travel distance disparities may work "in tandem with historical, social, and political conditions to produce a discriminatory result" that constitutes a violation of Section 2's prohibition on voting "abridgement." This was the first ruling, using the revised Section 2 language adopted in 1982, to identify travel distance disparities as a relevant factor in assessing the "totality of circumstances" that impact the ability of a protected class (e.g., American Indians) to fully participate in elections.[48]

Not only did *Sanchez v. Cegavske* establish that travel distance disparities are relevant, the ruling buttressed legal arguments that differentiate between abridgment and dilution. Deputy Assistant Attorney Vanita Gupta in a Department of Justice brief (2016) explains the difference: "Section 2 vote dilution claims—for example, challenges to district lines—do not usually depend on allegations that a practice makes it more difficult to participate in the political process by casting a valid ballot. In that context, the district lines' imposition of an inability to elect candidates of choice becomes the more important touchstone in establishing injury. . . . By contrast, in a Section 2 claim focused on an abridgement of the right to cast valid ballots, that abridgement alone amounts to injury necessarily impairing electoral opportunity." According to *Sanchez v. Cegavske*, travel distance disparities in conjunction with economic and sociodemographic factors constituted abridgment.

Emerging Issues in Voting Rights

Two emerging electoral reforms—voting by mail and abolishing felony disenfranchisement—are garnering substantial interest. Again, their potential impact on American Indian and Alaska Native communities is being ignored. Vote-by-mail (VBM) reforms have been embraced by liberals, who want to increase access, and conservatives, who see it as a way to save money.[49] Researchers, however, have provided evidence showing that VBM results in large numbers of ballots being lost (Stewart 2010; Alvarez et al.: 2011), and there is evidence suggesting that the effects are particularly deleterious for Native voting. In contrast, reforming felony disenfranchisement laws could positively affect Native voting, although most of the attention has been on its impact on African Americans.[50]

Voting by Mail

Over the past twenty years, states have adopted various different reforms designed to make it easier for people to vote, but no reform has generated more interest than all vote-by-mail (VBM) systems. Since Oregon adopted all VBM elections in the early 1990s, an additional twenty-one states have passed laws that allow at least some all VBM elections. In addition to Oregon, Washington, Colorado, and Hawaii now have all VBM elections, while other states give county governments discretion over where to use all VBM. Counties typically adopt VBM in rural areas with low voter turnout, while still keeping in-person voting on Election Day in other areas.[51]

The evidence is decidedly mixed on whether VBM actually increases turnout. Some studies have found increases in overall turnout, but others have found no effect or a decline in turnout (Bergman and Yates 2011; Elul, Freeder, and Grumbach 2017; Gerber, Huber, and Hill 2013; Gronke and Miller 2012; Southwell and Burchett 2000). Some studies have found that voting increased among high SES groups that already had high levels of voting but often decreased among low-propensity voters (Bergman and Yates 2011; Berinsky 2005; Berinsky, Burns, and Traugott 2001; Karp and Banducci 2000; Monroe and Sylvester 2011).[52] The impact on Native Americans, arguably the most "resource-poor" sector of the electorate, has never been studied.

Vote by Mail in San Juan County

Consider the evidence from Utah, which gives county governments discretion over whether to institute all VBM systems. When San Juan County switched to a VBM system, they closed precinct-level Election Day voting but continued to allow early and Election Day voting at the county clerk's office in Monticello. Some voters on the Navajo Nation Reservation had to travel up to two hundred miles to vote in person. In early 2016, the Navajo

Human Rights Commission filed a lawsuit alleging that the county's election procedures violated Section 2 and Section 203 of the VRA and the Fourteenth Amendment. While much of the case was about travel distance and access to early voting, this was the first time that the impact of VBM was brought up in court. The commission argued that all VBM elections harmed Navajo voters, who were less able to get administrative assistance to handle problems, such as lost ballots, and they had less access to post offices and mail services.[53] Moreover, they claimed the VBM system provided no means for people with limited English to get help in voting (*Navajo Nation Human Rights Commission v. San Juan County* 2016). The case was settled with the county agreeing to provide in-person voter assistance on the reservation during the twenty-eight days prior to elections and provide three Election Day polling places on the reservation. They also agreed to take additional steps to ensure that assistance is provided in the Navajo language (Lawyers' Committee on Civil Rights Under Law 2018).

However, VBM will be an even less viable means of voting for people living on reservations if rural mail service is reduced. President Trump recently ordered the U.S. Postal Service to study ways to increase revenue. Reducing rural mail service, which does not produce much revenue, is being considered. The National Congress of American Indians has held meetings with postal officials about the importance of mail service in Indian Country and how the push for VBM makes the reservation mail service even more crucial.[54]

Trust in Voting by Mail

There is a strong relationship between trust and people's willingness to participate in electoral politics (Wang 2016; Hooghe 2018). In summer 2016, I was part of a team that surveyed more than 1,500 Native Americans in Nevada and South Dakota on their levels of trust in different government entities and trust in different forms of voting. Most respondents evinced low levels of trust for different government bodies, but local governments, which administer elections, had by far the lowest levels of trust. When asked about the degree of trust they had that their vote would count if they voted by mail, only one-quarter of respondents stated they had "complete trust" that it would count—a much lower level than for in-person voting at a polling place (Native American Voting Rights Coalition 2018).[55] If a person does not think his/her vote will be counted, why bother to vote? Voting is a learned behavior, where people over time become increasingly habituated to voting.[56] While it is likely that VBM reforms are going to continue being adopted, the needs of reservation populations will need to be considered, as the court required in San Juan County, Utah.

Felony Disenfranchisement

The impact of felony disenfranchisement laws on African Americans is well known, but the effect on Native Americans has not been examined.[57] Data on incarceration rates can be used to get a general sense of the impact of these laws. Native Americans have the highest incarceration rate of any population, as well as the highest rate of being under correctional supervision (Woodard 2018: 150).[58] Among the thirteen states (Alabama, Arizona, Delaware, Florida, Iowa, Kentucky, Mississippi, Nebraska, Nevada, Tennessee, Virginia, Wisconsin, and Wyoming) with the harshest form of felony disenfranchisement (i.e., those where at least some felons are permanently banned from voting), five have substantial Native populations that are overrepresented in the prison system.[59] In those states, Native incarceration rates are 2.2 to 6.3 times greater than among whites.[60]

But more than three-quarters of all felony-disenfranchised people in the United States are back in the community, either under probation/parole and temporarily unable to vote or permanently barred from voting (Sentencing Project 2018: 7). There is substantial variation between states in terms of how easy it is for felons to regain the vote. In Wyoming, a state with a high level of Native incarceration, only first-time offenders convicted of a nonviolent felony can get the right to vote restored, but they must wait until five years after the completion of their sentence.[61] Arizona, another state with a high Native prison population, allows first-time offenders to automatically regain the right to vote after completing their sentence and paying any fines.[62] Repeat offenders who have completed their sentence, parole, and probation and have paid fines must then wait an additional five years before they can ask a judge to restore them to the voting rolls. Judges have complete discretion over whether to grant such requests.[63]

Although the Supreme Court ruled in *Richardson v. Ramirez* (1974) that felony disenfranchisement does not violate the Fourteenth Amendment,[64] the administration of laws can be litigated, as occurred in *Janis v. Nelson* (2009). South Dakota law allowed felons on probation to vote, but when two Lakota probationers attempted to vote, election officials refused to allow them to do so. The state legislature then changed the law to disenfranchise all people convicted of felony offenses in either state or federal court. Only after serving their entire term of incarceration, parole, and probation can felons regain the vote in South Dakota.[65]

Although these laws are written in racially neutral language, there was a rapid increase in their adoption, which coincided with voting rights litigation following the passage of the VRA.[66] Whether aimed as decreasing minority voting or not, the laws have a disparate impact. For example, South Dakota's Native incarceration rate is 5.08 times greater than that for whites (Wagner 2014). Although now a reliably Republican state, until recently South Dakota had a history of also electing Democrats. Current battleground states such as Arizona, Nevada, and Wisconsin also have extremely high rates of Native American incarceration; one has to wonder about the electoral implications.[67]

Summary

The focus in this chapter has been on providing a framework for understanding the more subtle forms of second-generation voting rights discrimination resulting from laws and electoral procedures that dilute, suppress, and abridge the electoral clout of Native populations. The issues raised in litigation involving at-large elections, malapportionment, and redistricting plans that "crack" or "pack" minorities closely mirror those commonly raised in cases involving African American and Latino populations. Although other minority populations may be impacted by the VRA's minority language provisions, strict voter identification requirements, and travel distance to polling sites, there are aspects of each of these that uniquely disadvantage Native populations. Evidence of the unique barriers faced by Native populations can be seen from the development of "abridgment" as a new legal standard in *Sanchez v. Cegavske* (2016). Several of these factors come into play when one also considers potential reforms, such as all voting-by-mail elections and abolishing felony disenfranchisement.

CHAPTER 5

A Case Study of Jackson County, South Dakota

Introduction

Jackson County is a place that very few people have ever considered worthy of note, even though many have perhaps unknowingly traversed it. Every summer, millions of people travel to South Dakota, whether to view the breathtaking beauty of the Black Hills or to gaze upon the visages of presidents carved into Mount Rushmore, or perhaps to attend Sturgis's annual gathering of bikers. Almost none stop in Jackson County, a 1,871-square-mile tract of land located in the middle of the continent. The South Dakota AAA guide does not include any references to the county. Visitors speed along Interstate 90, which goes through the northern portion of Jackson County. Occasionally an adventurous person will wander off the freeway. What they glimpse is a snapshot of early twenty-first-century rural America. There are huge stretches of grassland, some with cattle, fields of wheat, corn, and hay or grass for feed, and towns with a few small stores where locals purchase livestock feed or buy groceries interspersed among vacant buildings that feel as though they have been shuttered for decades. Despite the obvious signs of economic distress, the county was able to spend thousands of dollars in the *Poor Bear v. County of Jackson County* (2015) case described in the previous chapter.

Yet 175 years ago, present-day Jackson County was the heart of one of North America's great empires. The Great Sioux Nation—which was composed of seven tribes whose people spoke the Siouan language, shared family ties, and had similar cultural values (Chomsky 1990: 15)—had a territory that stretched from Minnesota through the Dakotas to the Yellowstone River and into Nebraska.[1] The Dakota were dominant in the east. The Lakota, some of whose descendants still live in present-day Jackson County, were dominant in the west. The 1851 Fort Laramie Treaty, an agreement between the United States and a number of Native Nations, committed the U.S. government to halting all incursions into Lakota lands. Different bands of Dakota, living in what is now Minnesota, signed two land cessation treaties in 1851 (the Treaty of Medota and the Treaty of Traverse Des Sioux) and another in 1858 that ceded the remaining lands on the Minnesota River in exchange for annuity payments.

Treaty Violations and Armed Conflict

In the east, the Dakota's promised regular annuity payments from the federal government were often late. In 1862, when late payments left the Dakota facing starvation, some whites suggested they should "eat grass." This was one of several events leading to the Great Sioux Uprising, after which Congress passed the Forfeiture Act, which took the Dakota's lands and banished them to Nebraska and parts of South Dakota.[2] In the west, thousands of miners were taking the Bozeman Trail, cutting through Lakota territory and threatening hunting grounds.[3] The U.S. military constructed forts along the Bozeman Trail, including one in the sacred Black Hills (Paha Sapa in Siouan).[4] These actions precipitated Red Cloud's War of 1866–1868, which ended when the military withdrew and the Lakota burned the forts abandoned by the military.[5]

The subsequent 1868 Fort Laramie Treaty promised the Sioux an inviolate territory running from the Missouri River in the east to the Big Horns in the west and going from the 46th parallel in the north to Nebraska in the south. The Sioux territory included all of the Black Hills, but only a few years later in 1874 the 7th Calvary, under George Armstrong Custer, discovered gold in the Black Hills and the U.S. government began pressuring the Sioux to give up the Black Hills. When the Sioux refused to give up the Black Hills, Custer was ordered to subdue the "hostile Sioux" (Brown 1971: 268–272).[6] The ensuing war lasted six years, but the most famous battle—one often reenacted in white towns—is Custer's 1876 last stand at Little Big Horn. Congress responded to Custer's defeat by removing seven million acres from the Great Sioux Reservation.[7] Sporadic fighting continued until the 1890 Wounded Knee Massacre, where roughly 350 mostly unarmed and nonbelligerent Lakota were killed by the 7th Calvary. The Great Sioux Reservation subsequently was broken up into nine geographically dispersed reservations (Massey 2015a: 6).

The Wounded Knee Massacre site is just past the western edge of Jackson County. While whites honor Custer's memory, Lakota remember relatives dying in the snow at Wounded Knee. It also was the site of the seventy-one-day standoff between the American Indian Movement and federal law enforcement officers.[8] Twenty medals of honor were awarded to members of the 7th Cavalry who participated in the massacre.[9] One hundred years later, the 101st Congress passed a resolution expressing contrition for the massacre and a movement was launched calling for the medals to be rescinded—a move that is gaining increased support (Hayoun 2019; Hill 2013). In 2000, a state government body concluded the Wounded Knee Massacre had "poisoned the relations between the Sioux and whites for generations to come" (South Dakota Advisory Committee 2000: 4). This is the history that continues to shape white-Sioux interactions and serves as backdrop to conflicts over voting.[10]

A Snapshot of the County

Jackson County, which begins approximately 100 miles east of Rapid City, is split by the White River, with the eastern portion of the Pine Ridge Reservation occupying the land south of the river. That area used to be Washabaugh County, but in 1983 it was merged into all-white Jackson County.[11] County government offices, as well as nearly all businesses, are located off-reservation north of the river. Less than 200 Native Americans live off-reservation, and less than 125 whites live on the reservation. Most of the latter have ranches in the extreme southeastern part of the county.[12] The high degree of geographic segregation makes it possible for the two populations to largely avoid interacting with each other.

Scholars have found that levels of prejudice are inversely related to social contact among groups.[13] Sociologist Garth Massey, who spent time in Jackson County doing research for his expert witness report in *Poor Bear v. Jackson County* (2015), noted that people in the county go out of their way to avoid interacting with people not of their race, even when it means traveling further to carry out everyday tasks.[14] Despite some exceptions, Massey (2015a: 8) concluded that "the two groups live worlds apart."

Voting Practices

South Dakota law allows voters to cast their ballots at a precinct polling place on Election Day or to vote by absentee ballot.[15] The county auditor mails absentee ballots out forty-five days prior to Election Day. Late registrants can get absentee ballots from the county auditor until 3:00 on Election Day. These ballots must be returned to the county auditor's office. The auditor must receive absentee ballots with enough time to deliver them to the polling place before the polls close on Election Day.[16]

In-person late voter registration, which ends fifteen days prior to Election Day, is done at the county auditor's office. People can vote by absentee ballot then or return the ballot to the auditor's office at a later time. While it is easy for people in the northern part of Jackson County to register and cast an in-person absentee ballot, it is much harder for individuals on the reservation to travel to the auditor's office, which is in the Kadoka courthouse.

When absentee in-person ballots are turned in on Election Day, the county auditor determines whether there is enough time to get the ballots to polling places. If she decides there is not enough time, the ballots are not counted. Polling places for Kadoka residents are in the basement of the courthouse, but the reservation polling places are twenty-eight to forty-six miles away.

Voting Rights Activism

Native Americans in South Dakota have been at the forefront of voting rights struggles for more than four decades. Important first-generation vote denial cases from the 1970s and early 1980s involved people from South Dakota reservations. More recent struggles have focused on second-generation issues of vote dilution and suppression. After voters in the Shannon County part of the Pine Ridge Reservation secured satellite registration and voting through the *Brooks v. Gant* (2012) settlement, activists on the Jackson County side requested a late registration/early voting satellite for their part of the reservation.[17] The county refused, citing financial cost, even though funding through the Help America Vote Act had been preapproved (Woodard 2014), leading to the *Poor Bear v. County of Jackson* (2015) lawsuit.

Data Collection and Methodology

In summer 2014, I took a team of graduate students to Jackson County to study the impact of travel distances on the ability of people to register and vote. We also examined the "totality of circumstances" that affect Native American electoral participation.[18] Students were divided into groups; each group was responsible for different aspects of the project.[19] Geographic Information Systems (GIS) software was used to identify population concentrations and to analyze travel times and distances. The 2010 U.S. Census and American Community Survey (ACS) results for 2008–2012 provided economic and sociodemographic data. Our survey, which we administered to voting-age residents, included questions about how travel distance affected people's ability to engage in daily activities, such as shopping, and their ability to vote. There were no questions about racial attitudes, partisanship, or voting preferences, although many people volunteered comments about these topics.[20] We felt that including those questions would have made it much more difficult to obtain a representative sample and would potentially introduce bias into our results.[21]

We traveled to virtually every community: Wanblee, Kadoka, Potato Creek, Long Valley, Interior, Cottonwood, Cactus Flats, Belvidere, and Stamford. Surveys were administered in public places (e.g., outside of grocery stores, post offices, gas stations, a hardware store, and a café). Most people on reservations do not have street addresses, many lack telephones, and a significant part of the population is homeless, which made this the only feasible way to do a survey.[22] We surveyed 9 percent of the county's voting-age population, for a total of 177 people (85 whites, 83 Native Americans, and 9 mixed race/other). We analyzed only the first two groups.

Key Census Data

Census data provide a snapshot of the county's inhabitants, as well as aggregate differences between the two populations.

- Nearly all (96.5 percent) of the white population ages 25 and over have a high school diploma, compared to just 69.7 percent of the Native American population ages 25 and older.[23]

- Among the white population, the unemployment rate is 1.4 percent, but for the Native American population this number climbs to 44.2 percent.[24]
- The median household income for white households is $51,850, compared to $25,430 for Native American households.[25]
- Only 1.5 percent of the white population receives food stamps or SNAP benefits, compared to 75.1 percent of the Native American population.[26]
- The per capita income for whites was reported as $23,072 in the 2010 ACS, while Native Americans reported an unbelievably low $5,725.[27]
- In 2010, 7.5 percent of white families and 11.5 percent of white individuals reported incomes below the poverty line; 42.1 percent of Native American families and 52.9 percent of Native American individuals reported incomes below the poverty line in the same year.[28]
- Among the white population, 6.8 percent lacked health insurance as compared to 36.9 percent of the Native American population.[29]

In 1982 the Senate Judiciary Committee identified three key factors—inadequate education, lack of employment, and poor health—as arising from past discrimination and that tend to depress political participation.[30] The Supreme Court in *Thornburg v. Gingles* (1986) found a strong link between these effects of past discrimination and decreased electoral participation.[31] Native Americans in Jackson County have all of the factors identified by the Senate Judiciary Committee in its report.

Geographic Information System Findings

Jackson County's most substantial roadway is Interstate 90, which cuts across the northern half of the state. Along the freeway, access to businesses is infrequent but sufficient. Most of the off-reservation population live near Kadoka (population 654), which has a post office, hardware/feed store, grocery store, high school, library, and tavern, as well as government offices. The other northern townships have populations in the double digits or less and are located along Interstate 90. Interior, just outside of the Pine Ridge Reservation and the Badlands National Park, has two restaurants, a convenience store, and a post office. All roads leading into Interior are paved and well-traveled. Belvidere is accessible by paved road, approximately one mile south of Interstate 90. From the south, the unpaved SD 63 bisects Belvidere. Cottonwood, with nine residents, is accessible by the paved 14 freeway and other roads.

Road quality on the reservation is similar, with main roads bisecting the reservation and minor, unpaved roads serving low-population communities. BIA roads 44 and 73 run from east to west and from north to south, respectively. The county's largest town, Wanblee (population 725), has a small grocery store, service station, post office, and school. Long Valley (population 229), where nearly all of the whites live, is off BIA 73. It has a school, convenience store, and post office. Potato Creek, located just off BIA 44 to the west of Wanblee, includes a cluster of rundown homes off dirt roads with no discernable services. Hisle, Lost Dog, and Eagle Nest are even less populated and accessed via poor-quality roads.[32]

There are few services on the reservation. The reality of daily travel on unpaved roads and the effect on gas mileage and vehicle wear are notable, but access during the summer was acceptable. Interviewees stated that road maintenance and snow plowing were ongoing issues. A tribal police officer spoke at length about conflicts between state, county, and tribal governments over which of them is responsible for road maintenance. Several interviewees stated that the road connecting Kyle (in Oglala Lakota County) to Potato Creek was rarely plowed, which raises concerns about travel, especially in the winter.

Differential Impact of Travel Distances

As is common in rural areas, many Jackson County residents have to travel substantial distances in order to shop, visit doctors, and go to work or school. While travel distance affects all residents, Native Americans are less able to bear travel costs. Their per capita income is approximately one-quarter of the per capita income of whites. While a person with a monthly income of just under $2,000 (the white per capita income) may complain about the price of gasoline, the adverse impact is much greater for the typical Native American whose monthly income is less than $500. The average price of gasoline just prior to the 2012 elections was $3.865 (Johnson 2012). Given that the average gas tank holds 16 gallons of fuel, the price of a fill-up is $62 or roughly 13 percent of the average monthly income for a Native American.

Travel distance affects electoral participation.[33] To utilize late registration and early voting procedures, people must travel to the auditor's office in Kadoka. Two-thirds of off-reservation residents live in the Kadoka Census Bureau subdivision and, according to GIS satellite mapping, are clustered close to the center of town. Some off-reservation people do face travel distance barriers. The 9 residents of Cottonwood live 37 miles from Kadoka, and the 94 residents of Interior are 31 miles away. The difference is that everyone on the reservation is a substantial distance from Kadoka. Among the reservation communities, Wanblee (population 725) is the closest (28 miles away). The next closest at 29 miles away is Long Valley, where most of the white population lives. Potato Creek and Hisle are 46 and 57 miles, respectively, from Kadoka.

A rough estimate of the financial cost of traveling to the auditor's office can be calculated. While it is impossible to know the average gas mileage for the vehicles driven in Jackson County, the Ford F-Series truck topped the lists of best-selling new and used vehicles in 2012 (Neff 2013). The average gas mileage for new 2012 F-Series trucks ranges from 12 to 19 miles per gallon (United States Department of Energy 2012). If one picks the middle of that range (15.5 miles per gallon) and uses it to calculate the round-trip gasoline cost of traveling from reservation locations to the county courthouse, the cost ranges from a low of $14 for people living in Wanblee to a high of $28 for those living in Hisle. For middle-income Americans, the cost of these trips might be an annoyance, but for people whose average monthly income is less than $500, the opportunity cost is considerable.[34] This, of course, assumes they have access to vehicles.

Postal Services and Absentee Voting by Mail

Since absentee voting by mail has been suggested as a way for rural residents to overcome the travel distance barrier (Dyck and Gimpel 2005: 539), we examined postal services in the county. There is limited residential mail delivery, so people use post office boxes, which have an annual cost of $86.[35] While neither traveling to the post office nor paying the fee for a box is an obstacle for most Americans, it is a barrier for poor people.[36]

There are two off-reservation post offices in Belvidere and Kadoka and two on-reservation in Long Valley and Wanblee. The reservation post offices, as well as the one in Belvidere, provide limited services and have limited hours. The Kadoka post office has twenty-four-hour access to post office boxes. The irony is that Kadoka residents, who do not face the travel distance barrier, have the best mail service.[37]

Requests for absentee voting require the submission of photocopied identification documents with a picture or a notarized statement that the person has verified under oath that everything in the application is accurate. While notaries cannot charge for this service, they can charge for traveling to notarize the request. There are no notary services on the reservation. Taken together, these facts make it unlikely that many Native Americans will use absentee voting by mail.

Survey Responses

We were able to survey people from Kadoka, Wanblee, Interior, Cottonwood, Belvidere, Potato Creek, Hisle, Long Valley, Eagle Nest, and East Pass Creek. The characteristics of these communities never varied more than 5 percent from the Census Bureau population parameters.[38]

Travel to the County Seat

The question about the frequency of trips to Kadoka garnered very different responses among the two populations: whites generally visited the county seat every day, but few Native Americans did the same. A large portion (39.8 percent) of Native Americans said they had not gone there in the previous month (see Table 2).

Impact of Travel Distance

We also asked questions about how travel distances affected participation in typical activities: shopping, going to work/school, getting the mail, and voting. Respondents gave responses, using a 1–5 Likert scale, with 1 being not at all affected and 5 being affected a great deal. The responses in Table 3 show travel distance has a much greater negative impact on Native Americans than on whites. For every one of the activities, a large portion of Native

Table 2. Frequency of Visits to County Seat

How often did you visit Kadoka in the last 30 days?

	Frequency	*Percent*	*Cumulative*
Native			
Every day	9	10.84	10.84
A couple of times a week	13	15.66	26.50
Once a week	7	8.44	34.94
A couple of times a month	10	12.05	46.99
Once a month	11	13.25	60.24
Not in the last 30 days	33	39.76	100.00
Total	83	100.00	
White			
Every day	74	87.06	87.06
A couple of times a week	2	2.35	89.41
Once a week	1	1.18	90.59
A couple of times a month	2	2.35	92.94
Once a month	1	1.18	94.12
Not in the last 30 days	5	5.88	100.00
Total	85	100.00	

Americans said there was a substantial negative effect. More than a quarter (26.9 percent) of Native Americans said it has a great effect on their decision of whether to vote, while only 3.9 percent of whites gave that response.

Registration and Voting

When people are asked questions about socially desirable behaviors, there often is an issue of bias in that people overreport doing the behavior (Cahalan 1968; Loftus 1975). Researchers have found that overreporting of voting ranges from 11 percent to more than 50 percent, depending upon the population (Silver, Anderson, and Abramson 1986; Bernstein, Chadha, and Montjoy 2001; Cassell 2003). This is a concern in this study, since nearly all of our respondents (89.71 percent of whites and 85.5 percent of Native Americans) said they were registered to vote. Nearly all whites said they registered at the local courthouse as opposed to only 26 percent of Native Americans. The most common way in which people registered was through a voter registration drive.

Table 3. Effect of Travel Distance on Typical Activities

How much do travel distances affect your decision to engage in the following activities?

	1	*2*	*3*	*4*	*5*	*Total*
Shopping						
Native	21 (25.61%)	4 (4.88%)	8 (9.76%)	11 (13.41%)	38 (46.34%)	82
White	40 (47.06%)	9 (10.59%)	14 (16.47%)	9 (10.59%)	13 (15.29%)	85
Work/School						
Native	24 (35.29%)	4 (5.88%)	8 (11.76%)	9 (13.25%)	23 (33.82%)	68
White	52 (75.36%)	2 (2.90%)	6 (8.70%)	1 (1.45%)	8 (11.59%)	69
Voting						
Native	38 (48.72%)	9 (11.54%)	6 (7.69%)	4 (5.13%)	21 (26.92%)	78
White	62 (80.52%)	9 (11.68%)	3 (3.90%)	0	3 (3.90%)	77

Of whites registered in 2012, 90.1 percent recalled voting that year, but only 79.7 percent of Native Americans recalled voting. There is likely to be a significant bias in these responses. Precinct-level data from the 2012 elections showed turnout in white precincts ranged from 63.8 to 83 percent and turnout in Native American precincts was approximately 20 points lower.[39] The reported means of voting in 2012 are summarized in Table 4. It is notable that no Native Americans said they used some variant of absentee voting.

Qualitative Data

After completing the survey, respondents were asked to provide additional information relevant to the survey. A total of 110 respondents provided comments. We also spoke with tribal and county officials. The following sections summarize typical comments.

Table 4. Mode of Voting in the 2012 General Election

How did you vote in the 2012 general election?

	Frequency	*Percent*	*Cumulative*
Native			
At local polling place	50	100.00	100.00
Absentee by mail			
Delivered absentee			
Total	50	100.00	100.00
White			
At local polling place	63	90.00	90.00
Absentee by mail	5	7.14	97.14
Delivered absentee	2	2.86	100.00
Total	70	100.00	100.00

Gas Prices and Travel Distance

Travel distances negatively impact both white and Native communities. A Lakota woman stated she had to drive 80–90 miles to her job. A woman living in Potato Creek said she hitchhiked 15 miles each way to work. Another traveled 32 miles every day taking her children to a Head Start Program. An elderly white woman said it was hard to access doctors and shopping. A white minister spoke at length about how being able to order products from Amazon and have them delivered by FedEx was transforming shopping for rural Americans, without considering that people without street addresses (i.e., those living on the nearby reservation) could not get this service.

Nearly everyone complained about gasoline prices. People mentioned wanting to shop in major stores in Rapid City, but gas prices made it hard to do so. An elderly white woman stated that her fantasy was for "gas prices to go down." A Lakota woman said the price of gas made it hard to go to Wanblee for groceries, much less to places that were further away and had lower food prices. An elderly woman from Hisle said having a car is good but that "it's hard when you don't have enough money for gas."

Poverty and Lack of Resources

Although the average white resident has substantially more resources than the average Native American, many whites said that providing for their families was hard, given the lack of decent-paying jobs and economic development. Several middle-aged whites worried about young people leaving to find work outside of the county. Quite a few Lakota stated they had no means of support, and those who were employed talked about how far they had to travel to low-paying jobs. A couple of Lakota mentioned people who had frozen to death because they could not afford the price of heating fuel. Although whites complained about the cost of travel, none discussed the possibility of freezing to death in the winter.

Perceptions of Racial Animus

Although the survey had no questions about race, respondents talked about race a great deal. Some made overtly racial comments: a white man in Kadoka proudly stated that he was a "racist." Others were more subtle: a grocery clerk said that "Indians don't like whites" and then warned against traveling on the reservation. Another respondent stated that "white culture is best." One survey taker (a Latino) standing outside of the post office in Kadoka was confronted by a white man in a pickup truck. The driver poked his head out of the window and yelled, "Are you full Indian?" and then made derogatory comments about President Obama and pointed to an American flag decal on his window, stating, "This is the country we should support." The implication seemed to be that only whites are truly American.[40]

Many whites expressed fears of being attacked on the reservation. Quite a few stated concern for our safety when we said that we were going to do survey work across the entire county. Several older residents of Kadoka mentioned the 1973 Wounded Knee standoff as an example of anti-white violence. Others had more mixed feelings. An elderly white woman told us that it was really important to be nice to "all of God's people" but then went on to describe how when two Indians had come to her ranch, she had "pulled a shotgun on them, and they never bothered her again."

Tribal leaders described incidents of racial bias in Kadoka and other border towns. One said he had been called "Prairie Nigger" by whites. A tribal police officer told us that police in off-reservation towns racially profile cars with reservation license plates. One woman described Kadoka as a "racist" city where people look down on Indians "as if we are less than them." One elderly Lakota man said it would be difficult to register to vote in Kadoka. When asked why, he just said it was "an attitude thing." Several others, however, said they had never experienced racism in Kadoka.

Voting Registration and Turnout

The voting-age population in Jackson County is 2,125, with whites making up approximately 56 percent of that total. If we include children, Native Americans and mixed-race individuals comprise 57 percent of the total, which suggests that whites will soon be a minority of the voting-age population.[41] Since South Dakota has strict felony disenfranchisement laws, it is likely that some people of voting age legally cannot register and vote; those people are disproportionately going to be Native.

The county auditor's data for 2016 listed 1,965 people as registered to vote, but the secretary of state's website showed only 1,882 are registered.[42] I could not ascertain why these numbers were different. If the county auditor's figures are correct, the registration rate would be 92.5 percent, but if the secretary of state's figures are accurate, the rate would be 88.6 percent.[43] The sections that follow use data from both sources. Since the county auditor's list is used to determine whether a person is registered and qualified to vote, we used this list to compare registration levels across precincts. For turnout, we used the official secretary of state figures because those are the official vote totals.[44]

Voting Precincts

There are eight precincts (five off-reservation and three on-reservation). The off-reservation polling places labeled Precincts 1–5 are: Rangefield Station in Cottonwood, Interior School, Kadoka courthouse, Kadoka courthouse, and Fellowship Hall in Belvidere. The reservation polling places for Precincts 6, 7, and 8 are the Long Valley School, Crazy Horse School in Wanblee, and a private home in Potato Creek.[45]

There are fewer polling places on-reservation than off-reservation, even though Precinct 7 in Wanblee has more registered voters than the two Kadoka precincts. The county auditor cited the difficulty in finding qualified people to serve as poll watchers as a reason for not establishing a second Wanblee precinct.

Precinct Registration Numbers

In 2006 there were 1,006 registered voters in the five off-reservation precincts and 1,041 registered voters in the three reservation precincts. Ten years later, there were 971 registered voters in the off-reservation precincts

Table 5. Precinct-Level Changes in Registration, 2006–2016

Precinct	*Registered Voters in 2006*	*Registered Voters in 2016*	*Percent Change*
#1 Cottonwood Rangefield Station	58	60	+6.9%
#2 Interior School	179	169	−0.05%
#3 Kadoka Courthouse	387	359	−7.2%
#4 Kadoka Courthouse	260	251	−3.5%
#5 Belvidere Fellowship Hall	122	130	+6.6%
#6 Long Valley School	158	158	0%
#7 Crazy Horse School	697	672	−2.9%
#8 Potato Creek	186	164	−11.9%
Total	2,047	1,965	

versus 994 in the three reservation precincts. These numbers suggest that Native Americans were poised to control electoral outcomes, but that is not the case. Census Bureau data show that Long Valley (the Precinct 6 area) has mostly white residents.[46] In much of what follows the data from Precinct 6 are combined with data from the five off-reservation precincts.

From 2006 to 2016, the six predominantly white precincts had a drop of 3.2 percent compared with 5.3 percent in the two heavily Native American precincts. Given the Native population is younger, their numbers of registered voters would be expected to increase as each new age cohort reached voting age, while the white numbers would be expected to decrease as older voters died, but this did not occur (see Table 5).

The Removal of Voters from the Rolls

South Dakota law, as well as the 1993 National Voter Registration Act (NVRA), allows for the culling of voters. If a person fails to vote in two general federal elections, the local election official sends a prepaid, self-addressed return card asking the person to verify his current address. If the person fails to provide verification in the specified time period, he is removed from the list of eligible voters. While this provision appears to be racially neutral, there are two reasons why Native voters are more likely than whites to be removed. First, mail is more likely to be lost or displaced on the reservation. Second, it is a felony offense, punishable by a fine and up to five years in prison, to provide false addresses when registering. This creates a huge problem for individuals in unstable living situations, as is common on the reservation.

Voting Turnout in General Elections: 2008–2016

In the 2008 general election, the turnout rate among registered voters in off-reservation precincts (1–5) ranged from 68.5 to 86.5 percent with an overall average for those precincts of 81.5 percent. Among the three reservation precincts, there is a huge disparity between Precinct 6, which serves Long Valley, and Precincts 7 and 8, whose population base is almost entirely Native American. The turnout in Precinct 6 was 77 percent in 2008—roughly on par with the voting in the other heavily white precincts—but the turnout rates in Precincts 7 and 8 were 47 and 55 percent, respectively. This translates into Native precincts having turnout rates roughly 25 points lower than those of the white precincts.

In 2012, the pattern was similar with turnout rates ranging from 63.8 to 83 percent in Precincts 1–5, for an overall off-reservation rate of 74.8 percent. Precinct 6, with a turnout rate of 71.2 percent, again was an outlier among the reservation-based precincts. The turnout rates in Precincts 7 and 8 were 52.3 and 53 percent, respectively, roughly 20 points lower than those in the white precincts.

In 2016, the rates in Precincts 1–6 continued to be high, ranging from 70.6 to 78.3 percent, but the rate in the Native American precincts dropped significantly down to 39.6 percent in Precinct 7 and 41.3 percent in Precinct 8.[47] There was roughly a 35-point difference in turnout rates between the white and Native American precincts. One reason for the drop-off in Native voting is there was a large get-out-the-vote effort in 2012 and none in 2016.

The turnout rates in the county's Native precincts also were far below statewide averages. In 2008 the overall turnout in South Dakota was 73 percent, roughly on par with the rate in white Jackson County precincts. The same is true with respect to 2012 and 2016 when the overall South Dakota turnout rates were 69.7 and 69.6 percent, respectively, which is somewhat below the rate for the white Jackson County precincts but again far higher than that among the county's heavily Native American precincts.[48]

Voting Turnout in Off-Year Elections: 2010 and 2014

Turnout in off-year elections typically is lower than in presidential election years. In 2010, Precincts 1–5 had turnout rates ranging from 61.1 to 73.4

Table 6. Precinct-Level Turnout in General Elections, 2008–2016

Precinct	*Number of Voters and Turnout in 2008*	*Number of Voters and Turnout in 2012*	*Number of Voters and Turnout in 2016*
#1 Cottonwood Rangefield Station	45 (86.54%)	37 (63.79%)	43 (74.14%)
#2 Interior School	109 (68.55%)	112 (67.88%)	117 (73.13%)
#3 Kadoka Courthouse	292 (79.78%)	273 (82.98%)	259 (73.37%)
#4 Kadoka Courthouse	171 (78.44%)	155 (72.09%)	168 (70.59%)
#5 Belvidere Fellowship Hall	88 (81.48%)	81 (71.68%)	94 (78.33%)
#6 Long Valley School	111 (77.0%)	109 (71.24%)	119 (75.80%)
#7 Crazy Horse School	256 (47.0%)	284 (52.30%)	252 (39.62%)
#8 Potato Creek	76 (55.0%)	70 (53.03%)	66 (41.25%)
Total	1,148	1,121	1,118

percent, and Precinct 6 had a rate of 71.3 percent. Only 35 percent of the registered voters in Precinct 7 and 40.6 percent of those in Precinct 8 voted in 2010,[49] for a racial turnout differential of over 30 points. Again, as was true for the 2008 and 2012 statewide turnout figures, the turnout rates in the white precincts for 2010 were close to the statewide average of 62.3 percent, but the Native American precincts' turnout rates were much lower. For 2014, the white precincts had turnout figures ranging from 56.4 to 66.7 percent, but the two Native American precincts had turnout rates of 36.6 to 42.3 percent.

Concluding Thoughts

One can only speculate about what would happen if Native voters were as likely to turn out to vote as whites. At this point, Jackson County is one the

Table 7. Precinct-Level Turnout of Registered Voters in Off-Year Elections, 2010 and 2014

Precinct	*Number of Voters and Turnout in 2010*	*Number of Voters and Turnout in 2014*
#1 Cottonwood Rangefield	33 (61.11%)	35 (63.64%)
#2 Interior School	93 (56.36%)	88 (56.41%)
#3 Kadoka Courthouse	271 (73.44%)	217 (64.97%)
#4 Kadoka Courthouse	153 (67.70%)	143 (65.60%)
#5 Belvidere Fellowship Hall	75 (63.56%)	74 (66.67%)
#6 Long Valley School	107 (71.33%)	98 (64.05%)
#7 Crazy Horse School	182 (35.0%)	210 (36.59%)
#8 Potato Creek	56 (40.58%)	63 (42.28%)
Total	970	928

most heavily Republican counties in South Dakota. In 2016, 65.9 percent of county voters cast ballots for Donald Trump. That probably would not have happened if Native American turnout levels equaled white levels. In Oglala Lakota County, which includes the western part of the Pine Ridge Reservation, Donald Trump received only 8.3 percent of the vote; it is hard to imagine there are big partisan differences between the two parts of the reservation. While Jackson County would not switch from red to blue, it would certainly become a place where both parties would have to compete for votes.

This might mean that county officials would pay more attention to people on the reservation. County services, such as road repair and snow removal, might improve and there might be fewer complaints about racial profiling by the sheriff's department. When the county librarian was asked about the possibility of bringing books to the reservation, she said it had never occurred to her that they might want books—before noting she was struggling to keep the building's doors open and couldn't help Indians.[50] One can only hope that Massey's "two groups that live apart" will find ways to come together and address the very real needs in their county.

PART III

GRASSROOTS PERSPECTIVES

CHAPTER 6

Lawyers and Native Voting Rights

Introduction

The material in this chapter comes from in-depth interviews with four lawyers who have litigated many Native American voting rights cases. I used general questions about the trajectory of their lives as prompts, but those only served as starting points for their stories. The interviews were recorded and then transcribed. Copies of the transcriptions were sent to the interviewees so that they could correct errors or delete material they decided, upon reflection, to not make public. Their stories provided insights into two general topics: first, what led individuals who could have pursued much more lucrative areas of law to choose the nonlucrative field of voting rights work, and second, what are the opportunities and challenges involved in pursuing voting rights in Indian Country. Without prompting from me, each person explicitly framed the stories of their lives as being part of the broader narrative of this country's struggle over civil rights and social justice for all citizens.[1]

As Truesdell (2017) notes, oral history is "grounded in memory, and memory is a subjective instrument for recording the past." Given the inherent subjectivity of memory, scholars typically triangulate sources by comparing information from different interviewees and comparing material from interviews with information gathered using other methods (Creswell and Miller 2000; Golafshani 2003; Jasso-Aguilar 1999). The recollections of public events that figure in the stories collected here are consistent with materials available from public sources (e.g., court cases, newspaper accounts, etc.). Much less subject to verification are the unique experiences that led up to their choosing to become involved in the voting rights issue. But these provide much of the richness in the stories and illuminate the character of the lawyers, who have been at the forefront of many of the legal cases discussed in the earlier chapters.

Oral History: A Shared Process

According to Moyer (1999), people "organize their memories" into stories, but people's lives have many different facets, so interviews must start with an "understanding of the issues to be addressed" (Oral History Association 2009). It is a shared process where the person being interviewed is telling his/her story, which means it may go in unexpected directions.[2] These often provide new insights that had not previously been considered. Oral history allows one to view events from the perspective of grassroots participants as opposed to more elite commentators. According to Rogers (1988: 568), oral history is a "critical source" in researching social movements where written records often miss the individual and collective consciousness of grassroots activists.

It is, however, impossible to avoid subjectivity, starting with who is asked and then agrees to be interviewed. I was fortunate in that people generally were very willing to be interviewed. Many were extraordinarily gracious and went out of their way to welcome me. But obviously there were people I could not interview because I was unaware of them or lacked the resources needed to travel to where they were. I also made initial choices about what material to include and how to structure the flow of stories. In a limited number of places, I included transitional or clarifying language to make it easier to follow the flow of events. In keeping with the spirit of oral history as a shared process, drafts of the stories were sent back to the individuals. Nearly everyone made changes, often adding back in material that I had deleted to save space but that they considered important and sometimes changing phrases to better reflect their thinking.

The four stories that follow can be viewed as broadly being grouped into two categories. The first pair of stories are the recollections of two white southerners, Laughlin McDonald and Bryan Sells, who thought they would spend their careers litigating civil rights issues affecting African Americans but ended up discovering that the voting rights issues affecting Native Americans are just as compelling. Laughlin McDonald is arguably the *éminence grise* of voting rights litigation, having spent nearly a half century taking on these cases as an ACLU attorney. Bryan Sells has a more varied legal career, having been at both the ACLU and the Department of

Justice and now has a private legal practice—but always doing voting rights. Neither expected to be litigating Native voting rights cases but were shocked by the hostility to Native voting in many localities. The second pair of stories recount the life choices of two Native women, Patty Ferguson-Bohnee and Natalie Landreth. Both knew early on that they wanted to do Indian law, although not necessarily voting rights. But at this point, they are among the most well-respected lawyers working in the field. Ferguson-Bohnee was introduced to voting rights litigation while at a private firm and now is a law school professor. Landreth, on the other hand, moved from a private firm, whose caseload had nothing to do with voting rights, to the Native American Rights Fund.

Two Voting Rights Lawyers Discover Indian Country

Although Laughlin McDonald and Bryan Sells are both products of the South, their backgrounds are quite different. McDonald came of age during segregation and was appalled by the racial caste system in the Deep South, while Sells is a product of the New South. He was born after the passage of the Voting Rights Act and grew up in Virginia, just outside of the Washington, D.C., Beltway, and much of his awareness of racial inequality was developed through his studies of history and social psychology.

Laughlin McDonald

> I was born on August 25, 1938, in Winnsboro, South Carolina. That's a historic town just north of Columbia in the Piedmont section. The town has the oldest striking town clock east of the Mississippi River. It also has things that were designed by the guy who did the Washington Monument. Prior to the Civil War, 65 percent of the county's population was slave. As a child, I realized that the community was really divided in three different ways, not just between black and white. There was the black community and the white community, but the white community was divided into two groups. The people who worked in the cotton mills were white people but were regarded by the townspeople as "potackies," white trash, rednecks. The townspeople thought they were superior to both the "potackies" and the blacks.

The people who lived in town thought they were aristocratic people, but they mainly were just the offspring of people who came from England, Ireland, and Scotland. This was true of my family. My father was Thomas Ketchen Elliot McDonald. My mother was a Davis from Clarendon County, South Carolina. The Davis family has been one of the biggest slave owners in Clarendon County. I never talked to my mother about slave ownership and I have no idea whether her close family owned slaves, but she was part of that family. My mother was a bright woman. She went off to college when she was sixteen years old and graduated from college when she was eighteen years old and then came to Winnsboro where she taught in the public schools. In Winnsboro, she met my father, who was a lawyer, and they had a relationship of some kind and ultimately got married.

I grew up in a house that was built in the 1880s and had four large rooms downstairs with a big hall going all the way from the front to the back so you can open up the doors, and then on top of that were four more huge rooms. I was born in the house. In fact, there were four of us children and we were all born in that house. The house was just on the outskirts of town, so it was still a rural kind of place. During the summer, I'd spend most of my time in the woods looking at the river and hiking around. Growing up, one of my favorite poets was William Wordsworth because he looked at nature as being a spiritual thing and I also looked at nature as a spiritual thing.

My father was deeply committed to racial segregation. While he was alive, no black people ever, ever came into our house, except those who were servants or people coming to do work. I remember one Saturday afternoon when I was six or seven years old. I was in the living room and heard knocking at the front door. I opened the front door and there was no one there so I looked out and there was this black guy standing outside the house. He had his hands and his hat in front of him and he said, "I'd like to see Mr. McDonald," and I said, "Just a moment, let me see if he can see you." I said, "Daddy, there's this black guy out here to see you." "Tell him to come outside around the back of the house." My father went outside because no black person ever came into the house unless they were a servant while my father was alive.

My father was on the State Board of Corrections and occasionally I would drive down with him to Columbia when he had board meetings. I would listen while he interviewed people seeking to be paroled. He was committed to the prisoners being racially segregated. My mother didn't oppose my father on racial segregation. But when my father passed away, things changed. My mother was appointed as the first woman to serve on the board responsible for social interest funding and the first woman to chair a state committee. This was in the late 1950s. There were blacks on that committee and they would come have dinner with us at our house. My mother was pretty progressive and very bright and very talented. I think that she became a little bit more herself after my father passed away.

So, anyway, I grew up in a totally racially segregated environment, as well as one with class divisions among whites. The schools were totally racially segregated. The mill kids went to grammar school in the mill village and then they were bused to high school in Winnsboro. The only real relationship the town people and the mill people had as kids was in high school. It wasn't socially. I had some friends who were from the mill village, but that was very unusual. The town kids would stay together and the mill kids would stay together except for when they went to school at the high school. They did get together on sports teams. Football was a big thing and basketball was a big thing. Me, I started the tennis team.

There were so many things that happened growing up that demonstrated to me that race was unfair, just hundreds of things. I was in high school when *Brown v. Board of Education* was decided in 1954, and I guess a year or two after that one of my teachers said, "I'd like to have a mock court on *Brown v. Board of Education* and who would like to represent the counties sued." And almost every hand went up in the senior class, and then, "Who would like to represent the plaintiffs that brought the lawsuits," and I raised my hand and that was it. And so, we had to read *Brown v. Board of Education* and a couple days later we had the debate. I got up and delivered my part, and the people representing the counties delivered their part, and after that we had to get up and go to a different class. As we were leaving the classroom, the teacher came up to me and said, "I just wanted to let you know that you did a very good job even though I know you didn't believe a single word that you said."

Growing up, it wasn't a question of being on the road to Damascus when understanding about the evils of racism dropped down from the sky. It was cumulative, just the experience I had growing up with racism and coming to understand how unfair it was. The first experience I had was when I was four or five years old. I went horseback riding with a friend who was several years older than me. We'd hooked up my parents' horse and the older boy was in front and I was in the back so I could hold on to him and we'd ridden around the neighborhoods. I knew we were racially segregated, but still there were some places that had these shacks that blacks lived in. When we rode by one of those, my friend said, "Look at that naked nigga over there," and it was a young negro boy with no clothes on, walking around the yard. We finished our ride and as it turns out, there was a couple from Pennsylvania visiting my family. The guy went to law school with my father in Columbia. When I came into the kitchen where they were all sitting down ready to have lunch, my mother said, "Well, how was your ride?" I said it was fine and we'd seen this "nekkid nigga boy." She said, "It's bad to use that word." Well, everybody used that word. Why is it bad to use that word now? It must be because these people from Pennsylvania are here. That was one of the first times when I realized that there was something wrong with the language and the attitude that whites took about blacks.

But, there was a constant stream of things. I'll give you one more example. When I was six or seven years old, my mother and I drove out to this place that was out in the country. It was a former slave plantation with small houses. We drove down to one house—they were all the same: two rooms, a kitchen and a sleeping room. And we picked up Mayzeta. She had just graduated from grammar school and wanted to go to high school. There was only one high school for blacks and that was in Winnsboro, but there were seven or eight high schools for whites that were all around the county. My mother said we'll make a deal with Mayzeta. She can come and live in our house and go to high school, but she'll have to be a servant. Mayzeta never had a meal with us, she cooked and cleaned up, she never sat in the living room, never met with us, never went with us to the movies, never did anything socially with the family. When she graduated from high school, my mother and I went to her graduation and afterward I asked her, "Where will you go to college?" because I knew how much learning meant to her. She just looked up and rolled her eyes and said, "We don't go to college." This was when I was like six or seven years old and that's when I realized there was something terribly wrong.

In high school, there were all these white guys who said they would go "nigger knocking," drive their cars through black neighborhoods and knock people in the head with bats. I'm not sure that they actually did that. So, I grew up knowing something was terribly wrong. And again, I saw this at a job I had. When I was sixteen or seventeen I got a job working at an ice and coal plant on Saturday during the school year and full time then during the summer. I got to know the blacks who worked there. The owner was a white guy and I was the manager, but everybody else was black. They drove trucks or worked in the ice houses. They became dear friends. When we weren't busy during the day, we'd sit on the ice house's porch and talk. We all made the same salary, $25 a week, and I said to myself, there's no way that black people can live on $25 a week.

When time came for me to go off to college, I applied to Columbia because I had read books written by people who taught there, I thought about Princeton because I had read books by people there, and I thought about the University of Chicago just because I thought it might be a different place. Anyway, I wrote to those places and got back their catalogs, but I applied only to Columbia University, and lo and behold I was accepted. When I got accepted I went to my high school English teacher, Miss Wiley, who had a doctorate but couldn't teach in college. I told her, "Miss Wiley, I got into Columbia." She said, "You don't need that, honey, that's a girl's school," and she was right, Columbia College, in Columbia, South Carolina. And I said, "No, no, the Columbia University in New York," so she walked away.

At Columbia, I was regarded as being bizarre because I wasn't from the Northeast. I think there were two of us from the South, one from Georgia and me from South Carolina. I grew up singing, so I joined the glee club and auditioned for the King's Men and got accepted. The senior member came up to me and said, "I just want you to know that one of our members is a black guy and I know that you're from South Carolina and I want to make sure you're not going to have a problem with that." So, I was thinking, why the hell would I come to Columbia if I have a problem like that? But I had really good teachers at Columbia. English was what I was really interested in. I just read constantly. My brother Tom was an English major, but I think I was just interested in literature.

I graduated from Columbia in 1964 with a degree in English and immediately got drafted into the army. I did basic training at Fort Jackson, South Carolina, before being sent to Fort Sill, Oklahoma, to do advanced training in the artillery. Then I got sent to Frankfurt, Germany, to serve in the artillery there. It was great being in Germany and being in the artillery. Then I decided to go to officer's candidate school. I thought they'd send me to the artillery, but they sent me to the infantry school, which was six months of the most demanding physical activity I've ever done. After getting my commission as a second lieutenant, I got sent to Washington state—Fort Lewis—and then my commander said, well, we're all being sent to Berlin.

So, we all went back to Berlin, where our task was to drive from Frankfurt to Berlin through East Germany to prove the right of NATO to cross Soviet-occupied territory. Funny as it seems, I was not scared at all. Maybe I should have been, but I was not scared at all. It was just our one small company that was being sent into East Germany. I was in the back, the last jeep driving across East Germany, and I just thought it was fascinating. When we finally got to Berlin, I was stunned to see the Germans there were waving American flags and cheering us, "Welcome!" They were shouting their pleasure and their great joy.

After getting out of the army, I went to law school. I think I was influenced by my father, but also I was not so much interested in being a teacher. I applied to Virginia, but my application was two weeks late, so I also applied to South Carolina, which accepted me even though I was late. I went there for the first year but decided to try to get back into UVA because South Carolina was still all-white back then. At the law school in South Carolina, I was having a conversation with this guy, who said, "You know I think it's terrible that they're desegregating these fraternities now." And I said, "But you're in a fraternity here and it is all white people. There are no blacks, so why is it a problem?" He said, "Well, what if we go to New York, or Pennsylvania, or some place and there'll be black people at the meetings there." That was one of the things that convinced me to go to apply again to UVA law school. I got accepted and that's where I spent my last two years of law school.

While I was in law school, I read in the newspaper that a six-thousand-acre place in Hilton Head had been purchased and they were going to open up a hotel and golf courses. I wrote them a letter saying that I can play the guitar and sing if you need somebody to sing in your bar. I got a response asking me to come down and audition. So, I drove down to Hilton Head and auditioned for the fifteen or twenty minutes and they decided to hire me. I worked there for two summers and when I graduated from law school, they hired me as a corporate attorney.

I didn't really decide to actually begin on doing civil rights work until after I had been at Hilton Head. During Saturday evenings, they had this black jazz group come up from Savannah and they would play. I would enjoy them very much and got to know them all. One Saturday evening, the guy who was the head of the band came up to me and said, "It's late, we got a lot of packing to do, we got a long way to drive, I was wondering if we could spend the night here." I went up to the manager and said these guys were wondering if they could spend the night here. This was now 1965, after the Civil Rights Act of 1964. He looked at me and said, "We don't let a nigger spend the night here," and so I went back to the guy and I said, "I'm sorry, but they won't let blacks spend the night here." The guy shook his head, packed up, and left.

I had heard that the American Civil Liberties Union was looking to hire a staff attorney. I didn't know exactly what they were, but I decided to follow up. The father of a friend of mine was a director of the Frogmore Institute, a place established after the Civil War to teach freed blacks how to read, write, and make a living. Its mission was still to help the black community. I arranged to go down there to play tennis at the time when this ACLU guy Chuck Morgan would be addressing an integrated meeting of high school newspaper editors. This was probably the only place in the state that would hold an integrated meeting at that time, so I went down and listened to Chuck speak. Afterward I told him I was interested in the job. But after that, I wrote to him, sent him my résumé, and then called on the phone. Finally one Sunday night around 11:00 I get this telephone call. "This is Chuck, how much are they paying you now? $9,000 a year? Well, I'll pay you $9,500." Anyway that's how I came to work for the ACLU.

I moved down to Atlanta and went to work at the ACLU. It was great work. The first case that I did anything on was *Washington v. Lee*, which was a lawsuit brought to desegregate prisons and jails in Alabama. So, here I was, a baby lawyer who had never been in a federal courtroom before, never participated in a trial, never had any part of a litigation at all. But Chuck Morgan couldn't go for this pre-trial conference before Judge Johnson, so I went down to Montgomery. I walked into the courthouse and was told to go into the court's chambers, so I went in, sat down, and in came the attorney general and his three staff members, deputy lawyers, and then Judge Johnson came in, so we all stood up. "Please sit down, introduce yourselves." "I'm Laughlin McDonald, your honor, I represent the plaintiffs." He turned to the other side and said, "Who are you all?" And then Judge Johnson turned to me and said, "As I understand the plaintiffs, the case, it is . . ." and then he outlined the entire case. I didn't have to say a word. And then he turned to the attorney general and said, "What's the state's case?" He folded up his arms, leaned back in his chair, and he made them present their case.

Judge Johnson was from Alabama, but he was very liberal, a very progressive guy. He asked me only one question. We said that racial segregation in prisons and jails violated the Thirteenth and Fourteenth Amendments and he said to me, "Do you really think that segregation in prisons and jails is a form of slavery that is prohibited by the Thirteenth Amendment?" And I said, "Well, your honor, we think it is a form of slavery that is prohibited by the Thirteenth Amendment and we'd like to keep that in our complaint, with all due respect." And he said, "We'll see about that." That was all that he asked me. I was convinced that either he thought this has got to be a baby lawyer or Chuck Morgan had called him on the phone and told him I had never been in court before. But anyway, that was my first case and we won it.

We argued that racial segregation in prisons and jails is in violation of the Fourteenth Amendment and *Brown v. Board of Education* applies. The state argued that the Fourteenth Amendment did not apply to prisoners and the court expressly rejected that argument and said the Fourteenth Amendment follows people convicted of crimes into prison and protects them against discriminatory treatment and requires the prisons and jails to be desegregated. We then filed a lawsuit challenging segregated jails and prisons in South Carolina, where my father was on the board, which meant he was named as a defendant. I called him and said, "Daddy, I just want to let you know that we're going to file this lawsuit challenging racial segregation in prisons and jails in South Carolina and the board of corrections and you will be necessary defendants." And I didn't know what he would say but he said, "Well, my career is just ending, yours is beginning so I'll just resign." I said, "Well, you can do whatever you want to but I'm not going to be representing the plaintiffs while you're going to be party," so he served out his term. After he resigned, I did get involved in the case. We entered into a consent agreement that desegregated the prisons, but there still were racially segregated road gangs in South Carolina.

People convicted of crimes were sent to work on these county road gangs. All of the prisoners on road gangs in Edgefield County were black, so we filed a lawsuit saying that they couldn't operate a road gang or a county lockup on a racially segregated basis. I called the county attorney and told him I'd like to come and talk to him and visit the road gang. We agreed that I would come at 1:00, but he made me wait about an hour and a half even though nobody was in his office. Then he said, "I just want to tell you one thing right now, that when you go down there you won't see any white people on road gangs because white people in Edgefield County don't commit crimes. It's only black people that commit crimes." I went down there and all the people on the road gangs were black. Then I went to the courthouse and asked to look at the criminal docket. It is a big, heavy thing that gives the names of all the people who were charged with a crime, their race, what the name of the offense was, whether they were convicted or not and, if so, their sentence and where they were sent. And indeed, I saw that there were a lot of white people who were tried and convicted of crimes, but none of them were ever sent to road gangs. At some point I told the county attorney what I had found. Anyway, we were able to enter into a consent agreement in which they agreed to desegregate their county road gang, but as soon as the order was entered, guess what the county did? It closed down the road gang. Rather than operate it on a racially desegregated basis, they refused to operate it at all. That tells you a lot about Edgefield County. It has one of the worst histories of racial discrimination in South Carolina.

Given everything, it is kind of amazing that I have never been threatened. I sometimes say to myself, "Why have I never been threatened?" because I read about people who had been threatened, never scared. Maybe because I was a McDonald and came from this old South Carolina family. I'm not really sure, but I never was threatened.

Also right from the beginning of my time at the ACLU, there were two general projects that we handled. One was Operation Southern Justice, designed to desegregate the instrumentality of justices in the South—things like the Alabama and South Carolina jail and prison desegregation cases. We had a lot of cases desegregating, grand and trial juries, law schools, and so on. The other project was called the Voting Rights Project, so that's how I got involved in voting rights. I honestly can't remember my first voting rights case. There were so many. In different ways, they were all memorable. Prior to 1980 we brought lawsuits challenging election practices that had a discriminatory effect. All you had to do was show effect, but in 1980 the Supreme Court ruled in *City of Mobile v. Bolden* that you had to establish that the purpose was discriminatory. That dried up the voting rights cases. None were brought up and the pending ones were dismissed. Then in 1982, Congress amended Section 2 of the Voting Rights Act, which provided that you could establish a violation when actions had discriminatory purposes or effects.

The first case that we got involved with on behalf of American Indians was *Windy Boy v. Bighorn County*. It was filed in 1984 on behalf of Crow and Northern Cheyenne Indians in Montana and we got a decision in 1986, finding that the at-large election system for the county commission diluted Indian votes and required them to adopt single-member districts, and then four weeks after that the Supreme Court decided its first case involving Section 2. We filed a lot of cases on behalf of blacks in the South and a lot of cases on behalf of American Indians in the West. This led to the Voting Rights Project becoming the central part of our work.

The *Windy Boy* case, which was the first ACLU litigation involving American Indian voting rights, came nearly twenty years after the ACLU was litigating voting rights cases involving blacks. The first case was actually filed by the legal director of the ACLU's state affiliate. He called me to see if I would be willing to get involved and help represent the plaintiffs. Anyway, I agreed to get involved and that was the beginning of the ACLU's real involvement with American Indian cases.

On a personal level, I had spent time in the West, including on reservations. I had read books about American Indians, so I was not ignorant about their problems. I knew their land was taken away and they were put on reservations. I knew that history so I was very pleased to be involved in this case. I'd previously been to Bighorn County in Montana, but I had never really had any real contact with tribal members. Through the case I became close friends with Janine Windy Boy, who was our lead plaintiff. She was one of the first Indians to get a Ph.D. and was president of the Crow Indian College. In working on the case, I got to meet and interview so many people. I spent hours talking with them. What's it like growing up here? What's your experience been? It was a way of learning more.

After winning the first case, I was pleased to file lawsuits on behalf of Indians in other states. Initially we filed lawsuits in five states. Progress has been made, but they still have so many problems. Government entities are closing down precincts in the Indian reservations. The people can't afford to get in their cars, or they don't own cars so they can't drive to polling places. If you have mail-in system, they don't have a post office box or they don't have cars to drive to the post office. And a lot of them are not English proficient, so if they get these mail-in ballots in English, they can't really read them. These are continuing, ongoing issues and we continue to be involved in cases with Alaska Natives and American Indians.

I think that first case was for me the most memorable. We got a big win and not only did we win, but we ended the system of elections whereby no Indian had ever been elected to political office—no school boards, no counties, no state, no nothing, ever in Montana. But after we won that lawsuit, an Indian got elected to a county commission for the first time in history. Now I think there are two or maybe three Indian members on the county commission. The sheriff is Indian. It's just terribly pleasing to me to know that you do this work and you not just win the lawsuit, but you can accomplish things for the people that you're representing. I saw Janine Windy Boy when there was a special program at the Montana ACLU affiliate. They gave me a little award and Janine was there. It was just so great seeing her. It's great being close to people, not being able to just visit the tribe, look at the history museum, but actually talk with them and learn about them. That process was repeated in all these suits. When you bring these suits forward, you actually have to talk to people and find out what it's like for them growing up in these places. That's been one of the great things.

There's still a lot to do, however. I would like to see Congress pass the Voting Rights Advancement Act, which would restore Section 5, but that's not going to happen as long as we have a Republican-dominated House and Senate and then there's President Trump. But I think we keep laying out our agenda, reintroduce the Advancement Act. And we need to take a stronger stand against racism, the KKK, and anti-Semitism. This is important for young people, not just those of us who have been around for many years. People have to be committed to racial equality and be opposed to these anti-Semitic and racist groups. They have to speak out against it.

I know we've seen things that were worse in the past, but this president is worse. He shifted the blame away from these white supremacist groups to other people in Charlottesville. I think the fact that somebody like him can get elected is a real condemnation of American voters. I am glad his approval ratings are down, but the fact that he got elected is very disturbing. How people in their right mind can vote for somebody like that. On the other hand, I find it encouraging that the ACLU is experiencing such an uptick in contributions and membership. That's very positive. I know the ACLU remains totally committed to equal opportunities for all people and enforcing the Constitution, so that's very positive. I find it very gratifying to be part of the ACLU.

Bryan Sells

I was born in 1971 in Alexandria, Virginia, a suburb of Washington, D.C. We lived there for the first three years of my life and then moved out to Loudoun County, Virginia, which was very rural back then. My parents moved out there so that they could have horses. My dad was a stockbroker at a brokerage firm in Leesburg. My mom was a stay-at-home mom for a while and then worked at my school. I think my childhood was pretty idyllic. I grew up on a horse farm, but there were houses nearby. Ours was one of the largest properties around. My friends would come over and we'd play football or soccer in the yard. I grew up on a dirt road and that means you can ride your bike all over the place, play without too much worry about the outside world. I guess you can't do that much nowadays, but that's how it was when I was growing up.

My parents instilled in me a well-developed sense of right and wrong, but they didn't talk about politics at all. Ford was the first president that I can remember, but I don't remember the 1976 campaign. I did know Jimmy Carter was elected president. Then I remember Reagan becoming president. I'm not sure I really paid any attention at all until 1988 when my high school did a mock Democratic national convention. To participate, I had to read up on politics. I was not old enough to vote at that time anyway, but I paid attention to a campaign for the first time.

I graduated in spring 1989 and started at Harvard in the fall. I was really captivated by psychology and ended up focusing on social psychology. Social psychology is really fascinating to me. One of the studies that really captivated my attention was Kenneth Clark's doll studies that were used during the *Brown v. Board of Education* case. I thought that was a very interesting use of psychology and doing something good for the world. Psychology has a lot of subdisciplines and I did a lot of social psych. At the time, there was an emerging field called social cognition, which applied cognitive psychology to social problems. Cognitive psychology is one of the more experimental subgenres of psychology. Researchers in cognitive psych try to get at the building blocks of the brain. It's almost neurology or neuropsychology.

A lot of cognitive psychology experiments involve looking at a computer and pressing buttons when you see words. In the field of social cognition, you're also often looking at a computer screen and pressing buttons when you see words about social concepts. A common finding was that stereotypes are primed. Let's say it says "black" on the screen; you might be primed for the word "poor" if that's part of the stereotype for black people, or lazy, or whatever the construct is in your head. For my senior thesis, I flipped the script a little bit and tried to determine whether people who are low on traditional prejudice scores had any priming of positive words, like "black and beautiful" or "black and proud." What I found is there is not a whole lot of positive association. It was a fun project.

I was big into social causes at Harvard. I worked a little bit at homeless shelters and then started a musical group, Harvard Musicians Against Homelessness. We put on benefit concerts. I can't carry a tune, so I played bass guitar and a little bit of keyboards. As I studied social psychology, I started getting more into race issues. Then I took a year off to work on the Clinton campaign. Clinton was the most charismatic politician we've had certainly in my lifetime. In the campaign, I was about as low down as you can get. They made me the volunteer coordinator in the Massachusetts headquarters of the Clinton campaign. I wrangled volunteers for the phone bank. We had volunteers who would come in and answer phones. My experiences in the campaign made me more of an activist. During that year, I had the opportunity to work with all different kinds of people. I lived in the south part of Boston, right on the edge between the South End that is white and Roxbury, which is black.

After graduation, I went back to Virginia and taught at a private school for a year. My title was "assistant to the headmaster." I did all kinds of stuff, but I ended up teaching a couple of courses, skills courses. I taught about racism and prejudice to sixth, seventh, and eighth graders. That was really interesting. First of all, kids at that age are incredibly perceptive and I was just constantly amazed at their observations of the world. That was really amazing. Parents were less amazing. Loudoun County, in general, is very politically diverse. It's kind of a purple county now, but has really red and really blue people. Obviously, there are some in the middle, but there are some very, very conservative people in Loudoun County. One family was absolutely livid that their child would be taught about race and racism and diversity. They thought that their child should be taught to be colorblind, but they said all sorts of disparaging things about black and brown people. Their son, however, was fine.

I had planned to be at the school for two years but decided to go to law school after one year. I don't really remember what my precise thinking was, aside from my being really inspired by the civil rights movement, particularly the lawyers who were a part of it—Thurgood Marshall, Charles Hamilton Houston, the whole list of them. At Harvard I took a class about the Warren Court from Mark Tushnet. He's a very famous law professor and he was fantastic. I thought that law was a good direction for me. From the beginning I wanted to do civil rights law.

I went to Columbia for law school. It was okay. Law school is not a fun experience. It's not supposed to be a fun experience. Columbia wasn't that hard edged, but there was a lot of studying, a lot of hard work. A lot of reading and a lot of boring stuff, like contracts. There was a really great civil procedure professor, Michael Dorf. There were a number of classes from adjunct faculty, which is one of the huge benefits of going to Columbia. I took a class from the legal director of the ACLU, Steve Shapiro, and a class from the legal director of the National Welfare Law Center. I took a class from the legal director of the NAACP's legal defense fund. All these guys taught classes at Columbia. Mostly I was at the library all the time, studying my ass off.

I got the opportunity to spend two spring breaks in New Orleans doing death penalty work and that was very fulfilling. It was meaningful, but it didn't entice me to do it for my career. I don't know if any of the men later got executed. The folks were on death row, but they weren't close to getting a warrant. I did little bits of research and writing and some jail visits. One guy was absolutely nuts. It's hard to imagine why he was on death row. He should've been in a mental hospital. We went to the Angola Prison, which was pretty impressive, and I don't necessarily mean that in a good way. Angola is in Louisiana and it's huge. It's a prison farm, just like the Parchman Farm in Mississippi. It really feels like a plantation because there are work gangs and almost all of them are African American. It's just a really bad place. We got a tour of the facility including the death chamber, and again, it was really impressive. I almost threw up, just the impact of it, totally wrenching my gut. It's a very vivid memory. But again, it didn't really whet my appetite to do that kind of law. I'm glad I had those experiences, but it's not what I ended up doing.

I wanted to do civil rights law. The hot topics in civil rights law at the time were voting rights and affirmative action. The Supreme Court had decided *Shaw v. Reno* in 1993 and *Miller v. Johnson* in 1995, which were voting discrimination cases. The Court also had just decided a major reverse discrimination case out of Colorado. Those were the two hot topics in civil rights at the time and I was mainly focused around those two areas.

During my two law school summers I worked at the ACLU Voting Rights Project in Atlanta. The story of how I got the job is that I was still dating my college girlfriend, who was a 2L at Michigan. She was on a journal called the *Michigan Journal of Race and Law*, which was putting on a conference while I was visiting. The keynote speaker at the conference dinner was Leon Higginbotham, who had written one of the books I read in a civil rights history class. I thought he was a tremendous figure and he looked like a tremendous figure, probably six-foot-five, James Earl Jones voice, sharp. At this dinner Higginbotham gets up at the podium and, as all good speakers do, he recognized dignitaries in the audience. One of the people Judge Higginbotham recognized was Laughlin McDonald from the ACLU. Judge Higginbotham said McDonald put together one of the finest records ever on voting rights and was a fantastic lawyer.

And I said to myself, wow, that's interesting; I better meet this Laughlin McDonald, so I went to his panel the following day. I don't remember exactly what the panel was about, but I'm sure it was about *Miller v. Johnson* and the whole line of cases. I think I said hello to him then. But shortly thereafter it came time to look for a summer job for 2L summer. I had a small stipend that Columbia gave to students who wanted to do public interest work. I wrote to Laughlin and said I saw you at this panel and I'm very interested in voting rights and I'd like to come down and work for you. Back then you wrote letters. He wrote back and said, "Yes." Not here's how you apply, not I'll set you up for an interview, just come on down to Atlanta. So, I spent my 2L summer at the ACLU working for Laughlin and I loved it. I loved Atlanta, I loved Laughlin.

Mainly I worked on a Montana case, *Old Person v. Cooney*. I thought I was coming down to Atlanta to do voting rights in the South, *Miller v. Johnson*, and I ended up spending my summer on Native American voting rights. I spent the summer listening to tapes of county commission meetings or redistricting commission meetings from Montana. Until I started working on the case, I had no idea at all that Native Americans face the same issues as African Americans in the South. It didn't take me long to figure that out. I was very familiar with Section 2 of the Voting Rights Act. It was a real eye-opener. On the tapes, there were white folks saying really awful things that they wouldn't get away with in Georgia, so that was shocking as well. I did some more of this work during my 3L summer, while studying for the bar.

I applied for various public interest fellowships for work after law school. The Skadden Fellowship is a very well-known one and there are a couple others. The way those fellowships work is you propose to do a project. I proposed a project dealing with Native American voting rights. This was in 1998. I'll never forget this. The director of the Skadden Fellowship program told me, "Bryan, voting rights is dead." She believed the *Shaw v. Reno* line of cases had killed voting rights or there wasn't anything to do with voting rights. "My funders on the Skadden committee, everybody reads the *New York Times*, they're savvy enough to know that voting rights is dead. Find something else to do." That's just a little bit of a tangent, but I ended up not getting a fellowship. I was trying to find a way to come back down to Atlanta to work with Laughlin.

I did end up getting a clerkship with a federal judge, Myron Thompson, in Montgomery, Alabama, for the year after graduation. One of the reasons why I applied to Myron Thompson was that he had virtually every voting case in Alabama on his docket. The short version of a complicated story is that these two voting rights advocates brought a challenge to the method of electing county commissioners in one county and then they basically expanded it to cover almost every county in the entire state. They brought it in the same court, almost like a class action kind of thing. Judge Thompson had all of these cases on his docket. He also had issued a huge number of very consequential voting decisions, all of which made working for him attractive to me.

During that year, I took the bar in Georgia because I knew I wanted to go to work for Laughlin and the ACLU. It wasn't a hard bar exam and the clerkship was great. There were a number of voting cases that I helped on and of course other kinds of cases as well. Being in Alabama for a year was something else, too. Montgomery is a really, really quiet town. It has a very suburban feel. But as a civil rights history buff, it was like being at the center of the universe. Literally where my desk was, my window looked out at the parking lot area where John Lewis got his head bashed in when he got off the bus as a Freedom Rider. When I was there, the Greyhound bus station, where he got beaten, hadn't yet been restored and my judge led the effort for it to be restored. Now it's a museum. Actually, where the buses pulled in was right underneath my window, so that was kind of cool. Within walking distance there's the Dexter Avenue Baptist Church and the Alabama state capitol where Martin Luther King gave the speech at the end of the Selma to Montgomery march. While I was in Alabama clerking, George Wallace died, Virginia Durr died, and Frank Johnson died and all three of those were major civil rights milestones so my year of clerking was just really steeped heavily in the civil rights movement. It was really fascinating.

I finished my clerkship without a job, but then one of Laughlin's attorneys had decided to leave, so a spot opened up and I applied. I don't remember if I was interviewed, but it took forever, absolutely forever for the job to come through. I stayed in Montgomery while I was searching for a job. But sometime that fall I got a job offer from the ACLU to go work for Laughlin. I moved to Atlanta on December 31, 1999, and I started four days later at the ACLU on the voting rights project.

My first big case was *Emory v. Hunt*, in South Dakota. It was District 28, I think, but it was Standing Rock and Cheyenne River reservations. The 1990 round of redistricting had created a single-member legislative district and then the legislature abolished it. We sued over getting it back and we won. Then I worked on a little case called *Bush v. Gore.* I also did some ballot access stuff in Virginia. The work was awesome. Well, it wasn't work because I loved it. Zero hours because it wasn't work. I was there without any family, so I put in a lot of hours.

I stayed at the ACLU for eleven years. It is hard to say what case was the most memorable. I had some good ones. Probably the most memorable was the *Bone Shirt* case. It was a big, big case and we had witnesses from both Pine Ridge and Rosebud, and we did a really—I think—good job of finding witnesses in the case and it played out very, very well in the courtroom. I think we had twenty witnesses. One of the significant issues in the case was whether the Pine Ridge Reservation was cohesive with the Rosebud Reservation. The state was arguing that they were not, so we put on a bunch of witnesses to show that they mostly were united. They may have had disagreements on some levels, but when it came to interfacing with the state, in particular with white people and white politics, they were more united than divided. They had similar experiences that they brought to bear on voting behavior.

As I think back on it, I met some great folks, some of whom I'm still friends with on Facebook. Just good people and there are obvious differences with their growing up on Pine Ridge and my experience. A lot of our witnesses were women, and I was struck over and over again how strong the women were in standing up for voting rights for other folks. We had some fantastic witnesses like Elsie Meeks and Charlotte Black Elk. Those two are just super impressive human beings and then we had just salt of the earth folks like Belva Black Lance as plaintiffs. Voting cases are all about numbers and maps, and we had that stuff down, but that particular case was about a lot more than numbers and maps. It was really about a common history of discrimination. How do you tell that story in the testimony of twenty people, and I think we did a really good job.

We spent a lot of time on the ground in South Dakota. Laughlin and I did a couple of trips where we just stayed and talked to people, interviewed folks, and asked who else should we contact. This is the kind of person we're looking for, just beating the bushes. It took a long time. I think we filed the case in 2001 and it didn't go to trial until 2004. This was a period of intense political activism in South Dakota. Things really heated up in 2003 and 2004.

Anyhow I was at the ACLU for eleven years. During that time I got married. My wife is a pediatrician. She started her own practice in 2006, just before the financial crisis hit. Up until that point I could have gone to other places, but opening her own practice set roots for us in Atlanta. The financial crisis impacted things at the ACLU. The Bernie Madoff scandal was part of the financial crisis and it wiped out a foundation called the Jett Fund, which was a big funder of the ACLU and specifically the Voting Rights Project. The ACLU was rocked by both the financial crisis and the Madoff thing. On January 21, 2009, we had our first round of layoffs. I don't know what percentage of folks were laid off, but one was the assistant director of the Voting Rights Project. This man had been at the ACLU for longer than I was alive and was Laughlin's number two guy. In February 2010 there was another round of layoffs. The legal director and the executive director came down to our office in Atlanta and said, "We wanted to let you know that we're not going to renew the lease for this office when it expires in 2013 and we're not going to guarantee you all jobs in New York and we wanted to give you as much advance notice as possible so you can act accordingly."

Around the same time, the Obama administration recruited me to move over to the Department of Justice voting section. The timing was good, so I left the ACLU and started as a manager in the DOJ's voting section in November 2010. When I took the job in D.C., I made it clear that I was going to commute from Atlanta. Initially I would be in the office basically full time, but after that I would tele-work from home in Atlanta. That was a bit of an exception because normally you have to come into the office regularly, so people only tele-work if they're only an hour or two drive from D.C. Things didn't work out that way. For the first two years, I was in the office full time and then I would try to fly home on the weekends. I just had a lot of litigation in 2011. There was three months when I didn't go home at all during that first year. My wife came up and she would see me when I came home at 11:00 on Saturday night. It got substantially better the next year, when I started working from home. I was able to be at home for four days a week. It changed my perspective a little bit. It felt more like Atlanta was home again rather than D.C.

At the Department of Justice, I supervised attorneys. We would open an investigation into some jurisdiction and attorneys would do most of the legwork on it. Then I would review their work and give them guidance on what to do. The amazing part was that I had the opportunity to work on some great cases and there's really nothing like getting up in front of the court and saying, "I'm Bryan Sells on behalf of the United States." Nobody gets to say that unless you work at the Department of Justice, so that was very cool. I learned some things and worked with some good people. But it wasn't all positive. I can't say too much about the negatives, but I'll say a couple things. The commute was very hard. What made it even harder was that there were large periods of time when we weren't doing as much as we could've been doing. It was very frustrating at times. I think we could've and should've done more.

At the Department of Justice, I spent most of my time on Texas redistricting. We had several trials. There was a Section 5 trial in D.C., when Section 5 still existed; that was in 2012. The Court found intentional racial discrimination in the drawing of the Texas House and congressional plans. Then after Section 5 was declared unconstitutional, we had to go to San Antonio and try the cases all over again under Section 2. There were two separate trials so we did a full week, more than a full week, of trial on each one. Those were hard but good. The redistricting plans were found to be defective in various ways.

I only did a little bit of work on Native voting while at the DOJ. We filed a number of "Statements of Interest," amicus briefs in cases such as the *Jackson County* and the *Wandering Medicine* cases. We weighed in, if you will. In both cases, we were rejecting the defendant's arguments. We weren't exactly saying the plaintiffs should win, but we were saying the defendant's arguments were no good. So, that was fun. Christmas Eve, December 24, 2015, was my last day at the Department of Justice. I was sick of the commute and I wanted to come home. I wasn't doing enough to make the commute worth it anymore.

Now, I am in solo practice in Atlanta. I took a few months off—not really off, but in stealth mode, set up my own practice and I launched it on March 7, 2016. It's been great. I love being home. It's gratifying that I've been busy. I'm doing the kind of work that I love. I'm only doing voting cases. One day maybe I'll branch out to other kinds of cases, but right now I've got a pretty full docket of voting cases. Currently I have six or seven cases. That's more than we did at the Department of Justice, where I had a team of twenty lawyers.

Even though I have a solo practice, I partner with other lawyers on the cases. Right now I'm working with Laughlin on a case in south Georgia. I have a team in virtually every case, either a local counsel or a co-counsel. Again, it is a much leaner operation than at the Department of Justice, but we get stuff done. I get paid if I win. There are fee-shifting statutes. The Voting Rights Act has a fee-shifting statute that says that a prevailing plaintiff gets fees from the defendant. It's a way Congress created an incentive for plaintiffs to bring the cases. And if I do ballot access cases, under Section 1983, there's a parallel fee-shifting statute. Sometime lawyers don't get paid when cases are settled. I've had some cases that settled, but they settled with fees. I have not yet been cheated out of a fee. I'm hoping not to be.

Despite the success I've had, I don't usually recommend that young people go into the legal field. The practice of law is changing and changing quickly. It's very hard to make it. Knock on wood, so far, this practice is working for me. The reason I'm able to make it is because I've put in fifteen years and become a nationally recognized expert in voting rights. I get cases referred to me. Someone starting out would have a hard time. Even though voting is now a hot issue, there are very few entry-level jobs in civil rights. It's hard. There are ways to have an impact on society, but I'm not sure being a lawyer is the best one nowadays. I had a lot of opportunities that no longer exist because of the transformation in the legal field and the economy. I hope people are inspired to make the world a better place and to realize there are still opportunities for doing that, but I'm not real enthusiastic about the legal profession right now.

I worry about voting rights. I could see myself getting put out of business by the Supreme Court. Really, we are one or two seats away from having five votes on the Court, from finding Section 2 unconstitutional. People used to say that Section 5 would never be held unconstitutional. I can totally see a world in which we don't have protections in the Voting Rights Act and I have a lot less to do. I just hope that the Court doesn't also wipe out the Fair Housing Act, the Fair Lending Act, all the other opportunities we have under the civil rights laws because then I'd really be out of luck. I am worried about that going forward, what that would look like for me and the country. If that doesn't happen, I think there are lots of opportunities for me to litigate under Section 2. The whole premise of my law firm, of my stepping out, is that there's work to be done. I felt that at the Department of Justice, we didn't bring many Section 2 cases, actually we brought zero while I was there. I started this practice with the belief that there are lots of cases out there. If there aren't I'm not going to survive. So, we'll see.

Two Lawyers with a Passion for Indian Law

Although the backgrounds of Patty Ferguson-Bohnee and Natalie Landreth are radically different, both focused on Indian law early on in their careers. Their commitment to the general field is rooted in their Native identities. But neither grew up on reservations, although Ferguson-Bohnee's family maintained strong cultural connections with their community, the Pointe-au-Chien. In contrast, Landreth grew up in the greater Los Angeles area and spent almost no time with her Chickasaw relatives as a child. As a member of a non–federally recognized Native Nation, Ferguson-Bohnee faced challenges in gaining access to programs designed to aid Native law students, but this did not deter her from her goals and she has played an important role in cases involving Native Nations in the Southwest. Landreth has been in the forefront of voting rights cases involving Alaska Natives, arguably the single most isolated group of people in the country.

Patty Ferguson-Bohnee

I am a member of the Pointe-au-Chien, a Bayou tribe. We are recognized by the state of Louisiana but do not have federal recognition. The lack of recognition impacts a lot of day-to-day issues, including subsistence fishing, protection of our land, and whether we have clean water. We are located in an area that has many environmental issues and the courts have decided not to adjudicate our land claims because we're not a federally recognized tribe. It also impacts education. Neither the state nor the federal government provided education to our people until the late 1960s. Before then, people from our tribe weren't allowed to go to high school. Nonrecognition impacts a whole bucket of fundamental human rights and it reduces our voice. We're also small, only around 750 people, which also affects our voice.

I was born and grew up in Louisiana but not in Pointe-au-Chien. I grew up a few hours away but spent a lot of time there. My family there are all fishermen of shrimp, oyster, or crab. My dad kept a small boat in Pointe-au-Chien. My parents took us to powwows and other cultural events. We lived in Zachery, a small town north of Baton Rouge. My dad worked as a clerk at the paper mill. It was a pretty stable job. My mom stayed at home and ran the four of us children around. I have a brother, an older sister, and a younger sister. We had chicken, sheep, geese, horses, and pigs, which meant we always had fresh food.

Even though I was born over twenty years after *Brown v. Board of Education*, our schools were just getting integrated when I started elementary school in 1981. We were the only Native kids in the school and realized right away that we were different when busing started. Older students on the bus started putting their hands over their mouths and making war whoops when they saw us. We were the only non-black students on the bus route.

I think the racial split in the district was about even, or maybe 60–40 with white and black kids. With integration, the white school became the elementary school and the black school became the high school. As elementary kids, we didn't see color. Some kids who played together in elementary school grew apart in high school. Teachers didn't know what bucket to put us in because you had the white or the black buckets in Louisiana. The teachers would say, "All white girls raise your hand," and all the white girls would raise their hand, "All white boys raise your hand," "All black girls raise your hand," and "Black boys raise your hand," and we wouldn't raise our hands so the teacher would get really mad because not everyone would raise their hands and the students would say, "Well, yeah." I would never make myself fit in a bucket.

My friends were a mixed group. I cheered with mostly white girls. I played basketball and ran track with mostly black girls. It was interesting. People saw me as race neutral. I think our class got along pretty well. As kids we didn't realize what was happening, that this integration was happening. I remember, though, one time a white girl in our class invited a black girl to have a sleepover, and that was not happening. Her dad did not approve. Kids don't understand this. But my friends crossed the color line and I didn't spend a lot of time worrying about racism.

I typically got along with everyone, but one incident sticks out in my mind. I went with a guy from my tribe to his homecoming dance. This guy was quite dark. When I was giving out my homecoming pictures, one of the guys in my class started saying, "You're a N lover" and other derogatory things. I said, "Well, what do you care, I can date whoever I want." I didn't even correct him and say he's not black, he's actually Indian. I was thinking, I'm not white, I'm not black, I can date whoever I want. There was a group of white female high school students who were hanging out with black football players. That was happening but not in public. Then, the principal told the football players it was not socially acceptable for them to date white girls. The story made the news and the principal was fired. Looking back now, there are a lot of things I didn't know at the time. The KKK was still around, but as kids we hadn't thought about those things. One of my friends, a white girl, was just talking to a black guy on the phone and her dad beat her. It was a very bad situation. When I saw her recently, I found that she had reconnected with the guy and they got married. Some of her family will not talk to her now.

I had some great teachers who really cared about the students. I always felt supported by the community. The teachers helped raise funds to pay my fees to attend cheerleading camp. At one point, a student club was planning a trip to D.C. The club was all African American except me, and all of the teachers were African American. The teachers knew my parents didn't have the money to send me, so they raised money for me to go. That was my first time being anywhere other than Houston or Mississippi. We went to Atlanta, where MLK's church was, and then we went to Washington, D.C. We went to Howard University and practiced track there. We met our congressman at the Capitol and experienced all kinds of things that I wouldn't have been exposed to without their support.

I participated in a lot of sports. Our school was seventh through twelfth grade, six or seven hundred kids in total, so when we ran track, we started varsity in seventh grade. There were some really good juniors and seniors who encouraged us. And the community encouraged us. In track, my specialty was 100-meter hurdles. I also participated in the long jump and triple jump. Sometimes, not by choice, I did the 4 x 100-meter relay. If the team needed it, I'd run the 4 x 4. I also played basketball. I wasn't the best, but I played forward. We had some growing pains, but after a couple of years we got pretty good.

Growing up in the country is really different. In Louisiana, during hurricane season, you can be without electricity for up to two weeks, but you're still going to school, you just adapt. Our parents raised us so that we could manage without going to the grocery store or relying on other people. My dad would shear the sheep and we would clean it and then Mom would put the wool on a big spinning wheel and make us clothes. One time, my parents said, "We're going to make lye soap today." I remember we poured or stirred and then cut the soap up. I don't really curse, but one day my neighbor and I were out back just saying bad words. My mom heard us and she washed our mouths out with that lye soap. When I was older, my mom washed my cousin's mouth with Dove soap and that didn't do anything. I said you need to get lye soap.

My mom's first language is French. Actually we speak Indian French, which is different from Parisian French and Cajun French. My grandma always spoke French, as did many in my family. When I was in Pointe-au-Chien, I learned if you want to eat, you have to be able to figure out "What are the words that I need to say in order to eat?" The French we speak is older seventeenth- and eighteenth-century French with Indian words in it. The word for raccoon is an Indian word, but mostly it's older French. The word for car is "char," which in Parisian French is "chariot." Because it's been spoken in isolated areas, our French has adapted differently. We just call it Indian French because it's unique to us.

During college, I had a Fulbright in France, where I was doing research on the history of French colonial relations with Louisiana Indians in the seventeenth and eighteenth centuries. My advisor wanted to check to make sure that I understood what I was reading. I had to show her what I had obtained from the archives and then translate the text. I was reading it, but one part was "char" and another part was "Les maringouins" so I said it was about a bunch of mosquitos and she asked, "How do you know this word!? That word doesn't exist anymore." I told her it exists down the Bayou in Louisiana. In Parisian French, mosquitos are now called "Les moustiques." I worry that we are going to lose the language if it's not reinforced other than when you go see your grandparents.

In high school, I started thinking about going to college. I only applied to schools that were trying to recruit me for track or basketball. Stanford wasn't recruiting me but I got something in the mail about their Indian program, so I applied. Then I got the acceptance from Stanford and that was a big "oh, my gosh." Some people made comments and questions like "Why do you have to go to school so far away, there are schools here, why California? There are gay people in California. They don't believe in God in California." People from Louisiana don't go that far away for college. The newspaper called the counselor to verify whether Stanford had really admitted me or whether it was Samford.

I went on a visit to Stanford and stayed with a host, who was Mississippi Choctaw. That made my parents feel good because some of my dad's family comes from there. But when I got my financial aid offer, it showed that I was going to have to take out $12,000 in loans. I couldn't comprehend being able to pay back that amount of money. At the end of the day, I took the opportunity. Now I realize it is not that much money in the larger scheme of things, but I really worried about paying back my loans. My parents had to pay for my food, which was around $1,000 per quarter so I didn't know how we were going to do that. But, I'm glad I did it.

At Stanford, I got to meet Native students from across the country. My first year I lived in the Indian-themed house called Muwekma; it's named after the Muwekma Ohlone tribe. There were six freshmen and a bunch of older students. The three of us girls shared a room. One of my roommates was from Blackfeet and the other was from Leech in Minnesota. I'm still pretty good friends with my classmates. Actually, the one from Montana was my roommate for the remaining three more years. Stanford didn't have a Native American studies degree, but they let me create my own degree in Native American studies with an emphasis in policy and law. I was required to take classes in anthropology, political science, and history as part of my core requirements. Sometimes I couldn't take the basic introductory classes for these courses but had to jump to higher-level classes and my reaction was, "Whoa, this is way over my head." But, it worked out.

When I first went to Stanford, I didn't know my tribe was not recognized. I knew I was Indian and that we were discriminated against. Obviously in Louisiana, you knew that you are not white. So, when I got to Stanford these other students were talking about being federally recognized. I didn't know what being federally recognized meant but wanted to figure it out. In my first year, I took a federal Indian law class at the law school and then another law class in my second year. I was mentored by some really great law students who are now fantastic attorneys. My thinking was always, "How can I better help my tribe," and that led me to law school.

Out of the six freshmen at Muwekma, three went to law school, one earned his MBA, another is doing energy work, and my former roommate is a doctor. The retention rate for Stanford Native students is high because there's a sense of community and support. Stanford's mascot used to be the "Indians," but they changed it to the "Cardinal" in the 1970s. The editor of a conservative campus newspaper kept trying to bring back the Indian mascot and alumni started coming to games wearing headdresses and feathers. We went dorm to dorm to express our concerns about the Indian mascot and we had posters with different ethnicities as mascots. It was empowering to see that our classmates mostly agreed that it was derogatory for Indians to be mascots.

I wasn't sure where I wanted to go to law school, but an Indian law program was one of my priorities. I deferred the decision while I was in France on the Fulbright. Then I heard from one of my classmates, who went to Columbia Law School. He told me, "Hey, you should apply to Columbia, we're starting an Indian law program." So I said, "Okay, I'll apply," and I got admitted. I knew that they would allow me to go back to France and take law classes and get credits toward the degree. When I went there I discovered they had no intention of starting an Indian law program. There was money for an Indian law program, but the dean decided to put it into a postgrad fellowship for people committed to doing Indian law. The program would pay for your loans. I applied four times but never got it. They questioned whether I was really committed to Indian law.

I was able to take an Indian law class at Columbia, mainly because we advocated for an Indian law professor. There was only one other Native in my class. The year below me had one Native and a Native Hawaiian. We had to really fight for things and learn how to work with other groups to get things done. We did things like have cupcake bake sales to get money to bring in a speaker. I was part of a human rights group and took a lot of environmental law classes. I got the certificate in foreign and comparative law. A bunch of the J.D. students, whom I had met while an undergrad, were now lawyers and could help me when I had questions. There also was the Pre-law Summer Institute for Natives interested in the law, but they didn't admit me because I'm not from a federally recognized tribe. It would have been helpful, but, at the end of the day, I made it through law school.

Career services at Columbia told me that I should aim for a district court clerkship because I wouldn't be able to get an appellate court clerkship. There was a Louisiana federal district judge I met at a mock trial involving Cajuns petitioning for an apology from the British government for their being driven out when they would not profess allegiance to the British crown. The whole proceeding was in French so the judge told me that he would be interested in having me clerk for him. But I had gotten married and thought I should be in Arizona with my husband. So I spent a year in Arizona, but I had a hard time finding a job. I secured a clerkship with an amazing appellate judge on the Ninth Circuit in Seattle, but I had a whole year between law school and my clerkship.

There were not many Natives in Arizona law firms when I started practicing. There were no Native partners at Phoenix firms when I started my job search. An alum from Stanford knew an attorney at Sacks Tierney and told them, "Hey, you should give her a job." I had already sent my stuff to their office like maybe a month or two before, but it didn't go anywhere. This person got me an interview and they hired me. I was thrown right into voting rights work. The first thing was redistricting after the 2000 census. It's not like I decided to be a voting rights attorney. It just kind of happened because that's what the firm was working on.

I had to come up to speed really fast. There were a number of hearings and the tribes were not necessarily all in agreement. The Navajo Nation, part of it was carved out, because the Hopis wanted to be in a separate congressional district. When they created the district, some Navajos were carved out as well. The court decided it was a political decision and they weren't going to force the Hopis into the same congressional district as the Navajos. On the state redistricting case, there were issues because the maps hadn't been pre-cleared. I think on the first day of litigation—maybe this was in the federal court case—the DOJ came in and said they were pre-clearing the maps, so that changed a lot in the case. And then there were Section 2 vote dilution claims. We could see looking forward that it would be better if the tribes could be together because they would have a stronger voice and participation. In 2002, there was a gaming initiative that the tribes put on the ballot and they did a lot of voter outreach. The end effect was this huge turnout because of the gaming ballot proposition and so it was hard to make the vote dilution argument because there was data from this one election. This was an anomaly and there was definitely racially polarized voting that you could show historically.

One of the cases was *Navajo Nation v. Arizona Independent Redistricting Commission*. There were other cases and some were consolidated. We're very aware of what the districts looked like, but the state legislative maps weren't initially pre-cleared because of the Hispanic population. I could be remembering that wrong. The next issue was the voter ID law. In 2004 the voter ID law passed by ballot initiative, but nobody really paid attention to it. Part of the law focused on why noncitizens shouldn't be entitled to use benefits. There was a lot of information about that, but no one talked about the voter identification part.

The law passed and then people were being turned away at the polls. This one older Navajo citizen sticks out to me. She was the main plaintiff in our litigation. The woman had voted ever since she legally had been able to do so. In Arizona, people who didn't read and write English could not vote until the 1970s. The woman had used her thumbprint because she doesn't sign her name. When she went to vote she was told, "No, you have to show your ID." She said, "This is my ID, it's my thumbprint." She introduced herself in the Navajo way, which identifies how you are related to others. She also explained this was her chapter and that her son was chapter president. The officials berated her and said she couldn't vote because she didn't have an ID. The woman was very upset and discouraged. They didn't even offer a provisional ballot, as required by law. The Navajo didn't have standard tribal IDs, so quite a few were turned away at the polls. Navajo citizens have an 8.5 x 11 inch certificate of Indian blood with your name and tribal number but no address.

The case started as *Navajo Nation vs. Brewer*. Three cases merged together, which becomes very expensive. Secretary of State Jan Brewer developed a list of acceptable types of identification. The list included Indian treaty cards and some people asked, "What is an Indian treaty card?" Nobody could figure out what that was. Secretary Brewer held a press conference where she said, "Well, we didn't mean to discriminate against Indians." Those weren't her exact words, but if we had discriminated against someone, and if we happened to include you, that's okay, too. That's not how she said it, but that was the gist of it. There was an election in 2006, and then the upcoming 2008 presidential election was around the corner, and this litigation is still going on. It's been going on for several years. We haven't had an evidentiary hearing. There's no trial. The *Gonzalez* plaintiffs appealed to the Ninth Circuit on the voter registration issue and got a positive ruling from a one-judge motion's panel. Then we get this unfortunate decision from the U.S. Supreme Court. It said you can't do anything when the election is so close. It's the *Purcell* Principle. Anyway, we had an evidentiary hearing on our Section 2 claims, and the judge has not issued a ruling.

The evidence showed, yes, Native Americans were disproportionately impacted by the voter ID law and, yes, Native Americans have fewer opportunities than others to elect candidates of their choice. By requiring them to have an ID to vote in person, you're subjecting people who need language assistance to heightened voter ID requirements because they can't get that language assistance by mail. These people don't even have phones in their home, so they can't call their recorder and ask, "Hey, can you bring me a ballot and I'll fill it out," if they even know that they can do that. There are people who didn't have electricity, who didn't have access to a car, and who didn't even get mail at their homes. For people in towns, like Phoenix, vote by mail is an easy option, but it's not an easy option for the elderly, non-English-speaking voters. It's also not going to be an option for people who don't get mail at their homes because even if they had phones and they could request a ballot, you may not get it in time and you don't have many early voting locations on reservations.

Those claims were not decided because of this *Purcell* Principle. They don't want to issue a decision before the 2008 election because it could change all the work that the county recorders have done to prepare for the election. We argued that wasn't necessary. You can just say, "No, you don't have to require an ID." It seems like a simple fix, but without a court ruling, a decision was made to settle and expand the types of IDs that are accepted for Native Americans on Election Day so that people could actually vote in the 2008 presidential election.

Inter Tribal Council Arizona and Navajo agreed to settle, expanding the types of identification to include something from the tribe that had their name and address on it. Or even something issued from the chapter or district with their name and address on it, and maybe they could issue two of them so that that person could use it that day to vote a regular ballot. Under the procedures, if you had any tribal ID with just your name, you could at least get a provisional ballot. That case was settled. The voter registration part went all the way to the U.S. Supreme Court, but the Navajo Nation was not part of that litigation.

After the voting ID case, I joined Arizona State University Law School. I had volunteered in the past to be a poll watcher, but Arizona poll watchers have to be affiliated with a party. It's a crazy law. You can't have nonpartisan observers at the polls. The parties never really coordinate to send people to Indian Country and protect the Native vote. I worked at ITCA with John Lewis and Travis Lane—we agreed that we should really be doing something to protect the Native vote, especially now with this voter ID law. We must have people in the field to assist people. We created a hotline with trained people. We decided to man the hotline with people familiar with the local county officials. We would be able to do outreach to them if a call came in. We had support from the Arizona Indian Gaming

Association, ITCA, and the Native American Bar Association of Arizona. ITCA encouraged tribes to have their attorneys volunteer on Election Day. If a tribal attorney calls the county, it might be dealt with differently than if a volunteer in the field makes the call. Then we stationed lawyers and law students at polling locations so that they could help people on Election Day. That's what we've been doing ever since 2008 and the process has improved every year.

In the 2012 election, people at Gila River were turned away because the addresses on their ID didn't match what the county had. We received these calls all day long about addresses not matching. So, for the 2014 midterm, we reached out to the county. We learned right before the midterm that the county changed everyone's address. If I voted in the District 4 service center, then the county showed my address as the District 4 service center. They did this for people with nontraditional addresses. But there is no way that my ID would match, there's no way that somebody would have an ID with the District 4 service center as their address. We worked with the governor of Gila River and their staff worked with the county. People should not be turned away when it's not their fault they have a nonstandardized address. We met with the officials in advance of the last presidential election to make sure their people were trained to accept these addresses.

The other counties accommodate nontraditional addresses, changing addresses when people don't have regular street addresses. However, the other counties weren't turning people away. What I understand from talking to the counties is that if you have an address listed as the corner of Baseline and Rural and then whatever your city and town is, you can have that address on your driver's license, but you also have a mailing address that is not on your ID. You may have your nontraditional physical address on your ID. When you go to vote, they don't put your physical address—the corner of Baseline and Rural—on your ID on the voter registration list. Instead they put down that the person had the District 4 service center address. If you look up the address, everybody who votes at District 4 is shown as living at that address, which makes people think it is fraudulent voting. But that's not the voter's fault. What some of the other counties do is that as long as you have something showing an address in the area, it is accepted as a reasonable match.

These are not standardized addresses like those that exist in towns. That was a huge issue.

Sometimes you have to litigate cases just to get people to talk to you. Other times you can resolve things through talking with officials. If you're going to be involved in litigation for four or five years, how are the voters being assisted during that time? Litigation is important, but it takes a long time and is expensive. If you need a Section 2 analysis or vote dilution analysis, you need experts and then you have to pay the expert and bring them out for the deposition. It's expensive and then the more people join in your lawsuit, the more costs add up and the process gets delayed.

During the last round of redistricting, we knew the tribes needed to get, on record, a plan laying out what they wanted. We came up with a redistricting guide. Then ITCA asked to have a hearing to get tribal leaders to testify about what they wanted. In Arizona, you can ask to be in the same community of interest with another group. The tribes worked really hard to ensure that the tribes in eastern Arizona counties were part of a majority/minority legislative district. I think Leonard Gorman from Navajo went to every hearing. It's important to get your views on the record. Commissioners who don't hear from you don't know how to include you. If you send a piece of paper, maybe they'll read it; but if you say it, then it's reinforced.

There are some places that didn't want to be in a heavily Indian district. For instance, Flagstaff is a large area, and for various reasons people there were concerned about being in a district that included Navajo. After the 2000 redistricting cycle, a non-Navajo, Ann Kirkpatrick, was running for state legislature along with two Navajos. People could vote for two at-large seats, so some people pushed for a single-shot approach. Some folks in Flagstaff encouraged voters to only vote for Kirkpatrick. It was interesting because the Navajo candidate of choice lost. She was an independent and the other Navajo, a registered Democrat, got elected. He got crossover votes from non-Navajo Democratic voters in Flagstaff. This raises other issues like, why do we have two at-large seats? Should there be two single-member districts? How would this impact other tribes?

Arizona seems to spend a lot of time trying to prevent people from voting. We have this ballot harvesting law that basically says no one outside of your household or your caregiver or your direct relative can bring your ballot to the polls. If someone else does, it's a class 4 felony. If you have two felonies in Arizona, then you can't even vote without getting your rights restored. The legislature passed this law a couple of years ago because the Democrats were so successful at canvassing. The Democrats called people who receive early ballots and then would go and pick them up for them. There was a proposition to repeal that law, but the legislature repealed the law on its own and after the DOJ asked for more information during the pre-clearance process. So then in the 2016 session, the legislature passed the law again but with no time for a proposition before the election. The law was not enforced in 2016, but it could be enforced. It doesn't prohibit someone from turning in the ballot, but that person could be charged with a crime. How does this impact Native people? If the post office is two hours away and you share your post office box keys with someone who doesn't live with you and they pick up your mail including the ballot, then that person may have committed a felony. That's outrageous because if you can't get mail at your home or if you don't have a car, you do not have a choice.

Some counties in this last election had open voting so anybody who lives in that county could vote at any precinct, but other counties didn't allow it. That's caused problems especially on the Navajo reservation. Voters called the hotline while trying to vote at their precinct, but machines weren't working. They had to wait for an hour and some left to go to work without voting. They're going to drive past numerous precincts. Data shows that Hispanics and Native Americans are disproportionately impacted by the lack of out-of-precinct voting. At Navajo where the chapter boundaries don't match the precinct boundaries, people go to vote for tribal elections and think they vote for state or federal elections at the same place, but all of the political boundaries don't match. When it doesn't match, then the vote does not count. Well, why doesn't it count? The county can allow it to count; it's up to each county. These things cumulatively impact and discourage Native voters. In this last election, we had people calling us on Election Day because they had been dropped from the rolls. They had voted in the previous election but were dropped from the rolls. I think purging the rolls is a huge issue. Do Native voters feel empowered and are they even feeling like participants in voting when there are so many barriers? When do they just give up?

I'm really passionate about voting, but I also work on other issues at the law school. I think, however, there is a relationship between issues. A big one for me is the zero tolerance policies that the schools have. They're criminalizing "kid behavior" and funneling them out of school into the juvenile justice system. When kids are out of school, they're getting in trouble. In Arizona minorities are disproportionately impacted by zero tolerance policies that criminalize normal kid behavior. In the old days, when a kid would get in trouble, you'd call their parents and maybe they'd get suspended. Now, they're calling the prosecutor and the kid could be sent to juvenile detention, where they are just learning how to be criminals.

There was a study done that showed that prosecutors have a lot of discretion as to when to charge and defer juveniles. There are very few Native lawyers, so you don't have Natives in these prosecutor jobs. What you find is that everyone has implicit bias and this impacts decisions made in the justice system. So, if you get on this road as a juvenile and you feel like you don't have any support, then as an adult you get in trouble and may continue to be in the justice system. If you have one felony, your rights are automatically restored at the end of it. But when you have two, the rights are not restored. You have to apply for them to get restored, and who's going to help you do that? We should try to support our young people. We shouldn't be trying to tear them down.

Remember, young people's brains are not yet fully developed. There's a documentary called *Tribal Justice* where there's this young boy whose mother is an alcoholic and his dad's not in the picture. The boy winds up in the juvenile detention for eight years and he's not receiving an education. When he gets out, his aunt, who is a tribal judge, decides to raise him. The boy is a couple years behind in high school, but he's doing okay until he has a mishap right about the time he turns eighteen years old. So, what happens? He gets sent to jail for two years for stealing something. So, yeah, I'm trying to raise awareness about this school-to-prison pipeline. Instead of sending a kid to jail, we should find out what's going on at home and try to help them that way.

There's so many things that I feel are important. I'm still working on my tribe's recognition issues. I don't know what it would be like to not be busy. These issues are so important. You need people coming together to talk and collaborate on finding solutions. That's why I feel the Native American Voting Rights Coalition is so important. We are collaborating to share information and address issues. I appreciate the opportunities that I have had and realize that my parents and grandparents did not have these same opportunities. My nephew just graduated from high school and we're all encouraging him because he has a lot more opportunities now than his grandparents did. My mom was not able to go to high school where she lived because of racism. My sister is working to complete her Ph.D. Thankfully, I came from a family that was really stable. I know that I have been blessed. I would make a lot more money in a big law firm, but having an impact and making a difference in people's lives is more important to me. Teaching students, I get encouraged by having the opportunity to volunteer and do pro bono work that makes a difference in someone's life.

I am reminded of the Navajo grandmother who was part of the voter ID litigation. She tried several times on her own to get her ID and she was just turned away. She lived in Chilchinbeto and we met her in Tuba City to get her tribal documents. Then we went to the nearest DMV and they said, "Well, we don't issue IDs at this DMV." The woman really wanted her ID so that she could vote. At that point, we've driven five hours already, but we drive south to Flagstaff, which is another couple of hours away. We go to the Flagstaff DMV and she has all the needed documents, but they rejected her saying that she doesn't have the required documents. So, I went to the counter and state, "Yes, she does have the required documents." She was born at home so she has something issued from Navajo Nation. They're required to accept it. I said, "You have to accept this. This is acceptable so you must accept it and issue her an ID." It's ridiculous that this elderly woman needed a lawyer's help to obtain her ID. It's just tragic. She was very thankful for our help. She did a video recording as a message about voting to the students. Of course, it was all in Navajo so it was translated but it was so powerful. If you work in the government, you should try to be helpful. Your mind-set should be these are my constituents and I should try to resolve this problem. It shouldn't be so hard to vote.

Natalie Landreth

I was born in 1974 in Portsmouth, Virginia, to a military family. I'm one of nine children and several people in my family still live in Oklahoma on the Chickasaw reservation. When my parents divorced, my mother, brother, and I stayed in California. My childhood was pretty uneventful. We lived in Orange County, in Irvine, through the time I was in elementary school. Then we moved to Chatsworth in the San Fernando Valley. Basically we lived where the schools were good. I was in the gifted schools from elementary through high school.

My dad did lots of different kinds of jobs, but my mom is from the mold where you started with a company and stayed there your whole life and moved up the ranks. She worked in credit at a construction company for her whole adult life. She never went to college. Nobody in my family had finished college when I was growing up. I think I was the first, although my dad went to college when he was much older.

I almost never went to Oklahoma while growing up. I only went there once, when I was seven or eight years old. Basically, I did not have much contact with my father, stepmother, or other siblings. Nobody taught me about the Native side of my family. My mother is white, so it wasn't until I was in college and basically an adult where I could fly back and forth on my own before I saw my relatives regularly in Oklahoma. I still go once a year or every two years.

I didn't experience racism growing up because most people didn't know I'm Indian. The first time I consciously thought, "That person is ridiculous and a total racist," was when I was in college. In my freshman year at Harvard, I had pictures of my family posted on the wall and there was a woman from Montana in the adjacent room. She came in and said, "Are you an Indian?" I said, "Yes," and she said, "I wouldn't tell anybody that if I were you." And that was the first time in my life. I thought that was really strange. The only other time was when I was in high school and got into Harvard. Although I had straight A's pretty much most of my life, people said, "You only got into Harvard because you're Indian." And I would laugh and say, "No, I got in because I'm better, that's why."

While growing up, I never thought about becoming a lawyer. It was not until my last week of undergrad final exams in 1996 that I even considered law. I'd seen a poster stating that Attorney General Janet Reno was giving a speech about the new Office of Tribal Justice. I decided to skip studying and go see what that's all about. The talk was at Harvard Law School. So, I went to the law school, listened to what they were doing, and thought it was really amazing. Afterward I went up to Janet Reno and said, "I want to work for you." She said, "Great," and gave me her card and the card of Herb Becker. He is from the Navajo Nation and was the first head of the Office of Tribal Justice. I followed up with Herb and told him that I wanted to work for him when I graduated.

Later I discovered they thought I was a law student, not an undergrad. The only thing they could give me was an internship with a couple hundred dollars' stipend. I'm sure I was the Office of Tribal Justice's worst employee ever. I didn't know my way around a law library. I didn't know what a case citation was. I just wanted to be there and help, but I never was anything more than an administrative assistant. After about four months, I said, "I want to go to law school," and the attorney general said she'd help with my recommendation. Even though I was the world's worst employee, Janet Reno and others from OTJ wrote my recommendations for law school.

Law school might seem pretty removed from my undergrad degree in art history. Art history doesn't mean you necessarily become terribly fluent in art, although I know a lot about it. You learn how to be very analytical with a limited set of information. For my essay for law school, I just wrote about how in art history you learn to perform an analysis and synthesize different sources and that it was a learned skill. It didn't matter what the subject was but that it was a learned skill. I guess that worked. But, yeah, I was an art history major. I even had been admitted to an art history Ph.D. program at Cambridge University in England, but I went to law school instead. I applied to Harvard and Stanford law schools and got into both, probably on the strength of the recommendations. I picked Harvard just to stay on the East Coast and be near my boyfriend.

Law school was a good time. I lived off campus with my boyfriend, now my husband. We had met in 1996 when I was still working in the attorney general's office. He moved to Boston with me and worked at Harvard. At the time, I was still very much from Los Angeles. My idea was to get a job at a law firm in Los Angeles when I graduate. I knew that meant going into entertainment law, so I took contracts and sports agency and entertainment law and copyright, trademark, the various forms of patent, intellectual property rights. I wanted to clerk for a judge and ended up getting a clerkship with Chief Justice Dana Fabe in the Alaska Supreme Court. The Alaska Supreme Court views itself as training people who will stay in the state. That means they prefer people who have lived in Alaska or intend to stay. As a young child because of my dad being in the navy, I had lived in Adak, out on the Aleutians, for a couple of years.

I didn't know how to get into Indian law. I didn't know much about how it worked until year three in law school. And by that time, I already had my clerkship set in Alaska. Year three was when I could take federal Indian law. In the first two years you have to take all sorts of mandatory classes. It was in year three that I really started to think, "I really want to do this," but I didn't really know how to get into it. And so when I graduated I went to Los Angeles and worked in entertainment law at a major law firm. I knew immediately that I had made the wrong decision. I started in October 2002 and by January 2003, I started emailing with my former boss about getting into Indian law. In June, she just sent me an email with a job announcement for the Native American Rights Fund. The application deadline was that day.

I told the people on my team that I was sick and going home. What I did was go home and work on my résumé and cover letter. In those days, you had to fax everything from Kinko's. We lived in Marina del Rey, so I had to go from my office in Century City to Marina del Rey and find a Kinko's and fax everything by 5:00 or 6:00. The next day, I'm at work and I get a call from my husband, saying Heather Kendall Miller from NARF had called and left a message basically saying, "If you want the job, call me in the next fifteen minutes. Otherwise, I'm going to the next person on my list." And so I called her right back. She said, "I want you to get on a plane tomorrow morning and fly to Boulder, Colorado, for an interview," and so I did.

They offered me the job that day or the next day. This all happened in the course of a week—apply, get the call, and go to Boulder. And that was okay with my husband, too. We were both okay with moving to Alaska. Just getting away from LA traffic. Everything happened very fast. I gave three or four weeks' notice to my firm. I was working on a major copyright case and needed to give them plenty of time. I started at NARF in Alaska in August 2003.

The other thing that happened in 2003 was that we got married. It was five or six years after we got together and we finally were getting around to saying let's get married, and then one day we get a FedEx letter saying that my boyfriend was being deployed to Iraq. Not only was he being deployed, he was overdue because the military had been sending deployment notices to the wrong address. He was in the reserves and was activated for sixteen months. In the reserves contract, activation is supposed to be only for six months, but they had suspended all of their own contractual limitations for the Iraq War. So we found out he was to be deployed on Wednesday, December 3, and we got married two days later on Friday. The military allowed him to stay and pack before flying out on Monday the eighth.

My husband was gone for sixteen months. He was an officer in an engineer battalion and beyond that I don't know a lot about what he did in Iraq. Military people who are deployed in situations like that tend only to talk details with other people who have been deployed. We used his combat pay to pay off my undergrad school loans and save for a house.

One of my first NARF cases was *AITC v. The State of Alaska*. It was an equal protection case against Alaska for discriminatory law enforcement services. There is a separate but unequal policing system in Native villages. There are no state troopers stationed in villages. Instead there are village public safety officers (VPSOs), who are not armed and have very limited authority. And they're the only people in the villages without a gun. The state's excuse is that it's just too expensive to pay for the insurance for VPSOs. It's a separate but unequal policing system. I don't care what anybody says, that's exactly what it was. But we lost that case.

One of my earliest cases was *Eyak v. Evans*, which dealt with five Chugach villages, Eyak to Chenega, Nanwalek, Tatitlek, and Port Graham, where the Exxon Valdez spill was. The villagers were suing over aboriginal rights in the Gulf of Alaska, arguing they had the right to fish for halibut where there were no halibut permits. That was a big case that went to the Ninth Circuit twice. I fully inherited the case when the other lawyer retired. We would lose at the district court, win at the Ninth Circuit. It would get remanded. Lost at the district court again and then the final piece was that it went to the Ninth Circuit, which issued a decision that we thought was in conflict with other circuit precedent. We did a briefing requesting rehearing en banc and got it.

At the Ninth Circuit en banc hearing, there were eleven judges. The hearing was in San Francisco in the old 1920s courthouse. So, it's you versus eleven judges. You're basically advocating for an aboriginal right to hunt and fish in the face of a federal agency (the Department of Commerce) that says we own all these waters and we get to decide. There was something disturbing about standing in a courtroom and asking complete strangers, who don't know anything about these communities or how they live, for permission to fish. People would ask me, "Weren't you scared?" And I said no, it really pissed me off because it felt inherently unfair. We had evidence from the eighteenth-century explorers Captain Cook and Russian Martin Sauer describing what they called Chugach people, which is exactly what they're called now, fishing for halibut in the area in the 1760s, 1770s, and 1780s. So, we had the smoking gun of evidence. The question was whether the court was going to let you assert an aboriginal right. No, it didn't scare me. It made me angry that people had to beg for that, to beg to be allowed to fish so they can eat. These were the communities damaged by the Exxon Valdez oil spill. They hadn't been able to fish for halibut for years because their boats were needed for cleanup and in that window, they lost all these rights that they were trying to regain. Their boats were loaned out for cleanup in 1988, 1989, and 1990. That was the first case I went through as lead counsel. I had some very experienced lawyers to help, a team of four or five, but this was the first time I had to lead.

My son was born on July 31, 2012, and because I'm a crazy type-A personality, I was checking my email on my phone while in the recovery room and I saw the decision that had come out. The only three words I saw were "Dissent by Fletcher." Fletcher knows a lot about Indian law, so I assumed we lost the case without my ever reading the opinion. I thought that I had lost 10–1 and I didn't read the opinion that day. I went on maternity leave and turned off my phone. Someone came to my house to bring a baby gift about two months later and said, "Oh, I couldn't believe that the decision was so close." I said, "What do you mean so close, 10–1?" She goes, "No, 6–5." So, I said, "6–5, I saw dissent Fletcher." And she said, "No, that's just a shorthand." They listed the dissenters by name, but the majority did not sign their names to it. I thought, wow, I lost by one vote. So, the fact that the Chugach don't have rights to fish for halibut in the Gulf of Alaska is, one could say, due to one person.

A case like that costs millions of dollars. Expert witnesses run to six figures. And if you figure attorney time, we have our overhead for the whole office, salary divided by hour, and you're counting it that way, it still came to almost two million dollars in cost for attorney time. That's the last case I lost.

The voting rights work started by accident. In late 2005, the D.C. NARF office said the Voting Rights Act is up for reauthorization and we need someone to write a report on Alaska. People in the office were concerned that Senator Ted Stevens was going to try to exempt Alaska from coverage. They thought, let's get some Alaska evidence. Census numbers show there's a large percentage of people whose first language isn't English, but nobody I spoke to knew whether materials or assistance was being provided. The initial report that we put out in spring 2006 concluded that there were widespread Section 203 language violations, equal protection violations, and Section 208 violations.

I came in to work one Monday morning in 2006 and found a congressional subpoena on my chair. It was really just a friendly letter, saying please come in. At that time, I had only been in court twice. I didn't even really own a suit that fit me properly and I had to be in the Capitol in Washington, D.C., for a hearing on Wednesday morning at 7:00 or 8:00. I had to take the red-eye that Monday so that I would have all Tuesday afternoon to sleep and catch up. On the way to the airport, I bought a suit at Banana Republic, just stuffed it in my bag. I realized on the plane that I was probably expected to write something, so I asked the flight attendant for extra napkins. I wrote my congressional testimony on Alaska Airlines napkins and then slept the rest of the flight. So, I get there Tuesday morning and typed up what I had on the napkin and emailed it in.

I go to the hearing on Wednesday morning and I keep making this bizarre gesture with my right arm because I hadn't removed the tag off this new suit and it's so itchy. The chairman asks me to read my statement. Even though I had typed the statement up before emailing it, I hadn't transcribed it for myself. But I had my airline napkins sitting in front of me and went off them. On either side of me were two old white guys. Sitting on my left was some very conservative person, and on my right was Bob McDuff, who's a legend in voting rights. He was talking while I was trying to reach for a drink. I was so nervous that the ice in the drink rattled in the microphone and Bob very subtly and quietly slid the glass to the edge of the desk so I could lean forward and drink without having to make any noise.

So I testified and got some pretty hostile questions about how there was no evidence of discrimination in Alaska. Later I was told that when I answered Senator Cornyn's hostile remarks, I turned my chair to face him directly and shook my finger at him like a parent and made like a very "don't fuck with me" kind of face—all without realizing I was doing it. There's a photograph of it somewhere. It was like that moment with *Eyak* where I wasn't scared. I was pissed off. Senator Cornyn never probably has ever been in an Alaska village. His question was something like, "Can you even identify a single instance where discrimination has occurred?" And my answer was, "When you're conducting an English-only election in a place that doesn't speak very much English, you're discriminating in every single election all over the state." The room became quiet. It's not something I practiced. It was that the legislators who are making the decision are so far removed from the actual people with the need.

That's how I got into voting rights. After writing the report, we sent a copy to the state thinking they'll fix it. What we found is that whatever remedies people would get in the lower 48 just would never make it up here unless someone forces them. Rights are not willingly given. People really, especially in the 1920s, 1930s, and 1940s, actively opposed Natives voting. Now they oppose them by ignoring them and not enforcing the VRA. There used to be very Jim Crow discrimination. Now, it's simply nonenforcement of the VRA. It's very different, but the effect is the same.

The first voting rights case in Alaska was born out of that report. After the report and hearing, Jim Tucker from the ACLU called and asked, "Do you want to bring a lawsuit on this?" He was a Section 203 expert. I said, "Sure," so Jim came up to Alaska and we spent the fall and winter of 2006–2007 looking for plaintiffs and doing interviews. It was odd because basically everybody in the villages told us, "We get ballots and stuff." Then we would tell them if you speak Spanish and you would go to vote out in LA, everything is in Spanish. They would say, "I didn't even know that was legal." They didn't understand what the law required. Nobody had ever done any outreach, so they presumed the status quo was the way that it was supposed to be—they thought the law required you to be fluent in English in order to vote and that you had to vote alone and the ballot could never leave the polling place, which meant disabled or bedridden people could never vote. All of these things were untrue, but no one had ever told them so they weren't even really aware their rights were being violated with every election.

At first, people downplayed the voting problems, but in every community we needed a translator. We stopped asking if there are any issues in voting. Instead we asked what language do you speak and what language is your ballot in. There was the answer. People didn't see the legal voting problems because they didn't know what the law required. They just knew it was really hard and only people who were fluent in English voted. So, we started asking different questions.

At first, Native people didn't really want to talk to us because (1) they didn't know what the law required so they didn't always realize this was a problem, and (2) they'd say, "I don't see how this is going to help us with subsistence and other things." We'd tell them, "Don't you realize that all your problems are tied to a lack of political power and if your villages, your tribes voted at 100 percent and in a unified way that you would control the results. It has everything to do with subsistence, hunting, housing, children's welfare. All the problems you have are caused because politicians are disregarding what you want because nobody goes to the polls. You don't think those things are related?" It took a while because people just sort of didn't see the connection. And so, Jim and I started to realize that we were asking the wrong questions. It wasn't about voting, but it was about politics. They weren't connecting the fact that the Voting Rights Act was being violated with the ways that their access to hunting and fishing was being diminished. It was impacting everything else, and it still is.

Our first case, *Nick v. Bethel*, was hugely contentious, very ugly. Some of the attorneys treated the plaintiffs very poorly. Some of the plaintiffs cried during their depositions due to the embarrassment of not understanding the intense pressure of the situation. The lawyers for the state and city asked questions about people's childhood, things about abuse. Questions that had nothing to do with voting or language access, questions that were cruel and designed to make people uncomfortable. Or yelled at plaintiffs in a way that the elders were never spoken to. Just repugnant. It was very contentious and very heavily fought.

We filed in June 2007 and I think the case ended in 2010. It was ultimately settled after we won a preliminary injunction. By the time it was settled, there were 768 docket entries, which is basically filing something every two to three days. Attorneys for the defense would file a notice to deposition, we would file a motion to quash because they would notice somebody living three hundred miles away or not give ten days' notice. They treated it like a major patent case for Microsoft. It was incredible, the force that was brought to bear, just to avoid translating ballots. It was the most heavily litigated Section 203 case ever.

I think the cost for the city of Bethel went into the millions. I don't know how that was funded but I think it is through a common insurance pool for municipalities. That enables them to spend a lot of money on attorneys for political reasons. It's ridiculous. The population in Bethel is roughly eight thousand people, but they went and hired outside counsel from Seattle. The city was so hell-bent on fighting bilingual election materials that they would find an attorney in Seattle to just really go after these people. They were way more aggressive than the state of Alaska.

The defense had a whole team of lawyers. There were three or four from the state and maybe three from the city. On our side it was me and Jim Tucker and Jason Brandeis from the ACLU and we still won. In some sense, it doesn't matter what kind of money you have, what kind of resources you're going to throw at it. If you're just wrong, you're just going to lose, and that's what happened to them. We stuck to merits, and when we filed the motion for a preliminary injunction, we won that. I think it was July 30, 2008, when we got the injunction saying that we were likely to prevail on the merits and it shifted the tone of the case. The way that the state started to litigate was to say, "Oh, we're making changes." They were trying to moot it out factually and avoid a decision on the merits. Interestingly, and quite rightly, the judge held that against them. Obviously, you could have done this sooner and you decided to only do this after you were sued.

The judge ordered a bunch of remedies so we ended up monitoring the November 2008 election when the preliminary injunction was in place. We got on a chartered plane. There were ten of us this time: five lawyers, five translators. We went out to the villages to see how the elections were going. We went to eight different places in one day. The plane would drop two people off, go to the next place, drop two people off, and then go around and pick them up in the same order. We saw people voting. We couldn't go in to the actual voting location, but we saw them coming and going from the building. When they were outside, we would ask them questions about the ballot and voting procedures. It was hit-or-miss, but state and city did not appear to be honoring the preliminary injunction. By this time, there was some recognition in Native communities that they were supposed to get translated materials and were not getting what they were entitled to. So we started collecting names, and afterward we moved to say they were in contempt of the court order. We did our own post-election report with thirty to forty affidavits of people saying, "We didn't see any of these materials at the polling place." We landed the plane and as soon as I walked into the terminal, the television said Obama was the forty-fourth president. All of us lawyers and translators started screaming and jumping up and down, and you could see some of the people working in the terminal were like, "Awwww shit."

We spent 2009 arguing with the defense attorneys about fixing things and settled in 2010. We got part of our attorney fees for Jim

Tucker's ACLU office in D.C., the NARF office, and all the costs. We had to turn in time records and the judge had to approve it. These were not estimates. These were court-ordered accounted time and receipts. I think it worked out to 68 percent of what actually was spent. I remember that the state sent the check in the regular mail. I've often wondered if they were hoping the check would be lost.

The next case was *Toyukak v. Treadwell.* After *Nick v. Bethel* was settled in February 2010, we assumed everything was fine. Then the 2010, 2012 elections roll around and Native people had been familiarized with the issue and they knew who to call. They called us and said, "We live in a village ten miles from this other village that gets these translated materials. Why aren't we getting these?" And so the situation in Toyukak is this: Yu'pik is spoken in three different Census Areas. Bethel only had villages from the Bethel Census Area. Census Areas aren't used for any law purpose other than voting and so nobody knows what Census Area they're in. We discovered that the state was interpreting the result in *Nick v. Bethel* to only apply to the Bethel Census Area and to not apply to all the speakers of languages covered by Section 203 in villages just north and south of it.

We were very lean and mean in *Toyukak.* We only had two hundred docket entries because we learned the first time around that they're going to slowly change little things along the way and we're going to file a preliminary injunction or we're going to motion for summary judgment within four or six months and the case will be over. We're done, win or lose. What we found in the discovery response was simply extraordinary. The state was deliberately providing materials in the Bethel Census Area only and their reasoning was that under Section 5—this was pre-*Shelby*—you couldn't make any changes to election procedures without DOJ pre-clearance. It was a fundamental misunderstanding of Section 5. All you have to do is write DOJ a letter and state these people up here speak the same language as those in Bethel, can we get pre-clearance, and you're going to get that pre-clearance. They never even requested pre-clearance. They used Section 5 as a crutch, saying we weren't allowed to make any changes, so they just never did anything except in the Bethel Census Area.

We litigated the case very differently, focusing on the witnesses, what they did and didn't have. We put the state officials who were in charge of elections in those areas on the stand and had them go through what they gave to the Bethel Census Area, the Wade Hampton Census Area, and the Dillingham Census Area. So we would put up a ballot with translations. Is it in the Dillingham Census Area? No. Why not? *Shelby County*. Is this in the Wade Hampton Census Area? No. Why not? *Shelby County*. We'd start seeing charts saying BCA (Bethel Census Area) only. And then there were the emails we got in discovery. We had twenty thousand pages come into the NARF office and we read every single page. People's emails would say things like, "Are you going to provide all these materials for the Yupik speakers in the Wade Hampton Area?" and the responses would say things like, "No, BCA only." There were even emails that said, "We're only going to do this for Bethel and we hope the lawyers for NARF don't see this, but if they do, oh well," with a smiley face emoji at the end. You better believe we put that on the screen in the courtroom. It showed intent and lack of concern.

The case was litigated differently because you weren't proving there was supposed to be language assistance and there isn't. You were showing that there was a deliberate choice to only provide it to the exact people whose communities were part of the earlier case. They were even trying to provide it only to the villages that had plaintiffs in *Nick v. Bethel*. It was this really crabbed interpretation of the settlement. It's the same language, it's the same statute. They're on the same list of covered jurisdictions for Section 203. There's no reason why they shouldn't be covered. We filed that in June 2013 and went to trial in June 2014. This was the first case fully litigated under Section 203 since the early 1980s. Our argument was if you're providing these for this area by law, you have to provide it to all the voters speaking that language in covered jurisdictions. Very simple case theory. The way the state litigated it was to say, and this is in the oral arguments transcripts, the division of elections gets to choose which materials voters get. Their defense was we give people information in those other two jurisdictions, just not everything that we provided in Bethel, because they don't need everything. One of their examples was, and I'm paraphrasing here, "We don't have to translate Republican primary election materials because they're all going to vote Democrat." That is actually not true, because Native people vote diversely just like everyone else, but it was really disturbing to have a statement in the record where the state says, "We're not going to give them what they want, we're going to give them what we think they need," and that's almost a quote. It was something very similar. That brought down the wrath of the DOJ—in the previous administration, of course.

That editing of material was unacceptable and the DOJ came in with a statement of interest stating, "It's a one-to-one ratio. If you provide it in English, you have to provide it in the covered language, and the only question is how: orally or written. For every question that they provide in English, we suggest the court have a chart and see what they're creating in that other language and if they can demonstrate where they provided it." That's how that case turned out. In response to the state's claim that they were entitled to choose what material would be shown to voters, the court's answer was an unequivocal, "No, you're not." The judge had set out the law of the case before the trial began. She had set out the law of the case saying you're going to have to prove one-to-one provision of the same information and they should've settled at that point. We all knew walking into that courtroom on June 23 that the state couldn't prove that they had all the materials translated and were providing them. We knew, they all knew it. It was nothing more than politics from the previous lieutenant governor, deciding I'm not giving in, even if I'm going to lose and even if I'm going to spend a lot of money.

The court issued a decision in September and the state lost, but the judge ruled on only one of the two claims at that time. She ruled they were violating Section 203 but hadn't yet ruled on equal protection. We argued the state purposefully was violating the Equal Protection Clause. What really changed things was that Bill Walker and Byron Mallot were elected in November 2014. The court issued an order saying, and again I'm paraphrasing here, "I want the new lieutenant governor to take a look at this case before I render a decision on the constitutional claim." The court directed a mediation or settlement conference, I believe. Our new governor is an independent and our lieutenant governor is a Democrat and an Alaskan Native. He is the highest-ranking Alaskan Native to hold a statewide office and I think the highest-ranking Native leader in the

United States. Lieutenant Governor Mallot seemed like he came in with the mind-set to fix this. He had grown up in a Native-speaking household, so he knew exactly what these voters were experiencing. He had likely seen it in his own home. He was pivotal in fixing this thirty-five-year-old problem and deserves credit for that. It took a couple months to iron out all the details. Of course with so many lawyers involved, that's going to happen. The DOJ also certified federal observers, so we now knew there would be actual oversight in the polling places. That kind of bird's-eye view is so valuable because it means these changes are much more likely to stick, be lasting and meaningful.

The problem now is keeping up messaging in the villages. There are so many things going on that voting rights maybe falls off people's radar. To keep up the messaging, that you've got to participate, that you've got to tell somebody when you don't see your language, or like last time that it's only for the villages from the *Bethel* case. Without Section 5, they might just remove things randomly. I think that it's a dangerous and precarious time, even though the remedies are there and the state is doing arguably a good job. Alaska is a large state, a lot of people, a lot of Native people, a lot of different languages, and right now the state is trying. For the first time, they're trying in this administration. That could change the moment there's a different lieutenant governor or when somebody doesn't care, no matter what party. Or, they just don't want to spend the money. We won big in terms of the changes that were ordered, but keeping it is much harder than the case itself.

Right now there are two issues. The most recent was early voting, which is part of Alaska voting but didn't really exist in the villages. People privately got it set up, like you'd have to go through a bunch of hurdles to get it. And Nicole Borromeo, a lawyer from AFN, the Alaska Federation of Natives, set that up. She went and did all of their paperwork and set everything up. People would run away from their fish camp to get their paperwork and fax it in. That's been the recent big issue.

But, the one now that is heating up is fights over bringing mandatory mail-in voting for everybody in Alaska. It violates the court order in the *Bethel* case, which requires language assistance and a translator at the poll. You can't do it all by mail even if you're going to write everything in the Native language because the literacy rate is low. You'll just create a different constitutional case, a different lawsuit. The other problem is that the people in Alaska do not receive mail regularly in rural parts of Alaska, it can be a week or more, and it's not easy to get stamps and not all the villages have post offices. The mail's dropped off at the airport in a bag and people go rifle through it and look for their stuff. So, it's not secure. How are you supposed to be sure to get your ballot? Who do you give it to and return it to? But there's also the trust problem. Many Native people don't trust anything they send through the mail because they see stuff get lost in the mail a lot. It's a real challenge. Some progressive organizations push mail-in voting as a panacea, and it just does not work in Alaska at all. We recently got information about people sharing post office boxes with three other families. Sometimes they don't get their bills because people just pick stuff up or somebody else will decide I don't have a ballot so I'll just take this one. Progressives who advocate for this all mail-in voting think they're doing good, but they're really harming people up here.

There is so much people do not understand about Alaska Natives. It's so infuriating when people say, "Why don't those people learn English?" or whatever. Alaska Natives have a hard time reading and writing because they're a product of a different kind of discrimination. When the United States purchased Alaska from Russia, they decided to not have schools in Native villages here. It wasn't until the 1970s that a bunch of teenagers sued the state of Alaska saying, "We're entitled to have schools in our villages," and the state fought them, saying that it was too expensive, just like what they said about village police. And those people won in a case called the *Molly Hootch*, but the state wasn't following it, so there was a follow-on case called *Tobeluk v. Lind.* The state really only started building high schools in rural Alaska in the 1980s, which means a lot of Yupik people above the age of forty are not fluent in English. They can speak enough to get by, to check into a hotel, to travel, or whatever, but they cannot read a ballot written in college-level English. They're having a hard time voting, because they were discriminated against in schooling. It's a state-created problem.

But voting rights is only part of what I do at NARF. I do a lot of things related to tribes; it sort of depends on the things that are affecting them and a lot of it involves Native people outside of Alaska. Right now, one of the things I'm working on is Trump's revocation of land in the national monument called Bears Ears. We also represent Rosebud Sioux helping to fight the Keystone Pipeline.

CHAPTER 7

Lifetimes of Activism

Oral Histories of Native Americans

There is a long history of non-Indian academics exploiting and misinterpreting information provided by Native informants,[1] which means any oral history process must be a collaborative one. It also must respect the role of oral tradition in the preservation of Native culture. Angela Cavender Wilson (1996: 7) notes, "It is through the stories of my grandmother, my grandmother's grandmother, and my grandmother's grandmother's grandmother and their lives that I learned what it means to be a Dakota woman, and the responsibility, pain, and pride associated with such a role." Along with the passage of cultural knowledge is the passing of stories and memories about the destruction wrought by Euro-Americans. Gross (2014: 29) describes this as "echoes of that trauma" in memories and stories.[2]

Framing the Oral Histories

With this history in mind, I have tried to "walk softly and listen carefully."[3] Many people from the Native American Voting Rights Coalition made suggestions and helped me identify people to interview. Without their assistance, it would have been impossible for this project to reach fruition. Although I sought a broad mix of people, there are no stories from young people. Whenever I asked for suggestions about whom to interview, I was sent to elders. It is a sign of the great respect that exists for elders. What this means is there is an opportunity for future research on young people, particularly those energized by Standing Rock and other protests. For this project, I interviewed a total of twenty-four American

Indians and Alaska Natives. Interview material is included throughout the book, as well as in the stories included in this chapter and Chapters 6, 8, and 9.

The oral histories that follow cover much more than voting rights, providing a window into Indian Country—and how the activism is embedded within daily life and flows out of personal experiences and the legacies of forefathers and mothers. Chapters 7, 8, and 9 are devoted to the stories of six individuals, grouped into pairs. The first pair, included in this chapter, are William "Snuffy" Main Sr. and John Lewis. While actively committed to voting rights, they see it as part of broader struggles for civic inclusion and Native self-determination. Chapter 8 is devoted to the second pair, OJ Semans and Barbara Semans, who are grassroots voting rights activists: they lead registration drives, organize get-out-the-vote campaigns, and advocate for voting rights. The final pair, Donovan Archambault and Johnnie Williams Jr., were plaintiffs in voting rights suits but had radically different experiences.

Decades of Social Justice Activism

The lives of the two men whose stories follow show the deep connections between the Red Power era and the current period. Each man spent decades engaged in politics, albeit within different settings. William "Snuffy" Main Sr. is an "old AIMster," with deep roots among the Gros Ventre of Montana. In contrast, much of John Lewis's activism is rooted in Saul Alinsky–style coalition building across different communities. Both view their lives as carrying out family traditions of activism and political leadership. As such, they are bridges not only to the Red Power era but to generations long past. Their struggles are both to gain their rightful inclusion as citizens of the United States, as well as for treaty rights.

William Main Sr.

> I was born in 1955 in Butte, which was a rough-and-tumble town at the time. My uncle Gerald looked in my cradle and said you have to be a pretty snuffy character to be born in Butte, Montana. The name Snuffy has stuck with me. My dad was a hard-rock miner, the kind who refused to work by the hour or the day. He got paid

for the amount of ore that he "pushed" each day. They had a competition each week to see who pushed the most ore. He was the top one or close to it every week. Then in 1959, he decided to go to work on the Glasgow air force base. A couple years later, we moved back to the reservation, and he was elected to tribal council. There were very few jobs, so when he decided not to run for reelection, he struggled but refused to take public assistance. He said, "A person should earn their keep. When I get old, I'll take my Social Security because I earned that."

On the Main side, our lineage goes back to our last traditional chief, Lame Bull, who was at the 1855 signing of the big treaty. My mother's great-grandfather, Bushy Head, also was at the signing. Bushy Head was a well-renowned war chief of the Gros Ventre. The treaty was with the Blackfeet Nation comprised of the Gros Ventres, Bloods, Piegans, and Blackfeet. The treaty established the "Blackfeet Territory," which encompassed about half the state of Montana. They called it a friendship treaty, which meant that you would live in peace with neighboring tribes and with white men. When they explained the living in peace part and being able to go everywhere, Bushy Head said, "I don't know why we'd want to sign this. We go where we want and when we want now." He left without signing the treaty. So I come from two very traditional families that have produced leaders.

Bushy Head's son White Cow married Lena Coleman, whose mother was Assiniboine from what is now Fort Peck. She was half white. I don't know if Lena was given to White Cow or what. Back then there were actually wives given to their husbands. They had just a couple children. My mother's mother—my grandmother—married a half Assiniboine, half Nez Perce man named Bill Brisbow. It's unclear how his father got here. It had something to do with the Chief Joseph Nez Perce battle in the Bear Paws. He had bullet wounds in both knees and was nursed back to health here and then married my great-grandmother. My mother is all kinds a mixture of blood. We are accustomed to talking about blood quantum because that's in our organic documents, which were forced on us by the federal government. Mostly, we are either Gros Ventre or Assiniboine, depending upon what your father was. My father was Gros Ventre, so that's my affiliation.

My grandmother on my mother's side was very, very kind. The older Indians were so kind, even in their tone of voice. It was calming to listen to them talk. She lived three miles east of Lodgepole in a two-room log house with no running water or electricity. She had a wood cookstove with a small fire box that burned out at night. She lived that way for years. Some relatives got mad at her because she had twenty cats. "Why do you have so many cats?" She said, "Because in the winter when it's cold and my fire burns out at night, my cats lay on my covers and keep me warm."

My grandmother on my father's side was full-blooded Gros Ventre. Even though she was deaf, my grandmother became a volunteer nurse and cared for wounded World War I veterans. Years later she would receive letters from guys thanking her for what she'd done for them. We used to laugh because they must have had different sanitation back then . . . must have had to use real hot water and wipe everything down. When she'd wash her dishes, she'd put her metal dishpan on the woodstove and boil her dishes. She'd take a fork with a washcloth and wash them off. Then she'd take her washcloth and wipe off her doorknobs, her bedsteads, everything, to sanitize.

My paternal grandparents were devout Catholics. I think my grandfather Tom Main had a sincere belief in God, but he also was heavily involved in ceremonies with our sacred pipe, which his grandfather Lame Bull kept until his death. The story behind that pipe is that it was given to us at the time of creation, so it came directly from God. My grandparents were fluent Gros Ventre speakers, but they never spoke it with the children. They walked three miles to church every Sunday to attend mass, but my grandfather also passed on to his children a lot of stories about Indian spirituality. I read a speech that my grandfather had given. The speech was about how he's reached the crossroads in his life, and there's a clash of two cultures: the old way and the new way. I think he chose this new society and believed that his children would be better-off if they went to Catholic school and graduated high school. He was married twice. His first wife died, and then he was diagnosed with bad heart disease and was not supposed to live very long. He allowed his wife's parents to take their three children. He went down to Oklahoma and started getting a little better before moving back and marrying my grandmother. They had nine children.

The traditional Gros Ventre way of conducting business is to have mass meetings. A lot of the meetings back then involved treaty claims. In 1935, the big issue was whether to adopt a government form supposedly modeled on the United States government. The Gros Ventres didn't want that or to incorporate with any other tribe. But they were tricked into adopting it. The Indian Reorganization Act laid out various ways of reorganizing as a tribe, one of which is a historical tribe. We've always been here, so we wanted to be a historical tribe. There's also this community concept, which is basically a created tribe. It was intended for places where there were fragments of tribes scattered in a geographic area. Those people would be scooped up, put on a reservation, and then recognized as a tribe. My grandfather was a staunch advocate of tribal sovereignty, and a created tribe does not have the same sovereignty as a historical tribe.

There were a few Gros Ventres with a little bit of formal education. They kind of understood what was going on and tried stopping it. My grandfather, an old man named Victor Brockie, and another named John Buckman were sent to Washington, D.C., to get the Gros Ventres recognized as a historical tribe. I tried to find the records of what happened. In the National Archives, the file on adopting the constitution has conveniently disappeared. There is a file on the adoption of the federal charter two years later. But there's a few items spilled over from those files. One is minutes from a meeting with the Gros Ventre and Assiniboine delegations, their attorneys, and some government bureaucrats. There's a handwritten note from one bureaucrat to another. The one bureaucrat writes, "Just tell the Gros Ventres that we're too far into the process. It will take too long to go back and get their own constitutions. By then all of the Indian credit money will be gone." The IRA established a loan fund that tribes could borrow from, but only if you reorganized. In the end, there was a vote and the new constitution barely passed. We became a community tribe with the Assiniboines.

Then in the 1950s, the Eisenhower administration was terminating tribes. In Montana, the process started with the termination of the Confederated Salish and Kootenai. Fort Belknap was next on the list. The rationale was, "They're a community. They no longer have their identity. They're losing their language. They're losing their culture. Therefore, they're assimilated." I keep telling people you need to keep your identity, keep your cultures. Keep those alive. It's a matter of survival. Once I started fully understanding this, back around 1988, I started advocating for separately getting the Gros Ventre and the Assiniboine listed on the federally recognized tribes list. But the BIA just fights it and fights it.

My dad was always involved in treaty affairs. He was on the Gros Ventre treaty committee and was instrumental in finalizing our treaty claims and getting Congress to pass a bill giving us our award in 1973 and again in 1983. I was four or five years old when he started taking me with him to talk to elderly guys. There were some famous Gros Ventres here—Rufus Warrior was one of them. My dad would take me down to see him. Rufus had a black-and-white TV with a ten- or twelve-inch screen. I remember watching Cassius Clay box and then the men would talk treaty business. In Butte, my dad and an old man named Al Buckman would talk treaty business. I was eighteen years old when I first got elected to the treaty committee. Those elderly people identify and groom someone to step into certain roles. And it always seemed like I was pushed in that direction.

My father always had a strong work ethic, but money was always tight. My mother did some work as a waitress and dishwasher, but she was mostly a homemaker. I always had to earn my own money. I shined shoes in bars, starting when I was nine years old. Couple of times when I was shining a guy's shoes, he'd get in an argument and fight. I'd have to wait until he was done fighting to finish shining his shoes. I also shoveled sidewalks in winter and did yard work in the summer. There was one elderly lady who told me that she'd give me an extra nickel for every dandelion that I could bring to her with the root intact. And she'd give me small spade. I'd try and try, but I never did get one. They always seemed to break off. Sometimes she'd give me a little extra for trying.

Then in seventh grade, in the summer, a rancher hired my brother and me to work on his potato and dairy farm. We worked there for two summers. Talk about a boring job. You walk through potato rows all day long and you look at the plants. If you see one with yellow leaves or wilting, you pull out that plant. The guy tried other kids the second year, but when it came time to go back out he came looking for us. He didn't want the other kids because they were pulling more healthy plants than sick plants.

The biggest discrimination in Butte involved class—economic class. Some of the higher-up kids kind of looked down on the rest of us. But I got along really good up there, especially with Irish families. I joke and say that I thought I was Irish until the principal spanked me for pinching a kid on St. Patty's day and told me I had no business pinching anybody because I wasn't Irish. There were a few people who had never been around Indians before. But I attributed their remarks to ignorance, no knowledge of Indians. In Butte, we were all just like one big family—most of us—because we were all families of miners. Whenever there was a cave-in and the whistle started blowing, the whole town would come to a standstill. Everybody wondering who it was and stuff.

When I was fourteen, my mother had emotional problems. My two older brothers were in the Marine Corps, so three of us older children were sent to Busby Indian boarding school on the Northern Cheyenne Reservation. Talk about cultural shock. The most exciting thing at night was to lie on the lawn and count trucks going by. I was there for eighth grade and part of ninth grade. It wasn't really too bad. There was a matron, who really liked me, and there was a cowboy who used to take me with him to team roping at rodeos. I played a lot of pool. I did learn some discipline there, about getting up early and going to bed early and making your own bed and doing various chores.

While in Busby, my dad got elected to tribal council. He moved my mother back to Hays first and then us. It was in Hays at St. Paul's Mission High School where my schoolwork improved. If you were struggling, there were old nuns who would help you. The sister who was the principal taught English, and she made it so interesting. She laid out the curriculum for that semester in advance. If you got done ahead of time, then you got free time. I would always do a lot more just to get free time. Later when I took my college entrance exam, my counselor called me in to find out where I went to high school. "St. Paul's Mission in Hays. Why?" He said, "Well, you turned in one of the highest scores here in English, which is unusual."

St. Paul's Mission High was only open for forty or fifty years. I was in the last graduating class in 1974. I was the only Indian male to have ever graduated from Mission in braids. When I was going to the earlier Catholic schools, we were required to wear uniforms and have our hair cut above the neckline, so as soon as I moved home in 1972 I grew my hair. Played basketball in braids. I boxed in braids. I was an undefeated boxer. Graduated high school in braids. There weren't very many men who dared to grow their hair long back then because people would make fun of you. I would get in fights in town in bars, and the braids made good handholds for the guy I was fighting to hang onto.

My mother said I was really a good kid until I was eighteen, and then I gave her an ulcer because I was always getting into mischief and ending up in the hospital. I got shot three different times. Just raising hell. One time I had driven a car to pick up my girlfriend off the boarding school bus. This cop started harassing me, so I almost ran over him. The cop started to pull out his .357 Magnum to shoot me, but he accidentally dropped it. He later caught and handcuffed me. He was tuning me up a little bit—zapping me with mace and stuff. I managed to get away from him, and then he pulled his gun out. I dove into his cop car and pulled it in drive and floorboarded it to try to get away. In the process I almost ran over the cop, who emptied his gun on me, but he only hit me twice—in each shoulder. Later they found a bullet lodged in the headrest. A fraction of an inch lower and I would have been shot in the head.

I was seventeen years old when Wounded Knee took place. My uncle and first cousin were going down to participate. I wanted to go, but my dad wouldn't let me. I was still in school. My father totally embraced the philosophy of the American Indian Movement (AIM) and got closely associated with Russell Means, Vernon Bellecourt, and other AIM leaders. He sponsored AIM conferences at our home out at Big Warm in the foothills of the Little Rocky Mountains. A lot of people don't understand AIM. They only see the militant side, but AIM started out as a spiritual movement. Its philosophy was guided by some old medicine men, who, to me, had actual connections with the Creator. These guys were really something. They were the real deal.

After Wounded Knee, I participated in a lot of the AIM stuff. One of their spiritual leaders, Henry Crow Dog, was about ninety years old in 1974 when he came to Northern Montana College, where I was a student. I was one of the few Indians there wearing braids. He was to give a talk and give a ceremony. Henry Crow Dog picked me, out of the three hundred people who got the honor of smoking with him, to sit right next to him. He whispered to me, "When you smoke that pipe, make a wish. It will probably come true." I started thinking, "Well, there's always money. No, I don't want that." My sister was having complications with her pregnancy, so I just asked for the baby to be healthy. He was born with crooked feet that got healed. Then he became a basketball star—all-state before being killed in a car wreck when he was twenty-five.

My dad really embraced the spiritual side. He had a real bad heart condition and his medical doctors kept saying he was going to die. He would leave the hospital and go see an Indian doctor. They'd have a ceremony. They pray and call on spirits to help with whatever is ailing you. Some use natural herbs and things to make stuff for you to either drink or chew. Afterward, my dad would go back to the hospital, and the doctors would be amazed that he was still even here. One time he had an aneurysm on his aorta, and the doctor said if it ruptured that he'd be gone. He went to his Indian doctor. My dad always told me that the Indian doctor said, "This doesn't work if you just want to try to do it because it's your last resort. This is something you really have to believe in and have your whole life in order for it to work. And believe in it." The next time he went to hospital, the aneurysm was gone. He lived for seven years after his medical doctors told him he was going to die. I visited him the night that he died. He told me a lot of stuff. "Snuffy, I don't think I'm going to make it this time, but I'm not afraid to die. It's just that I'll be lonesome for you guys over there. But if there's any way I can help you guys from over there, I'll sure do it."

I had a kind of mixed-up college career. I went to Northern Montana College shortly after high school and to a College of Great Falls satellite in Hays for one semester. Went to Long Beach City College for a while and Fort Belknap College. I have a cumulative total of about the equivalent of an associate's degree. I decided to take college seriously in 1980 when I was studying business administration and hoping to go to law school. But the tribe had some turmoil with the Department of Labor, which had a judgment against them. It started out like $3 million, and the final judgment was $1.7 million. The officers of the tribal council asked me to help resolve that issue, which I did. The $1.75 million eventually was reduced to about $70,000. But that was the end of my schooling.

Part of it was that I got married early on. My wife and I started dating in 1972, when I was a sophomore in high school and she was a freshman. On her father's side, she is Assiniboine and a little bit of Gros Ventre. Her mother is Japanese. She was seventeen and I was nineteen when we moved in together. One thing that I have noticed about the Indian women in our family is they don't get involved in politics. My grandma just raised the kids and took care of stuff at home. My mother was the same way. She'd get really angry but wouldn't say a whole lot about it. My wife is the same way. We had our first son in 1977. Five years later we had another son. Nine years later . . . no ten years later . . . we had a daughter. Year and half after that we had another daughter. Five years after that we had a son.

In 1976, I got a job working as a community health representative with elderly men. I'll never forget that experience. Even if I was helping them bathe, the men would tell me stories. One ninety-nine-year-old client told me about how the reservation was actually supposed to be farther west, but the line kept moving. Years later I did some research. The National Archives have many different 1886 maps of the Fort Belknap Reservation. The borders kept changing. What it looked like is that as homesteaders kept coming in, they just kept moving the line. At that time the Gros Ventres had an agency further west where they were making permanent agricultural improvements. Finally, the government completely cut out the area where the Gros Ventres agency was located. The Gros Ventres really loved the place. The people had fenced off little plots and had a few head of livestock. All of a sudden, government agents said they had to move. My dad said that when they left that area they had a broken-hearted dance.

I hold the BIA responsible. There was a BIA agent for each agency and a Montana state superintendent. In the 1851 Fort Laramie Treaty and the 1855 treaty with the Blackfeet Nation (comprised of the Gros Ventres, Piegans, Bloods, and Blackfeet), the Blackfeet Territory, covering half the state of Montana, was established. The territory was systematically reduced through executive orders and "agreements" negotiated after the tribes comprising the Blackfeet

Nation were decimated by smallpox, starvation, and warfare. In the 1860s, there was a really bad conflict between the Piegans and the Gros Ventres. I found the conflict was intentionally caused by government employees. There was a small encampment of Gros Ventres—six lodges, ten people per lodge, so sixty people—they were all wiped out. All killed. These government officials told the Gros Ventres that the Piegans killed them. So a Gros Ventres war party retaliated, and it just went back and forth until it was irreconcilable. In 1868, the government negotiated another treaty with the tribes belonging to the Blackfeet Nation. They divided the territory. The Gros Ventres took everything east of Sandy Creek, a few miles west of Havre, and sixty-six miles north and west of Fort Benton. Everything east of that line—north and south—is Gros Ventre turf.

After I helped out with the debt to the Department of Labor, there was a crisis with the Department of Housing and Urban Development and I was asked to go tackle that. They moved me over to housing as assistant director and then I became executive director of the housing authority. Then I got roped into running for council. I got elected to a four-year term. The second two years, I was elected chairman. I wasn't even thirty years old yet.

My wife, who worked in a Department of Labor program, was recruited to work in D.C. in the Division of Native American and Indian Programs. There was political turmoil here anyway. I couldn't get a job because I was coming off being chairman. Once you're out here politically, you're out. Other reservations recruit former chairmen to help with continuity. Here you're just an outcast. In Washington, I worked construction for a few months before being hired by the BIA to work on Indian housing programs for the tribes east of the Mississippi. I entered as a GS-11 and within two years I had made it to GS-13. But the group of elderly Gros Ventre ladies on the reservation were not satisfied with how things were going with the council and asked me to run for council.

I got elected while still in D.C. and working for the BIA. I got a waiver to commute to meetings. In 1991, I made nine trips driving back for meetings. Then my wife got some medical problems with her pregnancy, so we both came back until she had the baby. I got asked to run for chairman again. When I told my boss that I was thinking of running for chairman, he said, "Are you sure you want to do this? Tribal politics are very unpredictable." My dad told me, "You have to have rocks in your head to quit a good job in D.C. to come back here." I came back and got elected again to a two-year term as chairman.

We changed the constitution, reducing the council size from twelve to six members. This caused a big turmoil because six council members lost their seats. The night before the general election, I got warned there would be a motion to stop the election. I heard the chief judge was going to appoint an interim council and the BIA superintendent would recognize it. We earlier suspended the chief judge for not having a hearing on the issue before making a ruling to stop the election. We're governed by Robert's Rules of Order, so I sat up all night studying Robert's Rules of Order and found a rule that said, "If a motion is unconstitutional, it's out of order." At the meeting, this elderly man named John Capture stands up and says, "Mr. Chairman, if it's in order I'd like to make a motion that we stop this election." I said, "With all due respect, Mr. Capture, I'm going to have to call your motion out of order because it's unconstitutional." I could tell he was just put up to that. He said, "Okay." This one lady on the council and the vice president got all mad and said, "We'll see you at the polls tomorrow." We got beat by 100 votes out of 1,500 votes. Two years later, I was back for another term on the council and then another two more years. Afterward, I took a break. Then they put me at the tribal court system because the BIA was threatening to take it over. But the last five years I've just been doing contract work, helping people in tribal court. I function like a public defender.

I am the third generation. By that I mean there was my grandfather, my father, and now me living under this form of government that was imposed on us. My grandfather Tom Main was one of the country's most highly recognized Indian leaders, but the BIA viewed him as a troublemaker. A letter in the National Archives identified him as the only remaining Gros Ventre still making trouble. He was just advocating for his people. It was the same thing with my dad. He was the kindest, most hardworking, dedicated man. Yet there were so many rumors, untrue ones, about him.

This community concept government is a form of self-termination. A lot of these younger people really don't have a tribal identity. You ask them what they are and they say, "Fort Belknap Indian." There's no such thing. You're either Gros Ventre or Assiniboine. There has been a push to revitalize tribal culture and languages, but a lot is being lost in this process. A group of middle-aged tribal members who refer to themselves as "Young Elders" have borrowed customs and ceremonies from other tribes and tell the younger generation that these are Gros Ventre ways. Instead of gaining knowledge from our own elders, they have borrowed from other tribes. And the government just keeps fighting our efforts to get federal recognition for each tribe or to change to a confederation of tribes constitution, which would let us maintain our individual identities. They pay off people to talk against it. There is a word among the old AIMsters for tribal members like that. They are sellouts.

Voting has always been important in our family. Until his death in 1952, my grandfather advocated on the state and national levels for Indians to organize and do block voting. He believed the Indian vote could determine the outcome of state elections. Also as a member of the miners' union, voting was very important to him. As soon as we got of age, my dad always made us go vote. In the early days, we had to go to Harlem to vote. Then we had a polling place for Election Day voting on the reservation. Our first big voting push was on the school board elections. The board was all non-Indians. Back in 1987 we elected a majority Indian school board. It was kind of disappointing because we didn't get reforms that we wanted. There were still racist teachers. Then we had the "great white flight." Non-Indians living in our school district chose to transport their kids to school in Chinook, twenty-two miles away. But they only had to drive them halfway because a school bus came part of the way and picked the kids up. There was even a guy who served on the state legislature and whose wife was a schoolteacher who sent his children to Chinook. The non-Indian community just didn't want their kids going to school with Indians. After we got a majority of Indians on the school board, there were still the same teachers. We couldn't get them out because they had tenure.

I'll give you one example. It was nearing the Thanksgiving holiday, and this real racist teacher was giving a story about this wonderful Thanksgiving dinner and all this other stuff. My son Bill, who was in seventh or eighth grade, was sitting there shaking his head no. The teacher looks at him and says, "What's the matter, Bill? You don't agree with that?" "Nope. That's not what my grandpa taught me." "Why don't you tell us what your grandfather taught you?" So my son told him about massacring Indians and stuff. After he was done, the class kind of laughed—directing it at the teacher. The teacher told the laughing Indian kids, "Oh, why don't you go back to where you came from?" meaning the reservation. Bill looked at him and said, "Back to where we came from?" And the class all started laughing again. He sent Bill to the office. Imagine an authoritative figure like a teacher up there and you feel his dislike of you and having to go to that class every day. But it has slowly changed. There are a lot more Native American teachers and kids are treated better.

In the 1990s, we went after the Blaine County commissioners. The county commission was all non-Indian, even though the voting-age population is 50–50. We had ACLU lawyers and got a redistricted plan with almost 90 percent Indian in one district and 50 percent in another district. Then in 2012, I heard that Four Directions was looking for people to start an Indian voting rights movement and possibly do litigation. It is really hard to get Indians to vote. The state and county officials had gotten people believing they would stand a better chance of being selected for jury duty if they were registered to vote. Indians generally don't like to serve on jury duty. People just wouldn't register.

But I liked the idea of a registration and early voting satellite on the reservation. I thought it might really enhance voting and turnout. County officials threw every obstacle they possibly could. I identified three places that met ADA requirements including our courthouse that had just been remodeled and made ADA compliant. The officials said, "Oh, we'll come down and look at it," but they never did. They agreed to open the satellite. Then they turned around and held basically a secret public meeting in Chinook. Nobody here even knew about the meeting. They had sent a notice that the meeting was going to be held on a certain day but held it the day before. At this hearing, they decided, "No, we're not going to open one." They said the decision was based on the fact that there was no support for the office at the public meeting.

We were really upset about the decision. Not only did we have an Indian on the county commission, but a non-Indian who was married to a tribal member recently had been appointed after the death of the former commissioner. The tribal council and community members wrote letters of support for him to get that position over some tribal members who wanted the position. He had told us, "Don't worry. We'll get this done." When it came right down to it, both turned on us. My personal feelings are that neither is enrolled here. The Indian is enrolled on the Salish and Kootenai Reservation. My thought is that they like to have their elections just the way they are—status quo—because the people who are actually turning out to vote are a higher economic class of Indians. A lot of times, the higher economic class Indian looks down more on a lower economic class Indian than white people do. I think they were going, "If we have the satellite office, these guys are liable to get all these people out of these low-rent housing and projects, get them out to vote. They're liable to elect a person from their economic class."

Yep, so we ended up in court for the *Wandering Medicine v. McCulloch* lawsuit. I had to testify at the hearing in Billings. I wasn't a plaintiff, but I did all the groundwork. I had to get the ADA-compliant building secured, had to get the support of the tribal council, had to locate plaintiffs—certain types of people to be plaintiffs. The best type of person for a plaintiff is a veteran, somebody who would have to drive a long distance to the county seat. Several members of our tribal council signed on as plaintiffs. That's where Patti Quisno, Donovan Archambault, and Buster Moore came in. They all live forty to sixty miles from the county seat in Chinook.

The other part was coordinating meetings and stuff. The case involved three counties—Big Horn, Blaine, and Rosebud. When we went to Billings, the other side showed up full force with the commissioners, county attorneys, and some spectators. When I walked into the courtroom, I couldn't believe that there was a handful of us Indians sitting on one side of the room—OJ Semans, his wife, myself, Buster Moore. Less than ten. The other side was just full. I would say there were seventy to eighty people, all blond, real blond. I always joke and say, "And then there were a few dark spots sitting in there—including our Indian county commissioner and another Indian commissioner from Big Horn County." After Judge Cebull ruled against us, they were all high-fiving and laughing and stuff. It was a struggle all the way. In Blaine County, it was mostly Democrats, whom we fought. Blaine County Indian precincts vote 90–99 percent Democrat year after year.

I knew something was wrong with Judge Cebull. The law clerk was advising him on what to say. I don't know if the man was getting senile or what, but he definitely wasn't all there. It was just a circus to me, so the ruling was really no surprise. Then Blaine County started to act like they wanted to agree to a satellite office again. We weren't going to fall into that same trap, where they led us on all the way until just a few days before the election when it was too late to really do anything. We started appealing the district court decision, and the higher court got it sent back down to be reheard at district court but with a new judge. We ended up having an agreement to open a satellite office. I wish there had been a federal judge decision instead of an agreement because they are masters at trickery. When something is being done voluntarily, they can change it without telling us. For example, in the general election, they only had the satellite open one day in that thirty-day period in Hays and one day in that thirty-day period in Lodgepole. The rest of the days were at the Fort Belknap Agency, but Hays and Lodgepole are thirty-five to fifty miles further from the county seat than the Fort Belknap Agency.

Blaine County as far as I know is still in this voluntary agreement. The tribal officials in this past election had not been really active in the case and didn't understand a lot. Blaine County wanted a tribally designated contact person to work with on the satellite. Some council members recommended me, but I was posting some controversial stuff on social media and didn't get appointed. They chose the chief administrative officer, who signed off on anything the county sent. Hopefully, they will pay attention in the next go-round. The southern end of the reservation needs more days. Our population is pretty much evenly split so the access should be equal. There are two southern communities versus one community here. Down there it's Hays and Lodgepole, and up here it is just the Fort Belknap Agency.

We have potentially three thousand voting reservation members, but less than 50 percent are registered. We only have about a thousand people voting. We need to get those numbers up. We need to get people registered and voting. Organizations need to start cooperating on registering and get-out-the-vote stuff. Start early. Don't wait until the month before the primary election. Get some people working even if only on a part-time basis for six months leading up to the primary. Give them names of people they need to contact and get registered. Then they'll have that whole month to get them to one of the satellite offices. I think it can be done, but there needs to be resources. After Governor Bullock and a bunch of Democrats held a rally at the recreation center, they announced that people could still vote at the satellite office. When I drove by the satellite, there was a line over a block long of people wanting to vote. People hadn't even known about the satellite office. We put it on the radio and on fliers, but the door-to-door thing is really what needs to be done. It would cost maybe $1,000 a week for ten to twelve weeks leading up to the election.

I don't think the Democrats do a whole lot more for us than Republicans. If you had walked into my mother's house—even though she's now deceased—and looked at her sitting at the kitchen table, this is what you would see. Right above her on the wall was a big old felt poster of the American flag draped down over JFK and RFK. That's how people still envision the Democratic Party. It's no longer the party of the Kennedys and . . . Mike Mansfield, who was really an advocate for Indians. A lot of the older people think that party is still there. Indians, for the most part, have family heads who basically tell the family how to vote. As far as senators went, John Melcher wasn't too bad. Max Baucus was hit-or-miss. The one who really helped on a lot of Indian stuff and doesn't get any credit was a Republican, Conrad Burns. He was a staunch supporter of the tribal colleges even though he was lucky to get three to four votes out of the entire Fort Belknap.

I was on the council when Burns was in Congress. I was always able to go talk to him. He'd listen. When Hillary Clinton was going around trying to sell Bill Clinton's health-care deal, there was a meeting in Billings with tribal leaders. I was delegated to go down there for Fort Belknap. Congressman Pat Williams, who held Montana's lone congressional seat, was at the meeting. Montana used to have two congressional seats but lost one in the last census. Before that, Pat had represented the western district and Ron Marlenee the eastern district. Ron did nothing for Indians, but Pat helped a lot. They ended up running against each other in the general election and the Indian vote got Pat elected. At this meeting, Pat's job was to introduce all the tribal leaders to Hillary Clinton. When Pat got to me, he turned beet red. "I've known this guy for an awful long time, and I don't know his real name—only Snuffy." Conrad Burns also was there. After the meeting, these really redneck people were talking to him. I went by and patted him on the back and said, "Nice to see you, Conrad. Nice to have you on board on the Indian issue." He turned around, and his ears turned red. Out of the side of his mouth he said, "Get out of my life, Main."

I don't even think we have a two-party system anymore. Close your eyes and listen to two speeches. A lot of it is the same. They talk the same. I think Trump has figured that out. He's trying to keep people from voting. I don't know how to explain it. I've been involved in it for so long, and I see these cycles that come around. Periodically Indians will be high on the priority list, usually because of some catastrophe, and they will pump in money. As a response to Wounded Knee or Standing Rock or people dying in substandard Indian jails, there will be all this money for building jails but nothing for houses. A lot of it has to do with hatred and jealousy. The United States government wants people jealous of each other and constantly fighting among themselves. It is worse when you have two tribes that were enemies back in the old days and you stick them on the same reservation. In Montana, there's the Crow and the Northern Cheyenne right next to each other. In Wyoming at Wind River, there's the Arapahoe and the Shoshone fighting right now in federal court over some issues. I can't understand it. They choose to fight little nitpicky local battles among themselves instead of looking at the big picture of what is going to be left for their grandchildren.

The biggest concern here is water rights. I have served on the Gros Ventre Treaty Committee for nearly twenty-five years. Since 2000, we have been fighting to stop the Fort Belknap Community Council from finalizing a water settlement agreement with Montana and the United States government. The agreement is not a good deal. The treaty committee has very limited resources, $5,000 a year for most of the past twenty years, but we have managed to stop the finalization of the agreement so far. The tribal council, federal government, and Montana have spent millions of dollars in this fight. When the water rights issue was picking up steam, we formed a water rights task force along with the treaty committee. We operate on $10,000 a year for the treaty committee and task force. We have been fighting on the issue for seventeen years now.

The BIA has given the tribe $300,000–$400,000 a year to try to settle this water rights claim. We keep telling them they don't have the right to settle. The underlying issue is treaty based. The water rights issue hinges on their asserting that the reservation was established for agricultural purposes. Since Congress established the reservation for agricultural purposes, then you have a right to a certain amount of federally reserved water rights. But they're adding language . . . they're not saying it's based on the 1888 agreement, which is not even a treaty because Congress quit making treaties with Indians in the 1870s. Instead they said it is based on the 1855 treaty, but neither the Assiniboines nor the Fort Belknap Indian Community were party to the 1855 treaty and the community council is comprised of both Gros Ventres and Assiniboines, who are elected by members of the Fort Belknap Indian Community, which is a nontreaty, nonhistorical tribe.

Under the settlement agreement, the federal government is giving us this money, which we can only use how they say and mostly for agriculture. The last count I have is that we have thirty-nine members who are in the agricultural business. But they're going to spend $400 million to develop agricultural land. We have seven to eight thousand members, who have just as much claim to the water rights as the next guy does. The worst part of it is that you're settling the water rights, and you're giving up all past, present, and future claims against the government for water rights. The 1888 agreement that established the reservation does talk about agricultural purposes, but the 1855 treaty had nothing about agriculture. We weren't into agriculture then. We had hunting rights, fishing rights, and all these other rights that I think we're giving up a claim to if we enter this agreement.

We need to learn from the past. In 1973 when we settled our land claims, only seventeen people came to a meeting to vote whether to accept land settlement money. Only my dad and I voted against it. There was language stating you are giving up all rights to all past, present, and future land claims against the United States government. Okay. Years pass. There comes a boundary dispute on both the eastern and western boundaries of the reservation. We can't even go back and fight that boundary dispute because we accepted that 1973 agreement. I tell people, "So learn from that. You're putting the same waiver on the water compact. Twenty to thirty years from now if something comes up, you're not going to be able to go back and do anything about it." Anyway we managed on really limited resources to hold that off. The tribal community council approved the water compact in 2000. The state legislature approved it. All it has to do is go through Congress now and we've managed to keep it from passing for all these years.

This is why voting matters. It matters who gets elected to the state legislature, and it matters who gets elected to Congress. Had it not been John Tester in office when the water settlement was getting ready to be approved by Congress, it likely would have passed. But Tester understood. They had a hearing in Malta on it. It was supposed to have been a secret meeting with Malta downstream water users and Fort Belknap and congressional aides, but we found out about the meeting and attended, although we did not get a very warm reception. I gave a speech explaining that nobody on Fort Belknap has the right to negotiate any treaty issue under the 1855 treaty except the Gros Ventre tribe. After the meeting, John Tester's aides came over and talked to me for an hour. When the issue came up with Tester, he said, "It's a treaty issue" and refused to introduce legislation. He said, "Until you guys agree locally on what you want to do, I'm not introducing nothing." And I respect him for that.

My grandfather Tom Main had a vision or foresight about how important voting is. One article quoted him saying that "the number of Indians in Montana should control the balance of power in any election." That's true now because the country is so split between the Democrats and Republicans. If Indians would vote as a block, they could control a lot of these seats on the national level. It's just sad that people don't understand how important it is to vote. A lot of times one reservation will vote Republican and another Democrat, which dilutes the influence. A lot of it is that the first thing out of this other tribe's mouth is, "Nobody is going to tell us how to vote."

Let me end with a story about racism. When I was a young man, my folks spent many weekends in bars. I used to drive them around and play pool while they were drinking. Then I'd drive them home and make sure they got home safe. Indians just didn't go into some of the bars because they'd find a reason to kick them out. In fact, Kennedy's Bar in Harlem, when I was a kid, still had a sign hanging in the window: "No Indians or Dogs Allowed." That's right on the main street in Harlem. Anyhow, one evening, I was playing pool at a bar where a lot of Indians hung in Harlem. The bar had what they called a "bull pen." It used to be just an area in the back with benches and where people could buy a jug and drink after hours. Later on it became a place for the local drunks or winos to kind of sit around. Most of them were Indian.

One day I was playing pool by myself in this bar, and there was a wall with some holes that you could see through into the "bull pen." I could hear somebody in the back. I knew this old lady and her husband—harmless winos—had been back there. The guy, who was my grandmother's brother, must have left, but I heard his wife holler, "Snuffy!" Then I heard her say, "Indians don't do that." And I looked through that hole, and the son of a guy who owned a redneck bar down the street was trying to stick his penis in the woman's mouth. And I hollered at him, "Hey what the hell are you doing?" I run around there. I chased him out the back door and down the alley and into his dad's bar. He told his dad to call the cops and then ran out into the street. I caught him and beat the holy living hell out of him. Pretty soon the cops started showing up, and the first cop accidently caught a punch and ended up on the ground. By then all the people from the redneck joint/bar were all in the street kind of in shock, watching this long-haired Indian kid raising hell. Another cop shows up, and all the Indians from the other bars were in the street by then, hollering and jumping on cars and stuff. The cops finally got me subdued and stuffed me headfirst between the front and back seats in a cop car. This big cop, who weighed about 300 pounds, sat on me all the way to the police station. I weighed 135 pounds at the time.

At the police station, two cops held me against the concrete wall and this other cop took out a big long metal flashlight. And that's the last thing I remember. He whacked me across the forehead with it against that concrete wall. The other guys in jail told me the cops drug me in there by my hair and just kind of threw me in and closed the door. I got charged with assaulting a police officer. But my dad got this attorney and they were going to file a lawsuit because the guys who were in jail had witnessed what they did to me against that wall. They agreed to drop the charges against me if I would agree to not sue them. I agreed to get it over.

But I don't know if that event had anything to do with it or if it was AIM empowering Indians or what, but that was a turning point of Indians getting a little bit of pride and talking up for themselves in Harlem. All of the rednecks were shocked that an Indian would dare to do something like that in their town. The Indians over there down the street were all whooping and hollering and liking it. After that, things slowly started to change to where Indians could start going into any bar they wanted to in town. Of course, the economy started drying up then too, and a lot of people were moving away and stuff.

John Lewis

I was born on October 7, 1942, in Phoenix and mostly grew up in the Tempe/Phoenix area, which borders the Gila River Indian Community. My father is Pima and Tohono O'odham and a member of the Gila River Indian Community. My mother is Mojave and is a member of the Colorado River Indian Tribes. I'm enrolled at the Colorado River Indian Tribes, but my two brothers are enrolled at the Gila River Indian Community. Growing up, we spent quite a lot of time with our relatives at the Gila River Indian Community. My step-grandparents had wagons and horses. Once or twice a week, we'd ride in the wagon to get water that we'd carry back in a barrel. Near the water there was a store and it was exciting to go into the little store. It wasn't much thinking about it now, but it was fun.

A lot of the things we did were church related. Going back a long way, my family is Presbyterian. My great-grandfather was Presbyterian. My grandfather attended the Moody Bible Institute in Chicago and was a minister. He had churches in Oklahoma and around here in Tohono O'odham country. Gila River Indian Community has a large Presbyterian population. It all goes back to a Presbyterian missionary named Charles Cook, who developed churches there. The Presbyterians also started a school for ministers, the Cook Christian Training School. Initially it was located at Gila River, but then it moved to Phoenix. The school was interdenominational and brought in people from the Dakotas, the Northwest, from Alaska, New Mexico—creating connections from across the Indian Christian world. My father was a graduate of the San Francisco Theological Seminary and was an ordained Presbyterian minister. He had his church in Phoenix, where his parishioners were mostly Indian. He also taught at the training school.

There's a lot of things in Christianity that have moved toward tribal traditions. For many people it's integrated together. There's mutual respect. You do all this in different degrees, but still a lot of respect there and a sharing of both traditions and ways of life. They just add on to one's overall way of life. That's just integral to one's bringing up. I think when you see a resurgence of songs in our own language, those things are there and so one works on strengthening the language, strengthening the use of it. It flows to everybody and they draw from everybody to make it happen. It's not a big distinction.

As a child, I went to public schools in both Tempe and Phoenix. My Tempe school didn't have many, if any, other Indians. Everyone thought we were Hispanic because there was a large Hispanic population. In Phoenix, we lived in an Indian-populated area, right next to the BIA's Phoenix Indian boarding school. Some Indian kids, just a few, came to the public school with us.

Of course, there was racism. It was a time of racism, lots toward black people and Hispanics. There were "nigger" lines drawn, which meant there were certain places that wouldn't welcome you. Theaters, swimming pools, and other places. I'm not sure if it's changed that much. You don't have the blatant discrimination in public places, but you have attitudes about people of color. Arizona is ground zero for anti-immigration. When it comes to immigration, it's a color thing. If you're brown, you are discriminated against. At public hearings on immigration, there's just plain viciousness and meanness all around.

Just yesterday I was at a McDonald's and this guy came in and said, "I didn't get my order correct and I want to see the manager."

And it was a Hispanic lady he was talking to and she said, "I'm the manager," and he said, "You didn't get my order right. When I come in here, you need to be hiring people who understand English better and can speak better." You see that attitude in north Phoenix. Higher-income people live up there as opposed to south Phoenix, which is Hispanic. In north Phoenix, attitudes flare up. You never know when it's going to happen.

North Phoenix is where the BIA Indian school was located. The school was designed to be agriculturally self-sustaining, so it included a lot of land. The city took part of that land and built Central High School, with a student body that was 99 percent white. It's still a little mystery—how that land got taken. I guess that was Indian policy at the time.

Central High School worked out fine for me. My brothers and I played basketball. On the Indian teams, the position I played was center, but on other teams I was a guard. We hooked up with some Mormon teammates. A lot of Mormon places of worship have gymnasiums so that made it nice. It was a good experience. My community friends were Indians, who played basketball, too. Basically, my time was spent playing Indian basketball and organized school or league basketball. After I got into college and began to travel around the state, my friends were Navajo. One of my teammates was Peterson Zah, who later became president of the Navajo Nation. Basketball is gigantic in the Navajo Nation and we'd go up there and play in New Mexico, all over the state. Different tribes would have tournaments.

After high school graduation in 1960, I started college in Arizona and then went to the University of Tulsa, where my professors pushed me to study anthropology. University of Tulsa didn't have an anthropology department, so I transferred to the University of Oklahoma and graduated from there in 1965 with a degree in anthropology and history. My interest was in what is called "applied anthropology." It draws upon principles and thoughts from anthropology, as well as other disciplines, and then applies them to community development and community organizing. Edward Spicer was a well-known person in applied anthropology. After I got my bachelor's degree, I worked with my tribe and then went to the University of Arizona to study with Dr. Spicer for my master's degree.

Historically a lot of BIA/Department of the Interior people who had developed Indian policy had backgrounds in anthropology. With applied anthropology, you look at the strengths of communities and cultures, seeing those as positives and building on them. Part of my work was again working with tribes, mainly Tohono O'odham and Pascua Yaqui in the Tucson area. Tohono O'odham was heavy into mobilizing resources, accessing resources, identifying resources, and trying to work with communities. Same thing with Pascua Yaqui. What I did was help them write things up. The basic idea is to have in each community people who could identify needs, whether in welfare, agriculture, transportation, or health, and then try to bring in resources. With Pascua, it was building houses on a new community. They accessed some land through legislation and built a community called New Pascua. At the time, they weren't federally recognized, but they gained it in 1977.

By the time I graduated, Indian people across the country were really looking into improving communities on a much broader basis. With the Office of Economic Opportunity (OEO), a whole array of programs came into existence. In 1972 or 1973, I was hired by the National Indian Training and Research Center (NITRC) that was started in Tempe. It was funded by foundations and had different projects. The board included Indian professionals from all over the country. One of my projects was to look into what was happening with Indian child welfare. The Indian Child Welfare Act hadn't been passed yet when I started researching how states were dealing with Indian children. I traveled to different places to see what was going on.

By this time, I had connections with a number of Navajos, as well as Indian activists from all over. One of the people at NITRC was Sidney Bean. He got his master's in social work here at ASU but also was trained at Saul Alinsky's organizing school in Chicago. We worked together and then moved on together to work with Southwest Indian Development (SID) that was out at Window Rock. We set up a Phoenix SID office. SID had previously done lots of different studies, including one on the exploitation of Indians by trading posts. Trading posts were taking crafts and jewelry that people made and essentially setting up a company store, just like what used to be in mining towns. People trading there would be always in debt because they did not get paid much for their arts and crafts but were paying a lot for goods. Also the post office was located at the trading post, which meant checks and Social Security could be held onto.

The SID offices also studied education issues. People wanted schools run differently—public schools, as well as Bureau schools. Tribes were looking at self-determination, beginning with schools. At the time, Rough Rock Community School stood out because it had community control from the beginning. There were other schools, such as Rock Point, which was a Bureau school where people were pushing for community control. And then there were public schools that people wanted to change. That's where voting matters. There was a school board with no Indians, but that would change if Indians voted. The hardest piece was getting Indians to run for election, and the next hardest thing is to get out the vote. SID was doing all of these things. We used research as a way to look into issues, work on issues, and find answers.

I also got involved with broader Indian rights issues. The U.S. Civil Rights Commission spent a good part of the year—and we worked with them—in looking at issues, particularly in Phoenix and on Navajo Nation and other areas. In Phoenix, the big issues were education and access to resources. There are high dropout rates. There were lots of programs, but they weren't accessible to Indian people. We needed to be able to document things and then go to the city council. During this time, we began working with the Inter Tribal Council of Arizona (ITCA) and the Denver Research Institute, which is part of the University of Denver, on child welfare studies and employment studies.

When I went to social services offices in Arizona to ask about child welfare issues, they would say, "We know why you're really here. You're here because of Title 20." Title 20 was a change to the Social Security Act that gave block funding to states for social services programs. Before the change Arizona was getting about $12 million for social services, but Nixon was pushing block grant funding at twice that amount.

Arizona is a very conservative state and didn't want to pass on block grants to the tribes. Its position was that tribes are sovereign nations where they had no jurisdiction, so they would not give them Title 20 funds. I got involved with Title 20 activism, taking information to ITCA about federalism, block grants, and how tribes could access these streams of money. Tribes weren't getting anything from existing streams, so Title 20 was an opportunity. Along with ITCA and Navajo Nation, we worked on Title 20 disbursement in Arizona. That involved developing intergovernmental agreements with the state, which was a big effort, starting with a planning grant and going forward.

The Center for Community Change in Washington was promoting a lot of activism across the country in Hispanic communities, black communities, but we were probably the only Native affiliation. They had resources and access to people who were coming into positions at the Department of Health and Human Services in the new Carter administration. With the new administration, ITCA was able to be part of two Title 20 demonstration projects: one was to work with the state office and develop a system of allocating Title 20 funds and working on Title 20 programs with the tribes; the other was to look nationally at ways to change the legislation so tribes could get block grants just like states. We did not succeed in changing the Title 20 law, but we did build changes to different states—the Dakotas, Montana, the Northwest—and promote what Title 20 was so that they could start accessing it like we did it here.

Those were exciting times at SID. There was a thing called "revenue sharing," which was a chunk of new money that the IRS administered to the cities and states. We worked with Phoenix, so the city's Indian community got a share. The funds went to establish daycare centers, slots for employment and training. It just took a lot of meetings. There were a lot of committee meetings and negotiating with other ethnic communities to reach agreements about dividing up the pie. Then it had to be approved by the city council.

We provided documents to the state civil rights commission and the U.S. Civil Rights Commission. At the national level, tribes from across the nation were sharing information. That's where the National Congress of American Indians, the National Tribal Chairmen's Association, and different intertribal groups come in. There were efforts at developing comprehensive planning for health care. States were getting grants for health planning through Public Law 641. Navajo Nation was able to get its own 641 allocations, and we did a demonstration health-planning project with tribes. This was at Inter Tribal Council of Arizona because I left SID and went to ITCA in the mid-1970s.

My friend Sidney Bean also came to ITCA. He later moved to the Phoenix Indian Center, turning it into one of the largest urban Indian centers in the nation. The goal was to really bring together tribes and off-reservation communities—all Indian people. At ITCA, we developed an area steering committee for Phoenix Indian Health Service (IHS). We worked out an arrangement among tribes in Arizona, Nevada, and Utah to have a steering committee that would consult periodically with IHS executives on programs and budget.

I can say we have accomplished a lot. In 1975 when the Indian Self-Determination Act was passed, there was only one tribal social service program operation. Now, all the tribes have a social service department or office. We tried to ensure there were ways for federal and state funds to be allocated to tribal governments. ITCA set these systems up for health, Medicaid, transportation, just going down the line. But it's an ongoing effort because legislation changes, administrations change, everything changes. Always have to be on top of educating and reeducating and sometimes develop new legislation. Those are what intertribal councils do. It has to be the driving force in getting tribes engaged at the state and federal government levels. You need to have a voice and advocate for rights.

Voting is essential. If you want changes in education, the key is changing the school board, which means getting people to vote. In order to get people to vote, you have to make it easier and one way is by having polling places. There was an issue with a public school in Apache County. People wanted curriculum changes and an emphasis on hiring Indian teachers. Voting is how you influence the school board. Develop the vote, find ways of getting people to run for office and vote. Alberta Tippeconnic, Rosalind Zah, and others created a women's group to take on voting. These Navajo women went to the counties and pushed for polling places. They were successful in getting polling places, advertising votes, and eventually they got the school board changed and got changes in the schools.

After that effort, Alberta Tippeconnic started working with me on voting at ITCA. We needed people to understand how voting affects what state legislators do, how it affects members of Congress and increases our effectiveness when dealing with them. You need influence with your delegation and that comes through voting. You need to be connected with politicians from both parties. One way of doing that is promoting voting without being partisan. Just vote, get out the vote. Alberta, who later became assistant director of ITCA, focused a lot on voting. Also through the Center for Community Change, we hooked up with the Southwest Voter Registration Education Department and William Velasquez out in Texas. We were able to network and talk with them. They provided some money for promoting voting. In 1976 or 1977, we developed a voter's guide with candidate positions and that was distributed all over the Indian reservations.

Also it is important to see how the game is played and districts are apportioned. One state legislator was very effective on our issues, but redistricting took away his district. You needed to get oriented to all those different things. Remember Apache County. There were all kinds of issues about whether tribal people could run for office, where they could vote, and the carving out of new districts. The county commissioners wanted to make a new county up in the northern end where Indians lived and where no tax revenue was being generated.

In the midst of all this, there was a newspaper article about what we were doing and how important voting was. Right beneath our article was another one about Frank Harrison and Harry Austin, who had won the right to vote for Indian people back in 1948. I started asking, "Who knows these people?" A person from the Yavapai Community Center said Frank Harrison was Yavapai and still out there, so we decided to find him. We held a recognition event, a really nice event for him. All the tribes came and members of Congress. Bruce Babbitt came. The president of ITCA, Ned Anderson, gave a good talk on voting history. Harry Austin had passed, but Frank came with his family. We had that celebration and put together a slide presentation about the history of Indian voting rights, which was turned into a video. Frank was such a humble guy.

In the late 1970s we started a daylong voter education conference, involving all the Arizona tribes. Political candidates came, district legislative candidates, as well as people running for Congress and statewide office. People from the Democratic and Republican

National Committees pitched their respective efforts and candidates. We ran this for years. Even though it was quite expensive, tribes were willing to pay for food or make donations. But as tribes got more familiar with their legislative district people and candidates were spending more time going directly to tribes, there was less need for the conference. Times changed so we didn't need to do it anymore.

What we did was start participating in an annual tribal/state legislative day, where tribes go to the capitol and meet legislators. These meetings are an important mechanism for discussing legislation. It also gets Indians thinking about what people should be in the legislature. Who should you vote for? Do they respond to your issues? If not, what does it take to get a more responsive person elected? It gets tribal members educated on voting but also gets the state legislature hopefully more responsive to tribal concerns and issues. We also set up regular meetings in Washington with our members of Congress.

Right now one of the issues with Tohono O'odham, Apache, Navajo, and Hopi Nations is traditional languages and voting access. Much of it is going to have to be verbal. Tribes have some written language, but it's not practically of use in voting. Six tribes, including Navajo, have radio stations, television, cable, and other things that people listen to and can be used to provide information about issues and voting. Some counties are hiring Indian people to do the outreach and those are things that are changing.

But some people's attitude about minority voting, including the Indian population, is still something to overcome. The Republican Party is trying to curtail minority voting, particularly with the Hispanic population and on immigration issues. This directly impacts tribes, because we are people of color and many of us have Spanish surnames. Tribal governments need to continue developing their own efforts to get out the vote.

Counties and the tribes need to work together on voting. The biggest thing that needs to be resolved is addresses. How to handle people without street addresses and who use post office boxes. Sometimes the county lists a central place, like the district center, as the address on record for people and you get problems when trying to vote and there are fraud accusations. That happens on a lot of reservations, maybe all reservations. If one doesn't really know the people and the community and comes across something like this, at best the voters get a provisional ballot and oftentimes provisional ballots aren't counted. The tribal governments and state governments need to work on it because it's an ongoing concern.

Challenges can be used to drive away voters. Being challenged about whether one is entitled to vote gets very discouraging. It only takes one time for a person to be discouraged in voting. There needs to be some common understanding about residence addresses, and driver's licenses, and voter registration cards because they can all list different street addresses.

With the voter ID, we ended up in the Supreme Court, where we won that particular case. But it goes back probably to the 1980s with a reapportionment case where Gila County tried to split the San Carlos vote through redistricting. In the 1980s, the 1990s, we were able to get ITCA a voice in reapportionment. Then in 2000, there were special hearings about reapportionment for tribes. That shows some improvement and engagement with tribes. Navajo Nation has generated good data and came up with their own models for reapportionment. They used this effectively in negotiating a lot of things.

Again, with the 2004 lawsuit on voter ID, tribes learned about the legal aspect. The other aspect is attitudes. While the case was going through the courts, one court ruled in favor of the ITCA side. Arizona quickly appealed to the Supreme Court, but for twenty-four hours we were on the winning side. On talk radio shows, there were really derogatory remarks about tribes and about ITCA. That's still there, but the tribes continue to just move ahead.

I was at ITCA for thirty-nine years, and throughout the entire period voting was a key issue and it still is. ITCA is still dealing with the Independent Redistricting Committee that came out of the reapportionment win. It just continues. I was a plaintiff in the case dealing with voter identification and how tribes did not have the required IDs. There are so many obstacles to voting. It affects everything. Some tribes align their tribal elections with general elections. They'd go vote in tribal elections, but when they go to vote in the general election, it's different. You can't just walk in and have your name on the rolls. They ask you for things, and if you don't have them it's so discouraging. Those things were happening. Voting is just a part of those things.

There's still nastiness out there. Tribes are doing their part, but the education system could do so much more. We began asking the ASU law school for help, and once we got some help we began to ask for more help, then asked them to recruit more Indian faculty and students and develop Indian courses. Now there's a whole program with Indian students at the law school. But the same thing has to happen in elementary schools and high schools. People need to work together to make voting simple and to really generate participation. There are a lot of tribal citizens out there willing to make that happen and have made it happen. Each tribe has champions. They just need to be recognized and supported by tribal government. Indian people are willing to do their part. The state, county, and political parties need to recognize the importance of working with tribal governments and citizens, so we can really bring about what they call a democracy.

CHAPTER 8

Grassroots Voting Rights Activism

A Passion for Voting Rights

Any recounting of grassroots activism on behalf of voting rights in Indian Country over the past two decades should pay substantial attention to OJ and Barb Semans, whose stories are covered in this chapter. Their accounts show how hard it is to push through changes in electoral laws in states with deeply entrenched opposition. Unlike Snuffy Main and John Lewis, neither OJ nor Barb Semans had a history of activism until they reached middle age, when a passion for voting was ignited. Also neither comes from families that have traditionally provided leaders for their Nations. Instead of formal education, Barb and OJ's education was achieved through life experiences both on and off the Rez with all of the challenges and complications that people encounter.

OJ Semans Sr.

My name is Oliver J. Semans—they call me OJ. I was born in Winner, South Dakota, on November 19, 1955. At that time, Winner was still considered part of the Rosebud Sioux Indian Reservation. It stopped being part of the reservation probably in the mid-1970s. There was a case called *Rosebud Sioux Tribe v. Kneip*, in which South Dakota took us to court in order to take reservation lands, and we basically lost reservation lands out of Tripp and Mellette counties, as well as Charles Mix and Gregory counties. I've been married to Barbara for thirty-nine years and we have seven children. The six living ones are grown and live in different parts of the country. For much of my life I worked as a police officer. Now mostly I practice law in tribal court and serve as a consultant for the tribe and Ho Chunk Inc.

I'm the youngest of seven children. My father went fishing, fell into the lake, and drowned before I was born. Mom was devastated. They had a ranch and once he died—because he was non-Indian and she was Indian—basically the whites took everything from her. This was when Native women didn't have any rights. My first memory is of living in Bad Nation, out in the middle of nowhere. We still had the outdoor toilets. We would use horse and wagon to get water. Back then a good rain meant a good shower.

As a child, mainly I lived with my grandparents. When Mom was around, I would stay with her, but she had a drinking problem. I never blame Mom for how she had to handle life. The fact is I would not have been able to do what she has done. But I was always going from one home to another home. Once when I found out Mom was in North Platte, I hitched a ride with the mail carrier heading up there. When I get to her place, she goes, "Jimmy?" I say, "Yeah, I'm here to stay, Mom." I lived with her for six months, and then she takes me back to live with my grandma. Another time, when I was ten or eleven, I was living with Mom in Rapid City, but social services put me in a foster home. The son was on the same baseball team as me. I even made the all-star baseball team for the state of South Dakota. The family were the furthest thing from being Native. The father worked for the utility company. His real connection with Indians was shutting off their lights or their gas when they got behind on paying. One day he told me that he had cut off my mom's gas. And I just said, "That's life."

When I was thirteen, the parents, Mary and Jim, sat me down and told me they wanted to adopt me. I said, "You know, I really do love you guys. I appreciate what you've done for me. But I can't let you do that. Mary, you are like my mom. But you're not my mom. I only have one mom. Jim, I've never had a dad. You're like my dad. But I cannot let you guys adopt me. It's just not who I am." Then they said, "When do you want to go?" I said, "Well, I'll go tomorrow—Christmas Eve." They loaded me up with presents, called a taxi, and sent me off to my mom. I still stay in touch with the family. At the time, Mom was tending bar in downtown Rapid City and seeing this guy. I go up there on Christmas Eve and they're doing okay. But pretty soon, they started drinking and get into these fights. Finally, one day I tell them, "I can't put up with this," so Mom sends me to live in Sioux Falls with my sisters.

At this time, I didn't do drugs. I didn't drink. I didn't smoke. I was a boxer. I was a baseball player. But my sisters and their friends were partying and fighting. Again I was the new kid in school. When the white kids got tough with me, I would fight them. The last time was when this red-headed kid called me "a dumb Indian." I go, "What'd you say?" And he said, "You're nothing but a dumb Indian." So I said, "You know what I'm going to do as a dumb Indian? I'll knock the freckles right off your face." And he said, "Try it. That's impossible." I hit him once. He got up, ran behind a teacher, and started saying stuff again. The teacher did nothing, so I knocked the kid down and started hitting him. My sisters decided to send me off to my brothers in New York.

I moved with my brothers to a little bitty town called Honeoye, where I got a part-time job milking cows at a dairy. One time the owner left me to take care of the cows when he took the family to the World's Fair in New York City. After they left, I was milking this one cow, and the cow slapped its tail around my face. And the tail was full of cow poop. I wiped it off, went back to milking, and the cow did it again. So then I shaved off the hair on the tail. And the owner came back and he goes, "What the hell did you do to the cow?" I told him and he said, "How is he going to kill flies?" So I went and took a fly swatter, and I taped it on his tail, so he could kill flies. He thought it was so funny that he didn't fire me.

I played football there, but my brothers decided to move to a nearby town. I got into wrestling, actually made it to state. But I got harassed for switching schools. I was small, like five-foot-six or seven, but I was really fast, and strong. Because of my size and the color of my skin, people thought I would be a pushover, but I never was. One time, a guy kept on pushing me to fight. Finally I said, "Alright, let's fight." I hit him once and shattered his jaw. I had never really, really hurt somebody before. I got called into the principal's office. The kid's parents were very upset, and one thing I can say about the principal is that he was fair. He told the parents, "We looked into it. Your son started it. Oliver tried to leave, and your son cornered him. It wasn't Oliver's fault."

At seventeen I decided to join the service. Natives are taught that you join the service and become a warrior. I took the aptitude test and then the recruiter asked me how far I went in school. "Well, I started ninth grade, but I never finished." "Well, that's not going to work," so the recruiter put me down as graduating tenth grade. Two days later I get on a bus heading out. At first in boot camp, every recruit is a seaman, so at roll call you go, "Seaman Smith." They'd come to me and I'd go, "Seaman Semans," and they'd go, "Do you stutter." "No, no, chief. I do not stutter." "Then who are you?" "I am Seaman Semans." "There you go again! Are you trying to fuck with me?" They would do that just for the hell of it. After two months, you make rank. I made fireman, so when the chief asks me who I am, I go, "I'm Fireman Semans, sir." And the same guy goes, "There's no hope for you. First two months all you could do was stutter. Now you don't know who the hell you are. Are you a seaman or are you a fireman?" The navy was full of little shit like that. But I saw the humor in it, so it wasn't so bad.

I was in the navy from 1972 to 1978. After boot camp, I trained as a hull maintenance technician. I learned how to detect radiation in case there was a nuclear attack. I also became a certified welder. We used asbestos to protect the pipes and prevent a fire when we were welding. Your face would get full of smoke from the burning asbestos. I also was a multicross firefighter, which means I could train others to combat fires onboard ships. Even officers, who wanted to make rank, had to get their firefighting or damage control sheet signed off by me. That was pretty cool. I had a good time in the service. Fell in love a thousand times, wherever we happened to land. Made a lot of friends. Seeing different countries and different people was a real eye-opener. I could really relate to the brown-skin ones, just trying to survive.

After being discharged, I came back home in Rosebud. There wasn't a fire department and there weren't any good welding jobs. Then one day, I see a tribal police officer and I decide to check that job out. I filled out an application and was hired within fifteen minutes. Next morning I was handed a badge, gun holster, handcuffs. No training whatsoever. I patrolled with another officer for a week. Really my only experience with cops was seeing the TV show *Adam-12*. One night I was booking a guy for getting drunk and fighting when all of a sudden he jets out the door. I take off after him. He's getting away, so I pull my gun out. His back is to me, and I think, "What am I doing?" It would have been murder, so I holster my gun and took off chasing him. I can't take a life for stupidity. I've had plenty of opportunities to take a life and chose not to. Those people were just at a time in their life where it just wasn't working out.

I never really think of myself as a tough guy. You don't have to threaten somebody in order to get to the truth. Ninety-nine percent of people want to tell you the truth. They did something wrong and deep inside they don't want to have that lie eating up on them. I knew how to conduct interviews, when to look them in the eye. I knew what tone of voice to use, whether it was a stern or joking. One time, we were interviewing a guy who goes, "May lightning strike me dead if I'm lying." And I jumped up and out the window. I told my partner, "Get out of the way. Lightning is going to kill him." The man cracked up, and told me what happened.

As a Rosebud tribal police officer, I was making $2.35 an hour with no overtime, so in 1978 I got a better-paying police job at the Bureau of Indian Affairs (BIA). I started out in Rosebud and moved to Sisseton and then on to Aberdeen and Devil's Lake. The BIA is all about politics, from your tribal chairman, to your agency special officer, to your superintendent, to the area director. In Devil's Lake, I reopened the case of a murdered police officer and we indicted eleven people. I also arrested twenty-two people for fraud, including four of the five tribal council members. Tension got pretty high and the FBI wanted us to move into town under protection. We wouldn't have it. We didn't want people to think we were scared, which was kind of stupid.

Then I got sent to Tuba City, where I investigated the murder of two police officers who were found burned up in the back of their vehicle. This Navajo investigator and I are heading to the crime scene when a car goes by. I get the funniest feeling that something is not right, so I told my partner, "Turn around. Let's follow that car." The driver then gets nervous and starts going all over the road. We pull him over and I said, "Hey, listen, would you mind if we take some prints of your tires and ask where you've been?" We got a full set of tire tracks and a written statement.

At the crime scene, the dead officers have some burned flesh but are mainly bone and skull. It turned out that kids were having a party. Thomas Clyde, who we had stopped, had been there. Everybody was pretty drunk when Officer Begay pulls up. He and Thomas Clyde get into a fight and Begay is disarmed. The kids make Begay call his partner. Then they handcuff and put him in the back of the unit. When his partner shows up, they shoot both officers. The kids planned to drive the vehicle over a cliff into Lake Powell, which is really deep. Well, it had rained the day before, and the unit got stuck in the mud, so they set it on fire. The autopsy showed that the officers actually burned to death. The tire tracks allowed us to arrest and convict Thomas Clyde.

Next I joined a six-person special BIA investigative unit, but I had made some enemies. I had gotten the son of a BIA captain for involvement in a murder. This meant there were people in the BIA trying to get rid of me and the other special agents. One day, the supervisors gave each of us five allegations of child sexual abuse to investigate but wanted the investigations completed in five days. We knew this was setting us up to fail. Child sexual abuse cases can't be solved in five days. When the supervisors had us report after five days, the other officers asked for more time. They got to me last and I said, "Well, two cases were unfounded, and I got three confessions."

The supervisors told me to write up reports on the cases. I wrote the reports but also sent copies to the U.S. attorney's office. I kept copies and turned the originals in to my supervisor, who kept trying to find any little errors. Sometimes he made shit up, but I made every correction he wanted. Then I passed it on to his supervisor, who would criticize the changes. I would rewrite the reports in the way he wanted. Then I'd take his corrections, staple it, set it to the side with my number, and the corrections. It went back and forth for three to four months until the supervisors called me in. "We don't know why you made special investigator. Those poor kids out there, they've been terribly injured, and you haven't even gotten a report out yet." I pull out all the copies of the reports and show them. And they said, "You know, you really think you're smart. What about those kids?" I said, "The guys pled guilty two months ago." The supervisors were just messing with me. They didn't realize those guys already were sentenced to prison.

This was when I started paying attention to politics. Barb and I had registered as Republicans and voted for Bush. It was after that when we decided to go back to South Dakota. I was just burned out with BIA politics and the stress of policing. I knew the legal system, so I started practicing as an attorney in tribal court. But I continued thinking about politics. What made things work? What really got us energized was that our school sucked. There might be one Indian out of five on the school board. County commissioners were the same. At elections, we'd have five Indians and one non-Indian running and we'd lose. I decided we'd have to increase Native turnout. In 1994, Barb and I started pushing people to register and vote but didn't see a difference because too many Indians still were running for the same office.

Then in 2002 the TV was full of news about the Senate race between Tim Johnson and John Thune. This got Barb and me thinking. When we were registering people, they all registered as Democrats, so we switched our registration. I called Senator Johnson's campaign office and I go, "Why aren't you guys campaigning in Indian Country? There's a lot of us. Why aren't you here?" And they go, "Oh, we're going to work on it." They didn't do it, so I call them again, "You guys are really starting to piss me off. Do you want us to vote for the other party?"

The Johnson people hired Barb to do GOTV—get out the vote on reservations. We didn't have any experience with field organizing. But I had plenty of experience chasing people down. At first, the Johnson campaign sent whites to the reservation to try to register people. They would knock on doors, but the Indians wouldn't answer the door. Then the campaign turned everything over to Barb. We did a version of Driving Miss Daisy with whites driving vehicles and Natives knocking on doors and giving out information about what Tim Johnson was doing in Indian Country. We registered about six hundred people.

The Rosebud Reservation is in Todd County, which has Mountain Standard Time (MST), but the county opened polls on Election Day an hour too early, on Central Time. This cheated us out of an hour of voting. We went to court and got the polls kept open an hour longer. Instead of closing the polls at 7:00, they had to stay open until 8:00 MST. During the extra hour, we went to work. As our people were coming in, we sent them back out to find people who hadn't voted. We had poll watchers with voting lists at every place. As we got the names of those who voted, we would put in the numbers at the time they came in and the communities. In that last hour we got an additional 530–540 voters.

When the count started coming in, Sioux Falls showed Tim Johnson up by two percentage points. As the results were coming in, moving further to the west, the margin started going down, down. Pretty soon you're in Rapid City, and it's dead even. And then it goes toward Sturgis and all of a sudden you've got a 3,000–4,000 difference with John Thune ahead. The last ballots to get counted are from reservation counties—Todd and Shannon—where people had to travel more than 100 miles to drop them off. That night Johnson went to bed knowing he'd lost and Thune went to bed knowing he'd won. It was 4:00 or 5:00 in the morning when the reservation votes got counted. The next morning Johnson had won by 524 or 525 votes. The senator was elected by the Native vote. There were people on TV saying, "Indians stole the vote," but to be fair, Thune stuck up for us.

After the election we went to Senator Johnson's campaign party. They treated us really good. The senator shook our hands. His wife was wearing earrings that Barb had given her. But what happened next was troubling. They started calling different campaign people up to the podium and whipping out Star Quilts and wrapping them around them. All in celebration. Our tradition is once we give you something it's yours, but those Star Quilts were given to Senator Johnson by different tribes. By taking that gift and giving it to other white people, they basically shut the tribes out of the actual victory. It signaled that the tribes no longer mattered. We came away thinking we can't work for a campaign that forgets our people after the election. A little later, we got together with Bret Healy from the state Democratic Party. We expressed our concerns and decided to start Four Directions, a non-profit that would keep the power of the vote with Natives and not outsiders. Bret is now a consultant with Four Directions.

In early 2004, Congressman Bill Janklow resigned from Congress after getting convicted of manslaughter for killing a man in an auto accident. For the special election, the Republicans put up Larry Diedrich and the Democrats ran Stephanie Herseth. There was only a little funding for GOTV, so we decided to focus on just the main reservations: Rosebud, Pine Ridge, and Crow Creek. As a 501 C4 nonprofit, Four Directions couldn't endorse candidates, but we could do a scorecard laying out candidate positions. Herseth had a background with the South Dakota Farmers Union that was pretty good. While in the state legislature, Diedrich voted to stop funding scholarship money for tribal members. He had more negative than positive actions toward tribes. We did door hangers with the scorecard and plastered the reservations. When Herseth won, she gave part of her acceptance speech in Lakota. It made people feel they were part of the victory.

Our main goal all along was to use the political system to improve the economic and social conditions on reservations. We had some success. Senator Johnson did earmarks for us, including a $10,000,000 earmark for the Rosebud Sioux Tribe to start a Native aid program. Herseth went in as a Democrat but with a Republican lean. In South Dakota you get what you can get. Neither Herseth nor Johnson gave our people jobs on their congressional staffs. Senator Johnson would take Natives as interns but not staff. It was frustrating.

In 2004, the Republicans proposed changing the voter ID law. We really worked our contacts within the state legislature and got language allowing tribal ID as valid identification. Also in 2004, the state legislature passed a law allowing in-person absentee ballots. The new law allowed early in-person absentee voting for the first time. Barb, Bret, and I are sitting around visiting, talking about how this would affect tribes, when we realized two things. First, in-person absentee voting required traveling to the county auditor's office. Second, you could actually register and cast your ballot on the same day. We started mapping out distances and saw Indians had to travel way further than whites. From our community of Antelope to the auditor's office in Winner was a forty-five-mile trip or almost a hundred miles round trip. To do GOTV, we'd need twenty buses a day going to Winner, which was impossibly expensive. Also Winner is a racist border town. Usually they'll have the highway patrol specifically patrolling just outside Winner, bordering the reservation. More than likely even if you weren't speeding, you would be pulled over.

Shannon County—now Oglala Lakota—and Todd County are unorganized counties, which means officials in adjacent counties handle our official business. We came to the conclusion that the distance in traveling to the auditors in those counties constituted unequal access to voting and violated the Voting Rights Act. We asked for satellites for registration and in-person voting on the reservations. We decided to take away the excuses about why it could not be done. Every county official would say, "We would love to do that, but we can't afford it." To take that excuse off the table, we needed to get money to pay for the building, the mileage, and the people they would bring in to be the deputy auditors. Bret took on the fundraising. I think he sold a cow or two—Bret has a ranch.

We started with Todd County, which has three white and two Native commissioners. We sent a letter asking to discuss a satellite office. The commissioners sent the letter to Secretary of State Chris Nelson, who sent an email saying, "No, you can't do it." I called Nelson up and asked him to point out exactly where the county lacked the authority to put up that office. He couldn't. Then Bret called him and used the white privilege of cussing and swearing and threatening. Nelson changed his position. We met with the commissioners three or four times. We came up with money for the mileage, office, and the hourly salary of the deputy auditor. Finally Barb just tore into Commissioner Crenshaw, "Hey, you know, you are white trash. Remember who you played with as a kid was us Indians. Now we are here asking you. Don't forget who your friends were growing up and who treated you well." Crenshaw flipped and once he flipped, the rest agreed to set up the satellite.

Politics in Shannon County are a little tougher, but we took off their excuses about it being illegal and no money, so they agreed. I always say we bribed them. It's like white people won't do the right thing unless you give them money, which I think is a funnier than hell expression. Shannon and Todd were pre-clearance under Section 5, so we had to get approval through the Bush administration. The DOJ had sent election observers in 2002 and 2003, and we became really good friends with them. I go to D.C. and take some of these observers to lunch. I say, "Listen we have a problem. We've got a Republican administration. And we don't want DOJ to drag their feet on pre-clearance because we only have a week before absentee voting starts." These guys started talking, and one day before early absentee voting started, DOJ pre-cleared the satellite offices. And it was like, wow, that was close.

Meanwhile Senator Tom Daschle was running for reelection against John Thune. Our daughter Donna was field director for our nonprofit's GOTV. She hired people who had worked on the 2002 Johnson campaign. They hauled people to satellites to register and vote at the same time. There were a lot of Natives without tribal or state ID, so we convinced the tribe to give us tribal IDs for $10 instead of the normal $15. Then we advertised that individuals interested in voting but without a state or tribal ID could get a free one. Over a thousand people came for the free IDs. With their tribal IDs, people didn't have to fear having their right to vote being challenged and didn't have to sign an affidavit attesting to who they are. The poll workers would never offer affidavits. The signs that they put up at voting places stated, "You have to have a valid state or government ID"—didn't mention tribal ID. "Without an ID, you must do this, this, and this." Then at the very end it said, "Or sign an affidavit," without explaining what that affidavit was.

Senator Daschle lost, but not because of us. We increased voter turnout in Pine Ridge by 110 percent and Rosebud by 140 percent. John Thune won by turning out white voters. His campaign put out a flyer that had a picture of a prairie dog with the words, "The prairie dogs are coming out of their holes." He was talking to white people about Natives coming out to vote. The Republicans also started following and harassing Indian voters. Daschle complained and a judge agreed, but it triggered backlash. Two years later, in 2006, the satellite offices on reservations disappeared because there was no funding.

In 2008, I got a call from Wizipan Little Elk, who was running Obama's Native get-out-the-vote campaign. Wizi goes, "OJ, the Native American Democratic caucus at the convention is going to be meeting with different tribes. They have no idea about voting. Can you and Barb come up here and give some training in getting out the vote?" We borrowed money and went to Denver. We were about to go home when Wizipan goes, "Do you guys want to go see Obama accept the nomination?" I go, "Geez, we've got a long ways to drive. Nah." Then we head over to our friend Don Ragona's house. Don is the head of NARF and we're getting ready to go, and Barb says, "You know they offered us tickets to see Obama accept his nomination." Don goes, "Really? So you guys going?" Barb says, "No. We've got a long drive." He goes, "Can you guys get me tickets because nobody can get them," so we got the tickets and went. When we heard Obama speak, we knew he was the right man for the country.

In 2010, there was funding to work with Nevada tribes on GOTV. I go there and lay out a plan, not take over from the tribes but help. Then we started thinking about South Dakota, how we wanted those satellites put back on Pine Ridge and Rosebud. I lobbied the county commissioners individually. We went back and forth until we had enough votes to get it approved at a meeting. Todd County adopted a resolution saying, "As long as it's legal to have satellites, we are going to do it." In Shannon County, we had the county council votes, but the state's attorney, who was also the auditor in Fall River County, was really causing problems. The man told Bret and me, "If you push this, all of Fall River County election individuals will resign rather than any provide election services to Shannon County." At the next council meeting, we got on the agenda, but the auditor goes, "Before we get into Mr. Semans's request for the satellite office, I want to present you with this." And he gave them the resignations of all the Fall River election officials. Their plan was to completely shut down all Shannon County voting, even voting on Election Day. They were playing pretty rough, so we brought in the ACLU and the Department of Justice and said the tribe would run the election. Two weeks later, the officials withdrew the resignations and put a satellite office without us paying. That was our first real major victory without going to court.

Then we head back to Nevada to help with GOTV. We worked with Darrel Crocker, the executive director of ITCN, and Arlan Melendez, the chairman of Reno-Sparks Indian Colony. These are very well-established guys. Very knowledgeable. Real nice guys. They held an ITCN meeting where Harry Reid asked for their votes. They told him, "We are going to support you. Matter of fact, Barb and OJ Semans are here and they are going to organize getting out the vote for you." Well, I had a couple problems with that. We never committed to getting out the vote for Reid. Our goal was to get people to the polls, and they vote how they want. Then Reid goes, "Do you need any money?" Again, here I'm thinking Four Directions is a 501 C4 nonprofit, so I go, "No." Barb and Bret about fall over. We helped on a straight get out the vote and kicked up the Native vote higher than ever before. No ifs, ands, or buts, we increase turnout.

Back in South Dakota, the tribes had written letters asking for satellites and had been turned down. That's when we filed the *Brooks v. Gant* case to get a permanent satellite on the Pine Ridge Reservation. We wanted some plaintiffs who were registered to vote and some not registered. The registered people needed to say, "I could vote if it were here." The nonregistered needed to say, "I can't register, but I could if it was here." The state fought the case all the way. The state's team of lawyers, headed by Sarah Frankenstein, kept running up the costs. Right up to when they knew that we would win. Then they set up those offices without a court order. That means we did not get costs recovered. Our attorney, Steven Sandven, is a solo practitioner and a member of the Sisseton Wahpeton Tribe. Steven put up his own money to do the case. Because the state set up what we wanted without a court order, the issue was moot. All the money Sandven invested in fighting the case was lost. He was out at least $100,000. South Dakota has an insurance pool, so the state and counties have basically an open checkbook. So we won, but our attorney lost. That was in 2010.

In 2012 Tom Rogers, from the Blackfeet Reservation, reached out, saying, "We saw where you guys won in South Dakota. We have the same circumstances in Montana. Can you look at it?" We toured the reservations and saw how far people had to travel. Then we set up a meeting with the Montana secretary of state. We thought, this is going to be cool. We've got a Democratic secretary of state, a Democratic attorney general, a Democratic governor. The secretary of state's attorney is a guy named George—I call him Jorge—Quintana, who is on the Democratic National Committee (DNC). Bret, Barb, and I show up. We brought our granddaughter because we wanted to show her how we do things. We're getting old, and we want people ready to take over. There were all kinds of people there: leaders from Fort Peck and Fort Belknap, Native state senators and representatives. We go in thinking we got this. And so we made the request for satellites and explained how it would improve voter turnout. Secretary of State McCulloch's response wasn't even "I'll think about it." It was "No. We're not going to do it. We're not ready. The Indians aren't ready to do it yet."

After the meeting, we decide to take it to court. Steven Sandven agrees to take the case. I head off to Blackfeet, which is the closest reservation, to find plaintiffs. I'm a veteran, so I thought nobody deserves equality in voting more than veterans. So I went in the tribal office . . . usually when you go to the tribal office, they have a special place just for veterans . . . plaques and pictures and memorials. I find out that a Native had just recently been killed in Iraq. Then I meet with the vice-chairman, who is a veteran. He sends me to the person in charge of veteran affairs and I talk with the veterans. I got veterans from World War II and the Korean War. I got Vietnam veterans with Purple Hearts and Congressional Medals and some from Desert Storm, Iraq. Then I met the mother of the soldier who was recently killed. She couldn't be a plaintiff, but we knew that by putting his name out there, they'd have to fight to get him off, which would make pretty good news media.

Truth is, being a veteran is why I do this. Veterans actually fought for this democracy and deserve to be a part of it. I did a short narrative on the plaintiffs . . . what war, what type of medals. One even had been a state senator. They were good plaintiffs. I explained things, so they knew what they were getting into. A lot of them had never known that the opportunity was there for them to participate equally. Bret met with the secretary of state, who agreed to open a satellite office up in Blackfeet, which ended the lawsuit. Well, it turns out, they did not really do it, and then the election went by and it was too late. They said they would do it, and they dragged their feet. Then right when it was getting close, they said they weren't going to do it. They gave it and then took it away.

After that, I wanted to just do a lawsuit with Northern Cheyenne and Fort Belknap, but Crow got added in. I didn't want a bunch of plaintiffs because it is hard to organize them. You have to think about depositions. Natives aren't used to doing these things. Bret went to Fort Belknap, while Barb and I worked the Northern Cheyenne and Crow. I reached out to Michael Lynn from Crow. The tribal chairmen wrote letters asking for satellites and we delivered them to the Rosebud, Blaine, and Big Horn County commissioners.

There were a whole bunch of meetings but no decision. Some state officials—Natives—told us the Big Horn County commissioners were willing to put a satellite office in Crow, so we set up a meeting. Just before the meeting, I get a call from someone at Western Native Voice. They are concerned that we'll take money from one of their funders. I told him that wasn't our deal. They agreed to stay out of the way.

So we go to the meeting in Big Horn County, where most of the commissioners are Crow, and show them the letters from the tribe. Then the chairman of Western Native Voice—who is a Crow—comes in and says that they oppose the satellite offices—the Crow are not ready to vote early. A majority of the Big Horn commissioners then decide against satellites. Rosebud and Blaine counties followed suit. Western Native Voice gave white commissioners an excuse to say "no." "If the Indians don't want it, why would we give it to you?" They called us outsiders trying to get the good local Indians riled up. Sandven filed a lawsuit. The plaintiffs were veterans out of Northern Cheyenne, Crow, and Fort Belknap, as well as council leaders. The defense brought in Sarah Frankenstein again. The secretary of state—McCullogh—brought in her attorney, Quintana, who is part of the DNC. While this is all going on, I'm calling the DNC and going, "What is the matter with you guys? Why are we fighting you when you're supposed to be the so-called liberator of minorities and equality?"

The district court judge was Richard Cebull, who was about to get in trouble because of his racist emails about Obama and his mother. Judge Cebull ruled against us. But we appealed to the Ninth Circuit and by the time it got there, the justices had learned about the emails. What was really cool is that the justices convinced Sarah Frankenstein to say, "How about we don't make a ruling on Cebull's order. We just set it aside like it never happened." We had been scared it would be ruled a moot issue because the election was over. This gave the appeals court a reason to set aside Cebull's order and for us to proceed with the hearing. Sarah was setting up to do depositions and we knew the game again was run up the bill. Run up the bill. But this time we argued it was a discriminatory tactic to intentionally stop Natives from voting.

Back in Jackson County, Natives were trying to get a satellite in Wanblee. Jackson County includes the eastern part of the Pine Ridge Reservation and Wanblee is the biggest community. While we were waiting for the Montana deal, we started visiting with the Jackson County commissioners. We didn't file, but we had to set it up in order to move forward. We go to the county commissioners again with a letter—this time from Thomas Poor Bear, the vice president of the Oglala Sioux Tribe, saying that they wanted a satellite office in Wanblee. We have several meetings with the county commissioners and again it's basically, "Let us think about it." At one meeting, the Jackson County auditor told Bret that Wanblee was too far from Kadoka. When driving back to Kadoka, the poll worker's car may have a flat tire, and the Indians would come with an acetylene torch, cut off the lock on the ballot box, and steal the ballots. We offered to work to find funding. We knew the state had HAVA [Help America Vote Act] funds that could pay for the satellite office. They said, "Well, we're not going to make a decision."

At a meeting with Secretary of State Jason Gant and the election board, we suggest using HAVA funds. The election board has five members—two Democrats, two Republicans, and Gant. The Democrats want to use the HAVA funds, but Gant says, "No, we need to table this and refer it instead to the Electoral Assistance Commission [EAC] in Washington, D.C." It was a delaying tactic because the EAC didn't have enough members for a quorum. Gant put it to a vote and it passed three to two. The media went crazy on him. Every South Dakotan with common sense saw this was an intentional delay. When they saw how sneaky Gant was, the public started turning on him. There were editorials criticizing him in the *Rapid City Journal*. Keep in mind the *Rapid City Journal* is not friendly to Indian Country. The *Argus Leader* came out against him, and then the *Argus Leader* had me do a podcast. We showed Gant for what he was—basically a racist. In the meantime, we filed a complaint with the DOJ. We did that on the anniversary of the day that they signed the 1965 Voting Rights Act.

We forced Gant to put Four Directions on the South Dakota HAVA task force board. Then at a joint meeting of the HAVA task force and the election board, we got a unanimous vote to utilize

HAVA funds for satellite offices on reservations. We created a formula where if you're so many miles away then you automatically qualify for HAVA funds. Despite having HAVA money, the Jackson County commissioners voted unanimously to not do it. That was even with an Indian on the commission, but basically he's just Indian to utilize the Indian preference on leasing land. This led to filing the *Poor Bear v. County of Jackson* litigation.

Meanwhile, we're still working Montana in the *Wandering Medicine v. McCulloch* case. Again we were called outsiders. I reminded them that they had a Little Big Horn monument that showed we Sioux actually lived in Montana. We weren't outsiders. We were buried there. They ran up the bill as high as they could and then settled. The case was sent to a magistrate court. The magistrate wanted to get rid of it because we were picking on his Democratic friends. They threatened to sanction our plaintiffs. "Settle it now, or I'll slap a $25,000 fine on each of you. You can appeal it all you want. It will stay. You're going to settle." The defendants ended up paying $100,000 to our attorney, which wasn't enough to cover his actual fees. In the end, only one plaintiff signed the settlement. The settlement specifically stated that Four Directions could not work with tribes on getting the satellite offices ready. We weren't plaintiffs. Yet because of the pressure that we put on the secretary of state and the DNC, they got our names put in the settlement and said we had to stay out of the elections in Montana. Never heard of that before. We never signed the settlement. That's the first time we actually got kicked out of a state.

Back to Jackson County, we are going through the same type of crap. We get students from Claremont Graduate University (CGU) out surveying people about how travel distance affects them in all kinds of ways. None of the students, nobody got raped, killed, or hit by a drunk driver, despite what some of the white South Dakotans told them would happen. There is so much paranoia. During the Jackson County case, Bret and I were deposed. It wasn't about getting a satellite office. Sarah Frankenstein's intention was to probe into our funding sources, to basically tear apart our organization and identify funders, so that they could go after them next. Our attorneys were pro bono folks from an Indian law firm. The attorneys were all Harvard graduates and they shut Sarah down every which way. They stopped her dead in her tracks. So we get Jackson County out of the way. The judge let them agree to set up satellites until they ran out of HAVA money. I didn't think that that should be a requirement of having equal access. If money wasn't there, they should still do it.

While doing the Nevada GOTV, we noticed that Nevada reservations had worse voting conditions than Montana and South Dakota. People on the Pyramid Lake Reservation didn't even have an Election Day polling place. They had to drive fifteen miles one way. They're Paiute and part of the Inter-Tribal Council of Nevada. Walker River are also Paiute . . . some tribes are Paiute/Shoshone. At this point, we had become part of the Native American Voting Rights Coalition, so there was funding for CGU students to do surveys on the obstacles that Natives in Nevada face in trying to register and vote. One of the students was a guy named Troy Mikanovich, whose mother worked for the state attorney's office for Washoe County. Troy explained to his mom how unfair things were for Natives trying to vote in the county. She raised it with others within that office. At the time I didn't know this, but I did know that Washoe was the one that wanted to settle the most. The survey data were a big deal in the *Sanchez v. Cegavske* case. We got a ruling establishing satellites at Pyramid Lake and Walker River.

You know, I don't see an end to Barb, Bret, and me doing this work. I don't see us waking up one morning and saying, "We don't need to do voting work no more." I guess the last thing to end it on is that as long as we're able to breathe, walk, and talk . . . that if there is a law or a state that is trying to deny our people access to the ballot box then we will do something about it.

Barbara Semans

I'm a member of the Rosebud/Sioux Tribe. I was born in 1946 at the Indian Health Service Hospital and grew up in Mission. I still live in there with my husband, Oliver Semans Sr. We have seven children; six are living since our daughter Bobbie committed suicide about five years ago. There's Steve, David, Marty, Howard John, Donna, and OJ Junior, all of whom are grown and doing well.

My dad was crippled. He had fallen off a swing when he was twelve and broke his hip that did not get set right. One leg didn't grow and was almost a foot shorter than the other leg. He never let that stop him. He worked as a gas station attendant. When I was little, we lived in a one-room house that my dad built. It was wood covered with tar paper. There were two windows, a front door, and a dirt floor. I would wake up in the morning and look outside at a cottonwood tree and then to the east I could see where my grandpa Jim lived. I think he was related on my mother's side. A lot of times someone might not be blood related exactly. I had a bunch of grandfathers because all of my dad's brothers were my grandpas.

Dad's grandfather had been a medicine man, so he could pass on spiritual things. But he and Mom didn't teach us the Lakota language because they didn't want us to get in trouble at school. They wanted us to learn white ways, but always to keep our culture. Once when I was about five years old, Dad woke us girls up at 2:00 or 3:00 in the morning. We could hear dogs barking and see things because there was a full moon. We could hear the dogs coming closer and closer and closer until they were fourteen or fifteen feet away. Then we saw a man floating above the ground, just floating in the air, being chased by the dogs. The man had no legs, just a torso and a long black coat and black hat. We watched him float by. Teaching us about things like that were important to Dad, important that we be kept in touch with the spiritual side.

Starting when I was a small child, I kept having a dream where there'd be a fire at our house and I'd be running for it, but I was scared, my heart was pounding. Then I'd wake up. In my early teens, the dream came almost every night. When I was fourteen, I was supposed to spend the night with Grandma Cherry. I went down there with my sister and our friend Rosie. Grandma said, "You two can stay, but Rosie can't," so we left to spend the night at Rosie's house. While in bed, something woke me up. I went to the window and there was my dream. Our house was burning. I started running toward the house, thinking my mom, sisters, and brother were there. I tried to open the back door and the heat hit me. I went to the windows and reached in. All I could feel was hot, stickiness. Then my sister and I ran around to the other side and opened a window and reached to the bed. Nobody was there. They'd spent the night at Grandma Cherry's house.

Nearly all of the house was burned. My dad had lit the wick on the kerosene stove. He tried to turn the gas down, but it jammed. Everything caught on fire. The insulation in our house was cardboard boxes that just took off burning. Dad barely made it out. The whole thing was just like what I had been dreaming. Dad boarded up the front of the house and we moved back in. It was burned, but not so bad that we couldn't live in it. The floor was okay, so we put the woodstove in there and we all slept on the floor. There was a clothing drive because we had lost everything and these white people brought things that I had never seen. Crystal cups! I told my sister Martha, "They brought us nothing but junk!" We never got any towels or things that we could use like a chair, a table, or a bed.

There were some really nice white people though. There were a couple teachers, Helen O'Brien and Dorothy Furrey, who took me under their wing. One time, there was a square dance and they bought me a brand-new outfit that was a little checkered black and white skirt, a white shirt, and shoes. I can still remember those teachers. A lot of years are just kind of blocked out of my memory. But I remember my friend Sharon Bristow, whose family were ranchers. We went all through grade school together. There were spelling bees and arithmetic contests and I always took first in spelling and Sharon always took first place in arithmetic.

By high school, a lot of the whites sent their children to school in Valentine thirty-two miles away or to Winner forty-two miles away. But I still had Indian and white friends. The parents of a white friend, Pauline Hoffine, owned the Checkerboard Café. I'd go to her house sometimes to spend the night. I thought the house was a mansion! And I look at it today—it's still standing—and I thought, "That wasn't even that big!" There was another neighbor who gave me ice cream for the first time. It was vanilla.

But we had our own desserts. My grandma would hitchhike fifteen miles from Okreek to Mission. She'd be wearing her old shawl and her long dress while hitchhiking. She always brought dried choke cherries and dried plums. Sometimes we'd go cherry picking and plum picking. We'd smash up the choke cherries and then dry 'em out there. We'd make choke cherry patties that we'd put in canning jars. In winter we'd have them for pudding—choke cherry pudding. That is kind of how I learned about my heritage—at home.

In school, I was one of the few Indians treated good by the teachers. I spoke up for myself when they tried treating me mean. Some teachers would call on students to answer questions and they'd just call on the white kids. If you got the answer right, there was extra credit. Well, I would study up on the subject, and if they'd just call the white kids, the other Indian students never said a word, but I would say, "I have something to say about this subject." I didn't let people run over me. In high school I was a cheerleader—the only Indian with a bunch of white girls. At tryouts, I did all of the cheers and I think they were afraid not to pick me.

Nobody ever told me that I should go to college. In high school, two teachers, Mrs. Bristow and Mrs. Anderson, told me, "Barb, don't you ever just marry anybody. You're so smart, you go on with your education." But here I went and got married, without finishing high school. I did get my GED after I got married. A teacher, Mr. Simes, drove me to evening GED classes. At the time, I was working, from six in the morning to six in the evening, at the Starlight Café in Mission for fifty cents an hour. My husband Larry was out of work a lot. When the Starlight Café closed, I went to work at another café. We had two kids by that time.

Larry and I moved around. We spent some time on the Seneca Reservation in New York and then went to Ontario, California. Larry got a job clipping cows and I started managing apartments. That got us free rent. Then the owner, Brian Sellers, asked me to do more work and pretty soon I was doing carpentry. I got so good at the carpentry that I redid a house for him. By that time, my husband had gone off to Montana. He was supposed to come back, but my sister called to tell me he was living with a girl in a motel.

I don't just automatically believe rumors, so I left everything in Ontario while I drove the kids and our Labrador dog back to the Rosebud Reservation. I picked up my sister, and we drove to the motel in Montana. When I knocked on the door, this girl answered and I said, "You tell Larry . . . if he wants to see his kids . . . to come down to this park." Then I left and pretty soon he showed up. It was nothing new . . . same old thing, so I went back to Mission without him and moved in with my sister. Then Larry showed up, and I told him, "Hey, why don't you go back to California, get a job, and send for me and the kids?" After he got to California, I ran to Legal Aid and put in for a divorce.

The Legal Aid attorney was William Janklow, who later became governor. On the way back from the courthouse, Janklow was doing a hundred miles an hour. The driver in a car ahead of us all of sudden signaled to turn left, and there was oncoming traffic. Our car was going too fast. It was either hit that car in the rear end or take the ditch. Janklow drove into the ditch. We hit the approach, flew over it, landed on the other side, and then continued on back to Rosebud. The next day my neck hurt so bad that I could not move. I rang Janklow, who sent an ambulance, and I ended up in a Catholic hospital in Martin. They put me in traction.

This nun showed up and told me, "Get out of bed. I'm changing the sheets." I said, "I can't," and she jerked me off the bed. When I hit the floor, she started kicking. "Get up." I said, "I can't." She says, "I said get up," and gave me a hard kick right in my side. And I said, "Don't do that again," but she did it again. Something came over me . . . I felt nothing but anger . . . and I jumped up and punched her right in the face. Then I got dressed, left the hospital, and reported her to the police. The police called Janklow, who said, "Put her on the ambulance, get her to Rapid City. I'm paying for everything. I have insurance."

In Rapid City, I was in traction for weeks. After I got out, Janklow said, "I'm not paying the bill. You're just like the rest of these Indians. You won't do nothing." I decided to sue him. I went to another attorney and signed paperwork to start the lawsuit. Whenever I'd ask, the attorney just kept putting me off until the statute of limitations expired. And Bill Janklow went on to become attorney general and then governor and congressman. I wasn't the only Indian who suffered with Bill Janklow. This girl named Jancita Eagle Deer said he raped her. Then Jancita Eagle Deer turned up dead along the road. Hit by a car. I just got stuck with hospital bills that ruined my credit, but I was alive.

Then my ex-in-laws took the four kids out to visit Larry for the summer in California. At the end of summer, Larry's mother told me, "You're never going to see those kids again. Larry's keeping them." I said, "Fine," because I knew they would be coming back. Sure enough, Larry sent them back and we moved to Sioux Falls. Social services connected me with an Indian program at one of the colleges. I got hired to counsel students at Akstel Park High School. I taught them how to bead and took classes in Lakota. Finally, I was getting a good paycheck. In the late 1970s I started taking business and accounting classes. By that time I had five children—four with Larry and one with Howard, who I lived with for five years. I had skills now and got hired as a secretary at Value Construction back in Rosebud.

This is when I met OJ. I had known him when he was little, but now he was all grown up. I am ten years older than him and remembered him as "Little Jimmy Semans" who left Rosebud when he was seven years old. But now my sister Beth called, "Guess who's in town?" I said, "Who?" and she said, "Little Jimmy Semans. He's a cop, and he's all grown up." OJ invited me to go with some people to his trailer house and I saw his uniform was missing buttons, so I sewed those on. In my mind, he was this little boy. We started walking over to the boarding school to see free movies. Walking back I'd go to my sister's, which was on the way, and he'd go on home. We kept this up for a while. Then one time he came to my sister's. And somehow, he leaned over and kissed me. Then I saw him in a different way. But I told him that I was too old for him.

Then OJ asked me to marry him. I said, "No, I'm never getting married again. I'm not having any more kids." He said that was okay because he couldn't have kids due to working around radiation in the navy. He's always taking away excuses. But then OJ said that he had applied for a job in Dresserville, Nevada. This was Saturday and he was going the next Sunday. On Monday, I told my friend Joanne that I wanted to marry him, but I'm scared, and she said you can always get a divorce! So Joanne and I went shopping. I bought a shirt and a dressy outfit. I packed the clothes away and come Friday, and OJ had his stuff packed up to fly out on Sunday. I said, "Is that offer still open?" He said, "What offer?" "For us to get married." And he said, "Yes," so we went to Pierre and got married before a judge. On Sunday he flew out to Reno and from there he walked and hitchhiked to Dresserville. He didn't have enough money for a taxi, so he got blisters on his feet.

OJ got the job, so I bought a used car, loaded up a U-Haul, and drove to Dresserville, where I got a job as the night manager at the local Mini Mart. One night, OJ and I had gone to the drive-in movies. We had John, who was three, with us, and OJ was bouncing him up and down until he got tired and fell asleep. Then OJ looks at me and he says, "Barbara, I love these kids but I'd like to have just one of my own." The next day I was really sick. It turned out I was pregnant. And I told him, "You know how you wanted that one of your own . . . just like that, your wish is my command!" Donna was born on April 14, and then our first-year anniversary was April 20. Then we decided to go back to Rosebud, where OJ had a job with the tribal police.

Then in 1980 or 1981, I was pregnant again, this time with OJ Junior. This is when OJ switched over to the Bureau of Indian Affairs (BIA). It was a great paycheck, about $3 an hour more than he had been making with the tribal police. Over time, he got gigantic paychecks. And then the BIA sent him to Winner, which is off-reservation. We spent two days looking at houses to rent, but none turned out to be available. The third day I said, "OJ, I'm not going in with you to look at houses. They're not renting because they see the Indian in me. I really show my Indian. You can pass for white." And he said, "Oh it's not that way. I'm a police officer." I said, "Yeah, but you can pass for white." At the next place, only OJ went in and they rented a house to him.

Then OJ got sent back to Rosebud as a BIA officer and we got a Bureau house. Living right opposite of us was the top BIA officer, Frank, who was from Navajo. He was a real by-the-book guy, just like OJ. Within six months Frank had promoted OJ to captain. And then a tribal councilman was in a car accident. One of the BIA officers investigated and cited the councilman, who raised hell about it. And so OJ investigated and he told this guy, "I'm backing my officer. He made the right decision." Then Frank investigated himself and agreed with OJ. Within a month, the BIA had moved Frank and OJ. They couldn't fire the officers for doing their jobs, but the BIA could transfer them out. OJ got sent north to Sisseton Wahpeton.

When he arrived at Sisseton Wahpeton, OJ discovered he was now a GS-11, which is a pretty high rank and has good pay. We bought a house and thought we would be there for a long time, but then OJ got ready to issue indictments against someone high up for corruption, so we got transferred to Devil's Lake up in North Dakota. The BIA kept transferring him further and further north, but with raises. At Devil's Lake, OJ indicted eleven people for murder after reopening a three-year-old case that had been covered up. That's also where I got shot at.

One night OJ was sitting in the rocking chair in the living room. He said, "Babe, I'm going to go to bed," so I sat down in the chair. And I just lean back in the chair and BING—somebody shot through the dining room window into the living room. The FBI came out and tried to take us into town to a motel for our protection while this murder trial was going on. And we said, "No way! We are Sioux! We don't hide from nobody!" We were prideful about being warriors. We still are. It was stupid. They offered us all this protection, and we refused.

In the midst of all that, I got a job with the Census Bureau but was told not to do counts on the reservation. It turned out they had never counted people on the reservation. I complained to D.C. and got to take census counts everywhere. One day I went to take the census in the jail. I said, "I'm Barbara Semans with the Census Bureau," and the dispatcher looked at me, and said, "You aren't coming in my jail." And I said, "Oh, yes, I am, lady." About that time, OJ walked out with their chief of police, and he said, "Oh, hi babe," and came up and hugged me. So I showed the dispatcher my credentials and the chief said, "You let her in there." I went everywhere, including the reservation.

At one reservation home, I'd just got started when people started running all over the place. "What's the matter?" They said, "That cop's coming! OJ Semans—he's coming!" They were some of the murderers out on bail, but I didn't know that. They hadn't caught my name. But I said, "Don't worry about it. That's just my husband." And I said, "Just sit down . . . he's just looking for me because it's late and the kids are probably home from school." Then I went out and OJ said, "What are you doing?" I said, "I'm doing the census." He said, "Barb, these are some of the guys that killed Eddie Peltier." I said, "So? I still have to do my job. I'll be home in a bit." I went back in, finished the census, thanked them, and left.

Then OJ got transferred to Tuba City, Arizona, with a raise to GS-12. In between that time, those eleven people were indicted and found guilty of the murder of Eddie Peltier. In Tuba City, OJ caught some more murderers and then was selected to be part of a special investigative unit being established in Albuquerque. Albuquerque is where we started voting for the first time—Republican. Before then I had never voted in white elections. My parents voted in tribal elections but not state and federal elections. Dad used to say, "We have a treaty with the government. We run our business, they run theirs." They stayed out of white politics, and I did the same. No Indians ever voted in white elections. The government came to the reservations and set up a polling place in Mission at the Catholic church, but that was for white people. We never went and they never asked us to vote. But in Albuquerque, OJ and I started thinking about politics. I mean politics beyond Indian stuff. I had done things before, voted in tribal elections and raised money for AIM during the Wounded Knee standoff.

In Albuquerque we registered as Republican because that's what everyone was. We thought it would be possible to get more done if you are Republican. We just saw that power started with voting. Then back in Rosebud, we became Democrats. We looked into registering in South Dakota and found out you have to get the registration card notarized. This became a thing when we started trying to register Natives. OJ and I weren't notaries, but there was a tribal judge named Vi Burnett who was a notary. She had arthritis really bad, and her hands were all swollen. On weekends we would go door to door registering people and Vi would notarize the cards. This poor thing was in pain, but she would notarize the cards. But it was really important. How would we change schools and stuff if we didn't vote?

Then in 2002, the Tim Johnson campaign was hiring people to register voters, but they were only hiring white people and not going to reservations. This wasn't right, so OJ calls them and says, "Why didn't you come to the reservations?" I had been doing voter registration for a couple years, but the campaign people said I had to apply and be interviewed in Sioux Falls. I got dressed up and did the interview. Then the guy in charge, Steve Hildebrand, told me, "We have to advertise it some more, so we are going to be down in the tribal building." They didn't want it to be just me applying. Then OJ said, "Let's go see who all comes." Two old ladies showed up and no one else. The next day I got a call saying, "You're hired. We selected you." Big surprise.

I set up an office at the community building and lined up local people to work. The campaign people said, "We are going to send some students and staffers out of D.C. You pick who you want and send the rest to Pine Ridge." I picked good people, some who are still our friends. The professionals started telling me what to do. Their plan was these white guys in suits would all go to the doors to talk with people. I didn't want to do it that way, so I told Steve Hildebrand, "Okay, how about I try it one day? And we'll let them report back to you." The white guys didn't get one person registered. People thought they were either missionaries or Mormons or Feds in their white shirts. They wouldn't answer the door or would start running out the back.

Hildebrand said, "You can run it the way you want to." I told the white guys, "I want you to drive the vans and have my Indian workers do the door knocking." After that, they registered a lot of people. Then the day of the election came. OJ checked all the polling sites while I stayed in the office. The Democrats sent a lawyer from Sioux Falls to work in the office on Election Day. The lawyer got all worried. "Barb, I hear the Republicans are buying votes in White River. What should we do?" And I said, "Nothing. Those Republicans want to pay the Indians, they can go ahead. But I know the Indian people. They'll go vote the way they want to."

We also had the issue of poll hours. Our part of the state is on Mountain Standard Time, but the counties initially were cheating us out of an hour of voting by having all the polls close early on Central Standard Time. Gregg Limbrich, an attorney from D.C., filed suit. At 3:00 or 4:00 in the afternoon, the judge ruled that our polls had to stay open until the Mountain Standard closing time. OJ did a pep talk and told our workers to get out there and find those votes in the extra hour. Native Americans are 99 percent Democrat, so we knew that votes cast in the last hour would be for Tim Johnson. At midnight, the TV announcers said that Johnson was behind by 3,000 votes. Next morning at 8:00 we found out that Tim Johnson won it by 524 votes.

In December 2002, I had a stroke. I couldn't move my leg and my speech was slurred. OJ took me to Indian Health Service. The staff in the emergency room tried to give me something for high blood pressure, but OJ stopped them. Somehow he knew they shouldn't do that, which was good because the doctor later said I could have died. I got sent by ambulance to the hospital in Valentine. They did a test for a stroke, but it didn't show up. IHS said send her home. The Valentine hospital doctor said, "We think she had a stroke. Sometimes a stroke doesn't show up for twenty-four hours." This is over the phone right in the room where OJ and I were. And they said, "Send her home." OJ then gets on the phone and calls our insurance company and gets them talking with the Valentine doctor and they agreed to my being admitted. I was in the hospital for three or four days. After that I forced myself to walk, dragging my foot around. My left arm was impaired and my speech. My memory was just like gone.

In March 2003, OJ and I got the Paul Wellstone Grassroots Award for our voting work. We were flown to Washington for the award. I wasn't back to 100 percent after my stroke. But I got up there and gave a speech. And then OJ gave a speech. We sat with Senator Johnson and his wife, Barb. Al Franken from *Saturday Night Live* was the entertainment. Oh, we enjoyed it. Franken came on after we talked and said he couldn't follow our act. Whatever. He made a joke out of it. Then just before it was over, I had to use the restroom. I hurried out of there as fast as I could use my leg. When I was coming back, Al Franken comes up to me and says, "I looked for you. You took my award." Then OJ and he exchanged emails. That's when I realized that I didn't know anymore what an email was. It was gone from my memory.

Back in Rosebud, OJ kept on with his tribal attorney job. Then this man who had worked on the Johnson campaign tells us, "Bret Healy wants you to come to the Senator McGovern's dinner in Sioux Falls, and he paid your way." That's where we first met Bret. He was the head of the Democratic Party in South Dakota and the main guy who had run Senator Johnson's total program. At the dinner, I just said, "Hi," shook his hand, and that was it. Bret and OJ, however, talked a bunch. Afterward OJ and I kept on registering voters. Then Bret told us about this law allowing early voting. We had never heard of it. Nobody had told us, not even Senator Johnson's staff. We decided to form Four Directions as a nonprofit with OJ and me as directors, and we hired Bret as the consultant. I don't remember all the legal stuff. I used to be able to do all this, but the stroke. Four Directions would give us a way to organize Native voting.

Stephanie Herseth, who was running for Congress, contacted us to run some of her campaign. Bret was back in the picture working on that campaign, too. We handled the campaign office in Mission. After Herseth won, we started working on getting early voting satellite offices on reservations. We started in on Todd County. We fought over that for a year. Maybe it was for a couple of years. Finally they gave in. Then we went to work on Fall River County, which handled elections in Shannon County. They refused to give Pine Ridge a satellite for early voting. I spoke up at meetings. The Barb rule is I tell it like it is. I wasn't gracious or diplomatic at those meetings. All we asked for was equality. Nothing more, nothing less. Just equal. And they came up with so many excuses. We ended up suing them. Meanwhile we were taking trips to Montana to help tribes there get satellites as well. Bret was there and we met with the secretary of state. There also were state senators and legislators at the meeting. Anyway, they refused us, and they were Democrats so we filed a lawsuit.

Indians need to vote. That is how we get heard. Why? Because we have to make sure whites won't steal all our land. That's sort of a joke, but I am being serious in a joking way. Our tribe made the 1868 treaty with the U.S. government and that meant we had our own president, our own council, and the white people or non-Indians had Washington, D.C. We stayed out of their business. We minded our own business. We followed the rules of the treaty, and that's how we lived. But as time went on, they took more and more and made more laws to change things that robbed us Indians. Now we are the minority of the minority. This is about survival. I've been in survival mode from the day I was born. Now it's our health care. People are dying in the ambulances. They closed our hospital. Medicaid finally recognized that it wasn't even up to minimum standards. That's why they were closing them. We've been forced to get involved in the voting system.

I saw Martin Luther King on television and thought it was terrible that black people were going through all this stuff when it was also happening to me, but I didn't even recognize it. Didn't even know about voting. But I knew there was something wrong. I knew there was prejudice. Anyway, I never dreamed that we are going through the same thing. But we started to wake up to it. We saw there was something we could do to make things better. And we kept on going with it from Senator Johnson's election to the present day, and we're still fighting. It's a matter of survival for our people. If we don't act, there's not going to be any Indians left. There will probably be no reservations. They'll steal that too. It's flat-out stealing. Whites don't appreciate that from the time they were Pilgrims and we saved them on the shore to the making of the treaties that we all could share the United States. And they treat us like we're the enemy. But we've always wished the best for the United States. They made us citizens in 1924. They didn't ask us. They made us that. Now it's life and death. I guess it's always been life and death. We just didn't realize it. The one thing I know is that voting affects how the country is run. The elected officials are responsible for the majority of things that happen. We've fought the state and the federal government, and you do it by voting.

CHAPTER 9

Stepping Forward

The Different Paths of Two Plaintiffs

While there are important similarities between the stories of Donovan Archambault Sr. and Johnnie Williams Jr., there are equally important differences. Both are military veterans who chose to be plaintiffs in voting rights cases—one in Montana and the other in Nevada. Although both men grew up on reservations, their childhood experiences were radically different. Like many Native children of his generation, Archambault was sent to a boarding school committed to "killing the Indian to save the man," while Williams spent his childhood on his family's ranch on the Walker River Reservation. For Archambault, the decision to be a plaintiff was just one step in a life rooted in political activism, dating back to the Red Power era. Williams largely avoided politics, but when asked to be a plaintiff, he served, just as he had many years earlier in Vietnam. Finally, as plaintiffs, they had radically different experiences.

Donovan Archambault

> My name is Donovan Archambault Sr. I am enrolled Assiniboine from Fort Belknap. I was born in 1939 and mostly have lived on the Fort Belknap Reservation, aside from boarding school, college, army, and eight or nine years working off-reservation. I've been married to Laurie for thirty years. She is a fantastic teacher, who could be a principal, but she loves kids and wants to teach. We have eight children and we are so proud of them. They're all sober and productive people who take care of their children. The most important thing is looking out for the next generation. Laurie had two

children when we got married and I had three—and we had another three together. They are all our children. My grandmother taught me that when you marry someone with children, there's no such thing as stepchildren. Those are your children.

My father was enrolled Gros Ventre, but his father, Sam Archambault, was enrolled Standing Rock Sioux. He was a woodman, who got paid for cutting wood for boats. Dad was born probably in 1909 and lived here in Hays, until he went to a boarding school. My mother was a full-blood enrolled Assiniboine from the Horn family. She went to boarding school at Flanders. How do you learn to raise a family when you spent your childhood in boarding school? It was a thing for me to learn how to be a parent. Sometimes I talk with people in parenting classes. I draw upon experiences from raising cattle. I tell those guys, "Go look at cows or a herd of buffalo. When their calves wake up in the morning, they lick them clean. They wash them and clean them up. Then they nurse them. Then they go play. There's always four or five mothers that stick around with the calves, when the rest go eat." And I said, "If you want to learn how to parent, go watch buffalo. They'll fight a grizzly bear to protect that calf."

When we were small, we were very fortunate to have our grandparents to go to. The people who affected my thinking the most were my grandparents. My grandma told me a lot of things. Had I listened to her, I probably wouldn't have had such an up and down life. My wife's parents separated when she was at a young age. My parents separated. I blame that on boarding school. Our parents didn't know how to do parenting. I had to learn how to parent. My wife and I, we learned a lot from each other.

I was ten years old when I went to boarding school in Pierre, South Dakota, which is five hundred miles from here. It was a cruel and brutal place, like jail or prison. There were three of us littler boys. There were grown men in the eighth-grade class. They were there to avoid going to the Korean War. Milk was served in a big pitcher, which the little guys couldn't lift. The bigger guys were supposed to help us. Those guys took anything they wanted from the little guys. "I want that meat." If you didn't give it to them, they'd beat the hell out of you. We gave them the meat or the pie. One day I refused and got beat up. I thought of something my grandma said.

"If you don't like something that's going on, you don't have to be there." I said, "Well, I don't like this, so I'm going home." I had been taught to not criticize, not run anything down. If you don't like it, you don't have to go over there. I remembered that.

We ran away out of sheer desperation. There was Joey Clyde, Rueben White Bull, Henry Cliff, and myself. I was only ten years old. The school was about half a mile to the Missouri River. All I knew is that we had to go upstream. At home we used to go out to the Missouri River and fish. I figured that when I get to Cow Creek, I'll know where I'm at because that's where we went fishing. We covered fifty-six miles in four days before being caught. We ran all night and hid during the day. We ate berries. There were plums and cherries and wild grapes and stuff along the river that we ate. By the fourth day, we really starved out. I hear traffic, so I knew there was a road nearby. We went up to the road and we got picked up. The guy said, "Are you hungry, boys?" We said, "Yeah." He took us to a café and said, "Give these guys whatever they want to eat." So we ate. But he went to the phone outside. I told the guys, "We're caught now." A little kid who is hungry has to eat.

Back at the school, we got paddled. They took all our clothes away and made us kneel on the cement step. You couldn't go down off the step. The vice principal would come by and kick you in the heinie and say "Get back on the . . ." if you moved. You knelt like that all during your spare time. One day they come by and say, "Well, are you gonna run away again?" "No." They gave us back our clothes and we took off again. Second time they really fixed us. I just made up my mind to tough it out. I was there for three years. Some kids stayed even longer. I used to pity the little kids, who would sit there and cry. Everybody else . . . you just steel yourself not to cry. If you cry, you're a baby. I would get paddled and not cry. I'd always think about something else that hurt worse to take my mind off it. Students made our own paddles in shop. I had thought we were going canoeing with these three-foot-long paddles. When we start drilling holes in it, I knew it wasn't a canoe paddle.

I did a lot of things later on, like drinking and fighting. But being that young and having to endure in that kind of stuff was bad. Then there was the sexual abuse. Some of the bigger boys and the priests, who were supposed to be teaching you about God and all they did was tell how bad God was going to punish you if you didn't do what the priest wanted. When I got older, and I'd see a priest, I didn't know whether to shake his hand or hit him. Today, I got all or most of the anger out of me.

I really put myself through a lot of difficult things due to all that anger. That's what it was—it was anger. I was mad at my parents for separating and sending me to boarding school. Mad at them again because I was getting beat up. Mad at the guy who's beating me up. Mad at the supervisor because he didn't stop it. Mad at the supervisor for beating me up. It was a total anger thing. It made you so you could not trust anyone. You didn't have a friend. The first thing you learn is not to trust anybody. It's very lonely, but we just toughed it out. Boarding school also did some good things. It made you very independent. Made you tough. Not so much fighting. It just made you be able to withstand a lot.

When I was thirteen, things got better. I came back to Fort Belknap for the summer and then I went to boarding school in Flanders, South Dakota. I lived there for two years. It was like heaven compared to Pierre. You could go downtown and work. From there I went to Standing Rock, which was even better. We had boys and girls in the same dorm. We cooked our own meals. I learned how to box and got on the boxing team. Hitting them big bags and having a fight every week took away a lot of the anger. I was a state champion a couple of times. I graduated Standing Rock High School in 1957.

From there I went to junior college, the State School of Forestry in North Dakota. I was on the boxing team there for two years. Then in 1959, I went in the army. I was on the 7th Army boxing team, along with being a communications specialist and teletype operator. When they built the Berlin Wall, I was crew chief there. We got the message that they were buzzing convoys going to Berlin. Everybody went on alert. We got our field gear and rifles and loaded up like we were going to war. About 4:00 they called it off and said everything was fine. I enjoyed Germany. It was a beautiful country. From where I was stationed, I could go to Switzerland and Austria. I also got to travel on the boxing team.

I got an honorable discharge in 1962. Just before Christmas I came back to Fort Belknap. I had a bunch of war bonds. In the service, every month you can buy a war bond with your pay. My brother-in-law and I stayed drunk for three weeks on the war bonds. Then my high school boxing coach invited me to a tournament. He asked if I was in shape. I said, "Yes. I'm in pretty good shape." He said, "We need a 132-pounder. How much do you weigh?" I said, "132 pounds" because I really wanted to go.

I trained for a couple weeks and then won the 132-pound division. That was the last time I fought as an amateur. I fought two brothers who had wanted to fight me before, but we'd never been matched up. They'd either get beat out of the tournament, or I'd get beat out. The older brother said he was going to "really fix" me. I knocked the younger one out, and beat the hell out of the other one because of what he was saying. Twenty years later, I was the director at the Red Bottom celebration at Frasier, Montana. I was going around taking the names of all the drummers. This one guy tells me his name. I ask, "Are you so and so?" "Yeah." "Are you Donovan?" I say, "Yeah." Then he said I had fixed him so bad in the fight that he quit boxing. I fought with a lot of anger and sense of revenge. Boarding school made me very disciplined in going after what I wanted. If I wanted to be a fighter, I could be that. If I wanted to be a drunk, I could be that.

The boxing coach owned a store in Fort Yates and a big ranch, with forty to fifty head of buffalo. He gave me a job, working in the store. I think he paid me $8 a day plus room and board. Then I got offered a construction labor job making $6 an hour, so I told him, "I really hate to quit you. But I've got a job over here, and it's offering $6." He said, "You're a damn fool if you don't take it. I just made that job, so I could keep you here." I took the construction job and then moved to another construction company that built big steel buttresses for office space. I did that for a couple years, before coming back to Fort Belknap, where I did really nothing but drinking. Then a friend talked me into going back to school at American College in Berkeley to be an x-ray technician. But I got sidetracked and just started taking general courses. I liked math a little bit and I completed physics. I was going to start calculus, and I thought, "What the hell am I ever going to use calculus for? I'll never use physics. Why do you have to know how to calculate the velocity of a six-ounce object dropping ten feet?"

Anyway, I quit and went to work for California doing job placement in the Oakland ghetto. That was when I got involved in the takeover of Alcatraz. I worked in the kitchen at Alcatraz, cooking and making sandwiches. One day this big labor outfit came out there and donated $5,000. We gave them a baloney sandwich for lunch. They give this big old check, and they get a baloney sandwich. Dennis Banks, Russell Means, and those guys were really good. I supported AIM's philosophy. I know Richard Oakes was probably the real key when Alcatraz started. He lost his little daughter, who fell off the third tier at Alcatraz. After she died, Richard pulled back out. Things started getting really violent, so I pulled out too.

By then I'd gotten married and had my first child. I just decided not to jeopardize their livelihood. Then in 1970 a job at UC Davis came up. I was the only nondegree applicant, but I got hired. The UC Davis boss was really good. He told me, "You need to get involved. Be here four days a week. You can have Friday to do whatever you want." Every Friday I would work outside the university. I'd go to Nabisco and get jobs for people. Then this march was coming up. My boss says, "Go to it, Arch." The march was for Deganawidah-Quetzalcoatl University or DQU, which I think was the first Indian university. We took over the army communications center at Davis. One morning, I was going to work and saw all the rush-hour traffic. I went, "God, what am I doing here?" so I came back home.

I had lived in California for six to seven years. I was there for the hippie days of the 1960s when Janis Joplin and them were singing in Golden Gate Park, and you could drink wine with and smoke weed with them. I never smoked weed, but I drank. Janis always walked around with a big quart of Jack. Those were really good times. It was during the civil rights period and the movement for equal rights for women. I always had to laugh because Indians always place women higher up than men. The old pipe men always had a special prayer for women because they're the ones who bore us. We always honor them. Why did women want to be equal with men when they're already above us? That's our Indian way.

I went to work at the tribe in planning, getting people jobs. Working for the tribe seemed like the only way to get anything done. It gives you authority to push your issues. Then in 1976, I ran for the tribal council and got elected to a four-year term. During that term, Frank Ryan, who was teaching at Harvard, came out recruiting people for their master's in education. I told him that I was short credits for my bachelor's degree, but he talked me into applying. I thought, "What the hell," and got in. Harvard was really different. There were all these tight-lipped and stiff-collared people. I was the only guy walking around Harvard Square with a cowboy hat, old crooked-heeled boots, and a vest, at least until Johnny Cash and Willie Nelson came to town. Next day, everybody had vests and boots. That's how Harvard is. It was great though. At the same time, I was glad to get out of there because people were different, not friendly.

While at Harvard, I got removed from the council for missing three consecutive meetings, even though they had passed a resolution stating I could go to Harvard. But there was a new chairman, so I thought, "Well, let me resign." I did that and got my master's degree focused on administration and social planning. After I came back, I did planning, mostly in education. I took the theory and applied it on projects. Later I got back on the council and then was chairman of the tribe for a stretch. I am really proud that I was able to establish a Fort Belknap insurance company. The state said we couldn't do it because they had exclusive jurisdiction, but we did it. My idea was to take workman's compensation and unemployment, establish our own little agency, so we didn't have to be qualified through the state. As it was, nobody ever could qualify. We had never qualified anybody for workman's compensation and it was very difficult to get unemployment. So I said, "Why do we have to go through the state? We're sovereign. Let's exercise our sovereignty." We started that 1990–1991. Today we have over $18,000,000 in that account.

Four years ago I got on the council again. As part of our treaty settlements, we had established burial funds for each tribal member. On council, I said, "We need to do something. $1,500 isn't paying for a burial anymore. We have this insurance company, so let's have a burial insurance fund. We can take the interest off some of these accounts, put it in there, and have the tribal governments throw in $20,000 each for three years. That will shore up our account so that we don't have to worry about it for twenty to thirty years." The council approved it. Now everybody gets $4,000 for their burial insurance. The next thing I want to do is take the tribal insurance company and have us insure every building that belongs to the tribe. Why are we paying Mutual of Omaha or Liberty or somebody $750,000 a year even though we've never had a loss? I haven't been able to get the insurance director to do it. But I think the risk would be very minimal.

Opportunities require taking some risk. I'd like us to do more economic development. People need to think a little bit outside the box on whatever you're doing, whether it's planning a schoolroom or planning an administration building or planning for ranch economic development. Why can't we buy this ranch, fatten our own cows on our own hay, process our own beef at our own plant—and we have one . . . we have a USDA-certified meat stamp that we get inspected every year—and contract with the air force base in Great Falls. It would put thirty to forty people in jobs. You could have ten drivers of refrigerated trucks, fifteen people on the ranch doing the irrigation. Get your own pellet plant. Learn how to grade wheat. We can do that. We have our own college. I was on the council when we established the college.

We only have two visible resources—our land and people. Education wise, we've done very well by our people. We just graduated thirty-one from the tribal college. We had lost a lot of land through the Dawes Act, but we have almost all back. We're the only allotted reservation that can say that. The rest of reservations that lost land through the Dawes Act are all checkerboard with white and Native ownership mixed together. When I was the first land committee chairman in 1976, we established a land acquisition program. We took half a million dollars and said, "We're going to spend this to purchase back land." About 95 percent of our land is individually owned by members or tribally owned.

Elections and voting have always been important. I started out thinking about tribal politics. My cousin—who's gone now, lost in a car accident—he used to call it Mickey Mouse politics. He worked for the Bureau of Indian Affairs. I said to him, "Wait a minute. We have a tribal council authorized by the BIA and we have sovereignty." That was when I started thinking about voting, running for council, and getting back our land. A majority of our land back then was leased and utilized by non-Indians. There was this issue of non-Indians coming on the reservation, committing crimes, and there was nothing we could do about it. In 1977 Senator John Melcher came here to a big meeting about political jurisdictions and I told him, "Senator, when I go off-reservation to Harlem, across the river, I have to abide by county law, city law, state law, federal law, and even tribal law. The tribe doesn't have any jurisdiction over there but how we act over there represents our people. We have a standard to uphold as an Indian. When they come over here, they should give us the same respect. But that isn't the case. They can come in here and run around and then run across the river and we can't do nothing." He said, "The simple reason is non-Indians don't make your laws over here, so they have no say here." I said, "What the hell makes you think I make the laws in Harlem? I have nothing to do with that, but I still have to obey their laws. Why can't they respect us when they come on my land?" We had the big argument, and it's still the same thing today forty years later.

That is why I decided to start getting involved in nontribal politics. I even thought about running for county commissioner. I thought, "As a veteran, I should have a right to vote in any election. That right should be made possible by the government. I have to support and defend the country. I should have some say so in it." But I knew the system was discriminatory. An Indian would never get elected because of gerrymandered districts. I just want a level playing field. Running for the school board and it's the same thing.

It happens with farming and ranching. We would have county agents ridicule us. "Oh, the government takes care of you guys," when we were trying to qualify for the subsidy programs that every farmer in the county qualifies for. Finally, one day I blew up. This woman agent asked me, "What are you guys doing here?" I said, "Hey, all I want to do is report my crop and qualify for the farm subsidies that everybody is getting." "Oh, you guys gotta go back to the BIA." The next year I went through the BIA, which said I could qualify, so I went back to the county agent and heard, "You're not qualified. You don't have enough oat base." I went home and planted eighty acres of oats for a base. Next year, I got, "Oh, you don't have the barley base. You need . . ." Jesus. Finally, I took myself to Senator John Melcher. He said, "You qualified three years ago, so you go back to Chinook, Montana, and there will be something there for you. I'll see to that." I got qualified and about three weeks later those two old ladies who were disqualifying Indians were gone. Maybe they were retiring, maybe not, but they weren't there anymore.

The discrimination back then was so bad. It's a little better now. It's still there, but not as blatant. There's still voting issues. When Mark Wandering Medicine started talking about a lawsuit, I gave it some thought. I thought why can't we have voting out here on the reservation? If we have to go to court, then let's go to court. I was on the tribal council at the time and said, "Let's do it. Let's go to court." I made a motion that we request that the secretary of state establish polling places on Hays, Lodgepole, and Agency so people at Fort Belknap can vote. The motion passed. The state fought it, said they could not afford it. Why do Indians have to travel a long ways when whites don't?

It wasn't a hard decision for me to become one of the plaintiffs. It was an opportunity. I felt that it's something that everybody needs to have. We all need to have that opportunity because it is a right. A vote is a right. "Oh, half the people don't vote . . ." Well, that has nothing to do with it. It should be a right for the people, who want to. And maybe if it was here, more people would vote. I've never seen the numbers and I don't particularly care. Politically, legally, socially, it's something that should be done. That's basically why I got in on the case. I feel as strong about it today as I did then.

In my sworn affidavit, I described the June 9, 2016, settlement conference: "Like the majority of the plaintiffs in the case, Mark Wandering Medicine and I were proud to serve in our country's military. Mark saw combat as a Marine in Vietnam and I was stationed with the army in Germany during the Cold War. We walked into the settlement conference as proud military veterans, wearing caps to honor the forces in which we served. We believed that as citizens who served to protect this nation, we had rights that should be protected by the law."

That is not what came out from the settlement. It finally boiled down to Judge Lynch, who was bullying us to sign this agreement. If you are going to negotiate, it should be negotiating and not bullying. I'll never sign an agreement that's going to give us less than half of what we come in for. Why even come in, if that's what you're going to settle for? That is what the judge was pushing in the *Wandering Medicine* case. [The settlement called for limited hours at a satellite at Fort Belknap, the Northern Cheyenne, and Crow reservations. Even on the days when the satellite was open, the hours were less than the hours offered for the days at the election office.] After proposing the settlement, Judge Lynch told us to go home and think about it overnight.

The next day, Mark and I went back to the courthouse. The following is what I said in my affidavit about what happened. "Mark had his Marine cap and I was wearing my army cap. Out of respect we took our caps off and had them sitting on the table in front of us. Judge Lynch asked Mark and I, if we had made a decision. Mark said that if this is all we were going to get, we couldn't accept the offer. Judge Lynch blew up. He became quite irate and red in the face. He said, 'I thought we had a deal.' The judge was standing behind me and I turned and responded: 'Your honor, you told us we could take this home and think about it.' Judge Lynch did not respond to me; he didn't even look at me or Mark. He looked directly at our attorney and pointed a finger at one of our attorneys and said, 'You better get this straight. I'll make it so you have to pay the costs of getting the state and county people, and their attorneys here.' Judge Lynch kept talking to our attorneys about costs and sanctions. He asked if Mark and I had $20,000, because if we didn't accept the offer, he was going to make us pay that. At that point, our attorneys asked if we could have a do-over. Judge Lynch still had his voice raised and his face was still red. He asked, 'Do you have $20,000 to pay these people?' On the reservation, no one has that kind of money. He said: 'Sanctions will be issued that will stick with the Ninth Circuit.' Mark and I were uncomfortable with this; we felt threatened. This was not negotiation. Judge Lynch was yelling and saliva was spraying from his mouth during his tirade. He then said that he needed a decision in ten minutes. Then he left. There was no discussion of the offer, just threats against us and our attorneys. At that point our attorneys told us maybe we had to take the offer. . . . There was no respect. The judge bullied us and we got next to nothing. I thought the judge was supposed to be impartial. I thought we could get justice; instead, it appears discrimination is still alive and well in Montana and couched in the robes of justice. As soldiers and citizens we deserve better." I refused to sign the settlement.

In spite of all the progress that's been made in the area of discrimination and equality, you can't legislate feelings. It's evident today. Look at Trump in the White House. Way before he was president back in 1990 or 1991, Trump called my wife, Laurie, "trash." We had gone to Atlantic City. I was in the casino and Laurie was outside, sitting in Trump Plaza. Laurie was sitting on the step and I think maybe she was nursing our son Hunter. Trump and Marla came down the steps. Marla ran over to get a little closer look at the baby and sat down on part of the stairway. When Trump came by, he said, "Get rid of that trash." So the security guy came up and said, "Ma'am, you're going to have to leave because you can't sit on the steps." It's a good thing that I wasn't there because I would have attacked that son of a bitch. I don't want nobody to say nothing like that to my wife. I'll protect her with my life. But he said that, and ever since then I know how discriminatory Trump is.

I say to young people, "Don't give up. Keep going. Be yourselves and be the best." I remember being in Rayburn, Saskatchewan, for a boxing match. My coach said, "We don't have a match, so you can wrap hands." So I went to dinner and had a big steak. I came back to wrap hands. Then the coach says, "Oh, by the way, I got you a match." "You did? Who is it?" "Ahh, a big tall skinny guy. Don't worry about it. You can take him." Then I found out he was the province's 132-pound champ. I was 126 pounds. I tell my coach, "I'm not fighting that guy. He's a head taller than I am and ten pounds more. He's a champion." He says, "God damn it. You're a champion too. You're going to fight him, or you're going to walk home. I'll tell you how to fight him. The guy is going to come and try to tear your head off. You go out there, take one step back, and throw a right hand." Okay, so I got the boxer mad. He runs across the ring, and in thirteen seconds I had him out. But if you tell yourself you can't do it, you can't do it. Another thing I tell kids is, "Don't let anybody measure you. You use your own yardstick. You're the one that has to live with yourself." If you did your best, and this is what you've got, then that's all you need.

Johnnie Williams Jr.

I am a seventy-five-year-old man, living on the Walker River Paiute Reservation. I am semi-retired although still ranching. We, my wife and I, grow alfalfa and ship it all over. Right now I got a load going to Reno and another one maybe to L.A. And, so even though I have been retired, I work harder than I had been working. So, that's about it. I have four kids: three girls, one boy. I don't know how many grandkids, and how many great-grandkids. It's a big family. The only one that doesn't have any kids is my boy. And the girls, the oldest girl has two boys and a foster daughter. The middle girl has a girl and a boy, and the third girl has two girls and a boy and then we have relatives all over. So, it's a big family.

I was born here in Schurz and have lived here almost all of my life. When I was a kid, it was all sagebrush. The dog and I would walk all through the brush and pick up arrowheads, beads, all kinds of artifacts that were left years ago. And, I rode horses a lot, mustang ponies with my cousins. My cousins live right across the way now; we were always together and that's it on growing up. I spent a lot of time with my grandparents. They only spoke Paiute. I used to be able to speak it, but I've been away from it. I can still understand Paiute. My grandmother was a traditional medical doctor. Between here and Fallon is prayer rock. When we went that direction, she would leave money or beads or something on the rock. I wish I would have listened more to her. She got me into petroglyphs and I still study them. Altogether, I had a pretty good childhood.

My dad worked as a cowboy, horseshoer, and my mom was a cook at the hospital. She was there for some thirty-seven years. I have one brother and three sisters. For grade school, we went here in Schurz. I went to high school for two years in Yerington. Then the state came up with the idea that we had to go to school in the county we live in. People on the reservation, we lived in three counties: Lyon County, Mineral County, and Churchill County. Anyhow, I switched schools and went to Hawthorne.

After graduation, I went to barber school in San Francisco. I barbered with a few breaks for twenty-some years, until long hair came in and that really hurt business. When a job came up in the school district, I started here in Schurz elementary as a janitor/bus driver. When an opening came up at Hawthorne school district at the administration for purchasing agent, I took that and I stayed there until I retired. But I always ranched. At one time, we had couple hundred head of cattle, seven or eight horses, and dogs. We also had goats and pigs.

The biggest stretch of being away from Schurz was when I was in the military. Shortly after I started barbering, I got called before the draft board. There were eighteen of us that got called and sent to San Francisco for our physicals. Only two of us passed the physical. The other guy got picked for the navy. My father had been in the navy in World War II. He served on the battleship *New Jersey* and was at Pearl Harbor and Iwo Jima. He was one of the sailors who had to dive in and get the soldiers with flames all over the ocean. That's what he was. Anyhow I wanted either the navy or the air force, but I got stuck with the army. It was funny because you were in a line, those that got eliminated went this way and those that got picked for service went this way. I get up there and was told, "Go right," and I was in the army.

After basic training at Fort Ord, I qualified for training in electronics, in hot missiles at Fort Bliss. From there I went to Furst, Germany, where the hawk missile battalion was. When I arrived, it was starting to become winter so they had a basketball team. I went and played a bit with those guys on the team. They were ex-pro players, college guys, but heck I decided to give it a try. Anyway, I went and practiced with them a few times. One day the coach came to my dorm and asked me, "Aren't you going to try out for the basketball team?" I told him, "No, I just wanted to practice." He said, "I'd like you to come out" and I'll be darned I made the army team. We played mainly in Frankfurt, but we played all the teams in Europe. We won the championship and I was selected MVP. One of the players on the team was—you may have heard of him—Al Attles, later he coached the San Francisco Warriors. I was asked to try out for the Warriors. So, I went to a two-week training camp. I sat and sat and got to play a little and after the first week, I just left. But, Al was there and he said, "Why did you leave?" I said, well, I was just sitting there.

Then it was getting, I guess around March, and these guys from Vietnam come in, so I volunteered for Vietnam. It was 1966, just when it was getting bad in Vietnam and I'm sent first to Cam Ranh Bay. We couldn't figure out what was going wrong. A bunch of us had never seen a M14 before, so we got trained. I had to break that M14 down, put it together, break it down. Then we waited and waited, pulled guard duty, and finally got orders. "You're going to Infantry, First Calvary Division." So, I went to Anh Kay and once I got settled and checked in, we just headed to the field. My platoon just headed north all the time. I never did see my base camp until we headed to Fort R and R. That was about six months or so after I arrived.

I was out in the field all that time. Probably in combat about seven months of my tour there and we just kept going north, north. We found a Ho Chi Minh trail, hack and hack and hacked. We spotted cloaked trucks. The trail, it was wide enough for trucks, hauling in ammunition, stuffing people in on bikes packing big packs. They were going to Laos, you know. So, we reported that and they called in the B52s. You know, the next day it was going again; that's how they are, that many. From there, I kept going north. I had a little stop in Da Nang; from there, they put us with the 101st Airborne and we worked alone. We had battled all the way and lost so many young kids. Weren't trained right. Couldn't take the heat. Couldn't take the hiking. You could go maybe from here to the top of that mountain one day, maybe carrying a 120-pound pack, depending on how much ammunition you want to carry and rations. I always had two packs and about ten or twelve ammo clips. So, that's where most of the weight came from.

Early on, some guys used to call me Chief. I don't know if they meant that because I was the Indian, but they meant it in a sarcastic way. I got into a few fights, then they kinda settled down. I said, "I'm not Chief, I got a name." So, that ended that. Then I got a good squad of young kids—one I knew was seventeen, but he said was eighteen so he could get into the service—most of them were eighteen, nineteen years old. I think I was twenty-three years old. When this stuff started, they were right behind me.

There was another thing. I would get sent out on point all the time because I was Indian. They said, "You know the terrain, it should be trained into you." Other Indians I talked to had the same experience; they got put on point all the time, so I decided to push back. I said, "Well, what about my squad?" and they said, "No, they're staying back." My squad refused to stay back. When I went on point, they went on point. We were the main source of weapons for the platoon. I was in charge of the weapons squad, machine guns, so this stuff ended. I also had some good first sergeants who backed me.

Mostly we just kept going further north, fighting all the way. Once we were pinned down for a week in this one island-like place, they had us surrounded all the way around, with rice paddies. So, finally one night we took off. It must have been 1:00 or 2:00 and the 101st was set up high so we got to there and we had to cross a big canal. They had it all planned out. We had to cross the canal, climb a rope, cross the rice paddies, wait for light and they saw us and they started shooting. We made it to the top of the hill. We lost a third of our platoon. Here I am now. Nobody likes to talk about the fact of being alive. There were three of us Indians from Nevada on that same hill. My cousin was one of them. He was in the artillery. A mortar blew his jaw up. Another friend from home was on point in another outfit, when we were being ambushed coming in. I couldn't believe it, he recognized me. "Run Johnnie run!" So, we all took off running and it was Christmas. The guys there were having their Christmas dinner when they got hit. There was another guy all bandaged and bloody. "Johnnie": this guy couldn't talk good, but I heard my name. I looked over and it was an old friend. It was terrible all around there. But that was something to see three Nevada Indians.

Then on the way to Hue I got a field commission to E6. At times I went all the way up to first sergeant because the rest get shot, but then they replenish and I'd go back to being a squad leader. Hue was in trouble. The VC went to the right side of Hue and we went through the entrance. The Marines were already in there. We went into Hue just a little ways because the Marines were already in there and got that taken care of. We finally got a batch of new troops come in—all the rest were gone—there were only six left in my squad. It was tough all the way. I got shrapnel in my leg. When it happened, I said, "Oh, I get a little vacation." They pulled out some of the shrapnel, put on some cream and gauze, and sent me back to camp, out in the field where we were. It took forever to heal because of the moisture, the sweat, the doctoring. Probably five, six years ago, I finally got rid of the last shrapnel in my knee. It was so close the bone, the doctors couldn't take it out. The shrapnel just worked its way out. The pieces are so jagged.

When my time was up, I got sent back to base camp and started processing out. The navy and air force were in charge of the base. They treated me so nice. First night there, I had steak. They had television, showers. I waited there for about three days for my flight to Cam Ranh Bay. I stayed at Cam Ranh Bay until about 1:30 in the morning and then flew out on a 707. It was a big plane and fully loaded with men. I think it was around 5:00 in the morning we hit Fort Lewis in Washington state and then I caught a flight to San Francisco. I was in good shape when I went into the service. I am six-foot-two and weighed 260 pounds. I came out at 157 pounds, just skin and bones. Before heading home, they fit you with a new uniform. But as soon as I got to San Francisco, I got out my civilian clothes. I knew what was going on in airports—how they treated you. "Baby killer! Baby killer!" We were never involved in anything like that. I had to sleep on a bench in the airport because my flight to Reno wasn't until 6:00. I boarded that plane and it felt so good—safe and free.

And I'll be darned, in Reno I ran into my cousin's husband, who was in the Marines. He was being shipped to Hawaii and my cousin—well, his brother-in-law—was there to drop him off. I got my luggage and I had a ride all the way to Fallon and then my brother and mother came into Fallon and picked me up. And that's how I got home. It felt so good. In the car, my mother and sister said, "Let's go up and have a drink in Schurz." I said, "Sounds good to me." I knew something was wrong when we pulled up into the parking lot because it was so busy. We went in and everybody hollers. All of my friends and family, all of Schurz was there. At least they welcomed me back.

That was my story of the war. I always wanted to be back in touch with the men from my squad. I forgot their names. There were all kinds of folks—not too many Mexicans but a lot of black guys. They were mostly from New York and New Jersey. Some from North Carolina and I always wondered what happened to them. The earlier ones that got killed, I look at the Vietnam Wall, but I couldn't pick out their names. I don't know how I could find them, but I got that Vietnam book. I'm thinking of putting an article in and seeing if I get a response. Some, you didn't get a chance to know them. They were gone before you could get a chance.

When I came back from the service, I went back to being a barber. My boss had kept my job. He was a young guy but with heart problems. He passed away and I took over the barber shop. And then guys that got their hair cut every week would go a month or longer. I said, "This ain't gonna make it." And the school district had this opening for a bus driver/janitor, so I put in for that and that's when I started in with the school district. When the purchasing administrator job came in, then I got that.

For a while, years ago, in the 1960s and early 1970s, I was involved in tribal politics. I was on the tribal council and then secretary of the council. Back then it was all men. Now it's mostly women. Times have changed. The younger generation has taken over, which is good. They've got to learn the ropes. Besides ranching, I volunteer for different things. My wife and I, we help the boys and girls club build their greenhouse, bought them a few plants and do different things. We donate, but mostly I'm not really involved in tribal politics. But voting, that's important. I've voted since I was twenty-one. Them days you had to be twenty-one to register to vote. I registered in Hawthorne. They say it is thirty-three miles from here, but it's a little further. My parents, they made sure I voted. They were nonpartisan, I think. Just like the service. I tried to join before the draft got me. That was one thing my dad tried to influence. You get your military service done and you don't have to worry about it. My brother was in the navy. I looked forward to that, and the voting.

Voting is still real important, especially when you realize what's going on. Well, you know, talking about wars like Korea, the fights in this place and that place that's going on all the time. Like the wars, they better do something before that missile situation gets too far. Either beat them to the punch or they're going to beat us. But I'm sure there's something to stop them rockets if they ever are fired, you know, intercept them. Another thing that really got me was the deal in the Dakotas, people standing up. It wasn't just Indians, it was non-Indians that went there to Standing Rock. Maybe eight people from here went to Standing Rock, mostly young people. They carpooled up there.

Back when I was first voting, there was no polling place on the reservation, not even on Election Day. We had to go to Hawthorne and cast absentee votes. It was difficult for the elderly people to get there. Maybe ten or fifteen years ago we got a polling place here, but there still was no early voting here. During Nevada's early voting period, we would have to go to Hawthorne. If you had a driver's license, you could vote, but they would not recognize tribal ID. The elders are the ones that don't drive and don't have a driver's license. They can't register online to vote. They have to take their birth certificates and travel to Hawthorne. A couple years back, Elvita Martinez and I got ahold of a bunch of the older people, a lot of whom had never voted. We gave them rides and I think we got like a 35 percent increase in turnout.

Then in 2016, my cousin Alvin, who is originally from the Fallon tribe, introduced me to Bret from Four Directions. They were trying to get veterans to file a suit about unequal access, that we did not have satellites for early voting like other places in the state, and that's how Bob James, Bob Burns, and me got in. The girls, Elvita Martinez and Janet Davis, were real go-getters organizing all of this and getting people lined up for the case. We were really surprised when that meant we were going to federal court.

What happened is the secretary of state, the lady, she lied to the county clerk down here in Hawthorne. She told them not to sign anything pertaining to this lawsuit—that the county could not authorize setting up a satellite here, but they had the right to do it. Well, the kid, the county clerk, he was afraid of losing his job. It was probably his second or third year of his job and he said in the meeting that they had asked the secretary of state and she said no. Then she admitted to it in court. So, that's when everything went our way. The judge was Vietnamese. She was really good. We got almost everything we wanted and that's how it ended. Yeah, that was good. The judge then was telling us she was one of those Vietnamese babies that got put on the helicopters at the end of the war. I did some of that putting kids on helicopters in Chu Lai. It was right on the beach. Some guys would come running up to the bars of the helicopters with babies. Oh, it was a mess. Maybe I was one of those that lifted her up, but we were putting them on the helicopters. I wanted to talk to the judge after the trial ended, but she went to her chambers and I never got to that.

I'm getting the effects of the Vietnam War now, hands been operated on twice, and then my feet. The tendons in my hands, all got ate away. The doctors operated on the one hand twice and the other one once. They used that fiber optic on the one hand. The doctors used goat tendons on the other hand, but problems came back in ten years. But, now it's starting again. I had about 25 percent strength in my hands until I got it done. And then my feet are bad. I probably had six to seven hundred combat missions where I jumped out of helicopters. Sometimes you got to jump six or seven feet, which messes up your feet. The bones deteriorated on my arch and left a big crack and then small bones shifted underneath and left a big bump so I have to wear special shoes and I can't bend my feet. I take care of them. And the right one got an infection from a bone that grew through the bottom of my arch so they had to break my big toe to try to straighten it. The doctors put a steel rod in there. It was a good for a while, it healed up. It broke, so I still got part of the steel rod.

I get treated by the Veterans Administration doctors. My dad, uncle Tom, uncle Freddy, all of them fought in World War II. Except for my dad, all of them were in the army, in all the big battles over there. My one uncle got his feet frozen, hands frozen. He finally got his VA settlement, seventy years after the war, six months before he died. The VA sent some of the doctors from the big navy hospital to evaluate me. I can't work all day. I get out and do a lot of work out here, but on a schedule. I've got diabetes, I get tired, I come in, drink a V8 to get my blood sugar up. But I respect them, the doctors have helped me. They're busy.

I've had prostate cancer, colon cancer, along with the problem with my feet and my hands. They've taken care of me through everything. It is Agent Orange. All of the kids are infected with it too. Also I've got diabetes, heart murmur, and internal problems. There's supposed to be a settlement coming. I guess we should put in for it. It's such a rough time for me. I have to go to Reno, 120 miles for treatment. The doctors are all really busy. You wouldn't believe it. Used to be good when I'd go, they would take my blood, do the lab. It was first come, first served. But now, it's by appointment and get there or else.

CHAPTER 10

Why It Matters

Closing Stories from Indian Country

This book opened with two stories—the Standing Rock protests and the voting rights victory of Nevada Paiutes—so it feels appropriate to conclude with two stories that serve as reminders that winning a particular legal battle does not mean the struggle is over. Political scientist E. E. Schattschneider (1975: 16) in his classic work, *The Semisovereign People: A Realist's View of Democracy in America*, pointed out that losers in a political conflict can prevail by changing the scope of the conflict. While Schattschneider viewed this as a way for politically weak groups to prevail against more powerful groups, the strategy can be adopted by elites trying to derail victories of the less powerful. Two voting rights stories from the 2018 elections—one involving Sioux and Chippewa in North Dakota and the other involving Navajo in Utah—illustrate the incredible lengths that entrenched political elites will go to undermine equality at the ballot box. But even more importantly, the stories illustrate the resilience of Native people.

Reservation Voters in North Dakota

As noted in Chapter 4, the Supreme Court on October 9, 2018, rejected NARF's emergency appeal to stop North Dakota from implementing a voter identification law without a fail-safe provision to allow voters whose identification documents did not have residential street addresses to vote in the November 6 general election. The Eighth Circuit Court of Appeals in its ruling—the one the Supreme Court allowed to stand—noted that "some communities" might be disenfranchised but still allowed North

Dakota to implement the law (*Brakebill v. Jaeger* 2018). Make no mistake, the "some communities" are overwhelmingly Native American, including many who had voted earlier in the 2018 primary (Mask 2018). While other materials could be used as supplementary documentation, those had to have residential street addresses, not post office box addresses. This is a problem for Native voters, as many reservation roads are unnamed and streets are not systematically numbered. Even the headquarters for get-out-the-vote efforts on the Standing Rock Reservation in Fort Yates had no address. Standing Rock Sioux external affairs director Danielle Ta'Sheena Finn noted that people know their communities and that directions are given in the following manner: "Hey, that's so-and-so's house; you go two houses down and that's the correct place you need to be" (Astor 2018a). People may be arbitrarily assigned addresses that result in their having non-matching addresses in different government databases. The home of Leslie and Clark Peltier, who live on the Turtle Mountain Reservation, is listed with three completely different addresses in databases of the Rolette County election office, the Department of Motor Vehicles, and the secretary of state's office—a discrepancy that would preclude their voting (Stern 2018).

The Supreme Court's willingness to allow the Eighth Circuit Court's ruling to stand surprised legal scholars. It ran directly counter to the view that courts should not make decisions that alter electoral rules in the period just prior to an election. This view, known as the Purcell Principle, was derived from the *Purcell v. Gonzalez* case (2006) where the Court vacated a Ninth Circuit Court injunction that would have stopped Arizona from implementing a strict voter ID law on the grounds that changes just prior to an election cause problems for administrators and confuse voters. In *Purcell*, the Court's upholding the legal principle harmed Native voters in Arizona, as described by Patty Ferguson-Bohnee in Chapter 6. Now twelve years later, the Court was again harming Native voters but by undermining the principle.[1]

When faced with the possible disenfranchisement of thousands of voters, Native leaders and activists from the Turtle Mountain, Spirit Lake, and Standing Rock reservations, working with NARF, Four Directions, and the Lakota People's Law Project, mobilized. NARF's lead attorney in the *Brakebill* case told the group that either a new tribal identification card or even a "tribal voting letter" with an individual's name, date of birth, and a physical address could be used as supplementary documentation (Four Directions 2019). Tribal leaders agreed to provide voters with free tribal identification that would meet the law's requirements. At the tribal headquarters on Turtle Mountain, the machine used to print ID cards overheated because the demand was so high and it started to melt cards (Astor 2018a). But the ID cards needed to list street addresses, which generally meant obtaining addresses from local county officials.[2] As a backup academics with training in Geographic Information Systems (GIS) created addresses for some people living on the Standing Rock, Spirit Lake, and Turtle Mountain reservations. These were prepared for "tribal voting letters" as a fail-safe for individuals who had not obtained new tribal IDs with addresses (Astor 2018a; Four Directions 2019).[3]

In late October, Courtney Yellow Fat, a Standing Rock Sioux council member, predicted that the new law actually would spur people to vote. Spirit Lake's secretary/treasurer Lonna Jackson-Street also predicted high turnout—"numbers we've never seen before" (Astor 2018b). Leaders and activists at Standing Rock described the struggle to vote in 2018 as "another episode in an enduring battle to harmonize their tribal and U.S. citizenships—to protect their rights as North Dakota voters, while also defending tribal sovereignty" (Buckley 2018).

When social networks encourage voting, there can be a contagion effect that triggers even greater participation (Vonnahme 2012). The turnout on the North Dakota reservations in the 2018 midyear elections fit this model; they experienced the highest turnout ever, even surpassing the previous high-water mark of the 2008 presidential election. Much of the credit, according to OJ Semans, goes to Native youth, who used social media to mobilize their peers, parents, and grandparents (Reilly 2018). The 2018 Miss Standing Rock, Wanbii Waunsila Wi Eagle, filmed a public service announcement encouraging turnout. At Standing Rock high schools, age-eligible seniors were allowed to leave class to get free tribal identification and then to vote (Astor 2018b). At Turtle Mountain, the youth council led a several-mile march in the snow to the polling place on Election Day. The marchers carried signs reading, "Warrior Up," "Don't Disenfranchise us," and "We are the grandchildren of those you couldn't remove" (Reilly 2018).[4]

Navajo in San Juan County, Utah

Meanwhile, equally compelling events were taking place in a remote part of Utah. San Juan County, located in Utah's southeastern corner, shares borders with Arizona, Colorado, and New Mexico. The county encompasses 7,933 square miles with a population of 15,358, or 1.9 persons per square mile. A 120-mile stretch of land along the southern edge of the county is part of the Navajo Nation Reservation. Most residents who live north of the reservation are white Mormons, although there is a small part of the county that is part of the Ute Mountain Indian Reservation. American Indians make up 49.4 percent of county residents, while whites make up 47.4 percent with the remainder largely comprised of Latino and mixed-race individuals (United States Census Bureau 2017). The poverty rate for Native Americans is 42.9 percent versus 12.3 percent for whites (Data USA 2016). Most of the Navajo inhabitants live in isolated areas, often miles away from their nearest neighbors, while most whites live in the county's small cities.[5]

As was true in Jackson County, the two populations live "worlds apart" from one another (Massey 2015b: 30–32).[6] The town of Bluff, which is the gateway to Bears Ears National Monument, includes a monument to the arrival of Mormon settlers in 1880. Its inscription describes settlers as enduring forty years of attacks from "hostile Indians."[7] The county also was the site of Posey's War, the last armed conflict between the U.S. government and Native Americans (Utes and Paiutes). Utah did not eliminate laws prohibiting Native Americans from voting until 1957, and over the past four decades there have been many lawsuits charging governmental entities with discrimination against Navajo.[8]

Voting Rights Litigation in San Juan County

After a DOJ-initiated Section 2 case in the mid-1980s, the county instituted single-member district elections for commission and school board seats. This made it possible for Navajos to be elected for the first time.[9] Aside from minor changes to the boundaries of two white commission districts, the boundaries were unchanged. In 2012, the Navajo Nation sued, charging that the county had limited the opportunities for Navajos to be elected by "packing" Navajos into county commission District 3 (93 percent Native American), while Districts 1 and 2 each were only 30 percent Native American. The county argued the earlier consent decree prohibited them from changing the boundaries. Judge Robert Shelby disagreed and appointed a special master to draw up a redistricting plan (*Navajo Nation v. San Juan County* 2016).

The new plan gave Navajos an opportunity to elect majorities on the school board and county commission, leading some whites to claim they were now being "disenfranchised." Public attention has been mostly focused on the commission districts, which have the following proportions of Native Americans: 11.1 percent in District 1, 65.6 percent in District 2, and 79.9 percent in District 3 (Tanner 2018a). Given the history of racially polarized voting, District 1 almost certainly will continue to elect white Republicans and District 3 almost certainly will elect Navajo Democrats. The outcome in District 2 is less easy to predict because Native Americans have much lower rates of voting turnout than do whites.[10] Also in 2018, the county commission attempted to implement an all vote-by-mail system that would have decreased voting among Navajo and likely ensured that District 2 would elect a white but backed off after the Navajo Human Rights Commission sued.[11]

National Implications of Political Disputes in San Juan County

Normally, San Juan County Commission elections are of little interest to outsiders. These, however, are not normal times. Although few people have heard of the county, many have heard about Bears Ears National Monument, which is in San Juan County.[12] The Navajo Nation strongly endorsed President Obama's decision to create the monument, although not all Navajo agreed with the decision. The most prominent Navajo critic was District 3 commissioner Rebecca Benally, who publicly praised the decision to shrink the monument's size by 85 percent.[13] The Navajo Nation formally chastised Benally for appearing to speak for the Nation in public appearances against the monument (Coriz 2018).[14]

The Trump administration cited the San Juan County Commission's opposition to the monument as evidence that the local community wanted it cut back. This meant the 2018 election of county commissioners had national implications. All District 1 primary election candidates, including the victor, Bruce Adams, are white Republican supporters of President Trump. Since Republicans did not put up a candidate in District 3, the Democratic primary winner, Kenneth Maryboy, gained the seat. Maryboy, a supporter of Bears Ears, is a long-time board member of Utah Dine Bikeyah, whose mission is to "Preserve and protect the cultural and natural resources of ancestral Native American lands to benefit and bring healing to the people of the Earth" (Trahant 2018a).[15] This meant the District 2 winner would determine whether the San Juan County Commission had a majority in favor of or opposed to Bears Ears (Gehrke 2018).

The District 2 Race

In late summer, the District 2 race was thrown into disarray when county officials—all white Republicans—removed Democratic primary winner Willie Grayeyes, a big supporter of the national monument, from the ballot. A Republican candidate, Wendy Black, had filed a complaint, stating Grayeyes actually lives in Arizona.[16] Black stated that she had driven past his house and described it as "not livable" (Langlois 2018). Grayeyes provided county officials with a satellite image of his house in the Navajo Mountain part of District 2, a document showing he does cattle ranching there, his Utah voter registration record, and a copy of his birth certificate. The county Democratic chair testified Grayeyes had lived in his house for at least thirty-four years. The vice president of Navajo Mountain verified Grayeyes's residency but explained he traveled to Arizona to access the Internet. She also stated that Grayeyes has an Arizona post office box because mail service in Navajo Mountain is handled through that branch of the post office (Tanner 2018b).

County Clerk/Auditor John Nielsen, who removed Grayeyes from the ballot, claimed the county possessed evidence that "sufficiently rebuts the presumption of residency." The evidence included anonymous sources who stated they lived in the area but did not know Grayeyes or said he often stayed in Tuba City. There was a report from a sheriff's deputy who visited the residence saying that the dirt in the driveway did not show "recent tire tracks" (Tanner 2018c).[17] San Juan County Attorney Kenneth Laws, whose father (Kelly Laws) was the Republican nominee, asked an outside prosecutor from another county to investigate Grayeyes for possible election fraud charges. The prosecutor refused to do so. Grayeyes responded by filing a suit against the county, naming the county clerk, the original complainant, the sheriff's deputy, and the county attorney as defendants. In August, Federal District Judge David Nuffer granted Grayeyes's request for a preliminary injunction and ordered the county to place his name back on the ballot and restore his voting rights (Maffly 2018).

Even though Navajo constitute a majority of voters in District 2, their historical turnout rates lag behind those of whites, but not in 2018. Grayeyes defeated Laws by a margin of 817 to 648. Not only does this mean the

San Juan County Council will have a majority in favor of keeping Bears Ears, they also might adopt measures to benefit Navajos—such as funding basic services (e.g., running water, electricity, sewers, and road maintenance) that are lacking (Langlois 2018; Stevens 2019). Perhaps the national reporters who have covered the environmental and historical significance of Bears Ears might consider writing this equally important story of how Native Americans overcame political power and cronyism in a remote corner of Utah.

Political Engagement Going Forward

It is hard to imagine another time in the past quarter century where the need for Native political engagement has been greater. As Wizipan Little Elk (interview 2017) noted, Indian Country faces all of the same issues—health care, economic development, environmental issues, resource protection, global warming, housing, drug addiction, and education—as the rest of the country, but the adverse effects are "more intense and on a larger scale."[18] Another huge battle is looming due to the approval of a route for the Keystone XL pipeline that will adversely affect the Fort Belknap and Rosebud Sioux populations. But as the stories from North Dakota and Utah suggest, Native people are no longer politically marginalized. They have developed a rich web of cross-tribal coalitions functioning at the national, regional, and state levels with new ones being created as needs arise,[19] as well as leaders and politicians with a deep understanding of politics and a younger generation inspired to activism.[20]

Nearly seventy years ago, Snuffy Main's grandfather wrote, "If we stick together, we can influence about 10,000 Indian votes in Montana, which is probably enough for the balance of power in any election in the state."[21] Today the proportion of Native Americans in the Montana state legislature (ten Democrats and one Republican) is on par with their proportion in the population, but their influence is even greater. Twenty-five legislators regularly attend the Montana American Indian Caucus's weekly lunch meetings, where bills covering topics as diverse as the preservation of indigenous languages and the identification of missing and murdered indigenous women to Medicaid expansion recently have been discussed. Even individuals with troubled past histories of interactions with Native Americans recognize that the Indian Caucus is a political force not to be ignored. For example, Representative Geraldine Custer (R-Forsyth), who was one of the election officials sued in *Wandering Medicine* (2014), attended a recent caucus meeting to get feedback on legislation to require all vote-by-mail elections. While she did not gain too much support, it is telling that Custer reached out to the caucus (Ragar 2019).

In 2018, a record number of Native Americans ran for political office; many stated they were inspired by the Dakota Access Pipeline protests (Public News Service 2018). More than one hundred American Indians and Alaska Natives competed for nontribal political offices, including eleven who ran for Congress—four Democrats, four Republicans, and three independent or third-party candidates (Trahant 2018b).[22] And a record number of the candidates were elected, including such notable firsts as Sharice Davids (D-KS) from the Ho-Chunk Nation and Debra Haaland (D-NM) from the Pueblo of Laguna Nation, who became the first Native women elected to Congress.[23] Although it garnered far less attention, it is worth noting that the North Dakota legislator who was the lead sponsor of the voter identification law lost his race to a Native woman, Ruth Buffalo of Hidatsa/Mandan and Chiricahua Apache heritage.[24]

The Standing Rock protests also are serving as a catalyst for an entire generation of young Native activists, perhaps triggering a new era of Red Power. The Spirit Riders, the young Crow Creek Sioux men who patrolled the borders of Oceti Sakowin on horseback, are committed to continuing their engagement (Sazue interview 2017). After returning from Standing Rock, young Paiutes from Pyramid Lake and Walker River joined their elders in get-out-the-vote efforts in the 2016 and 2018 elections. They posted material on social media and put up posters and flyers, as well as going door to door, urging people to register and vote. Young people who had never given speeches began doing so, telling stories about what they had learned at Standing Rock. Some said the experience of being at Standing Rock transformed their lives, giving them a sense of purpose for the first time (Davis interview 2017; Martinez interview 2017; Four Directions 2019). A young Te-Moak Shoshone woman whose ill brother insisted on going to Standing Rock and died before returning home described Standing Rock to me as a "sacrifice," albeit one that created "renewable energy." After Standing Rock, the woman said, "I felt that even if we were grains of sand, we matter. We're something and we're getting people moving" (Ledesma interview 2017).

NOTES

CHAPTER 1

1. There is some archeological evidence indicating that indigenous peoples were in North America as early as thirty thousand years ago (Rollins 2004: 126).

2. It is far easier to simply consider the indigenous peoples as fading away. Nearly two hundred years ago, De Tocqueville (2005: 876) captured this sentiment when he described Natives as "an ancient people, the original and rightful masters of the American continent melting away daily like snow in sunshine and disappearing from the face of the earth" as "another race rises in their stead."

3. Prior to the Dakota Access Pipeline protests, few people had heard of Energy Transfer LP and its chairman/chief operating officer Kelcy Warren. Energy Transfer LP is one of world's largest pipeline construction companies, earning $54.1 billion in revenue in 2018. The company has a troubled history of regulatory problems, including multiple sanctions for spills. In April 2017, a drilling-related spill released 2 million diesel-contaminated gallons of liquid that coated a 6.5-acre wetland in Ohio (Leonard 2019).

4. The 3,572-square-mile Standing Rock Reservation is home to slightly more than 8,000 Lakota and Dakota Sioux. Although the Dakota Access Pipeline does not go through reservation land, it comes within a half mile of the reservation's current borders. The pipeline, which transports 450,000 barrels of crude oil every day from the Bakken fields in North Dakota to southern Illinois, was opposed by the Standing Rock Sioux from its inception. The Tribal Historical Preservation Offices raised concerns about the desecration of culturally significant sites—places that had been promised in perpetuity to the Sioux in the 1851 Fort Laramie Treaty—while environmentalists focused on the threats to the Standing Rock Reservation's main drinking water supply, Lake Oahe. What makes this even more of a travesty in the eyes of the Sioux is that Lake Oahe, which is an artificial reservoir with a power plant that provides electricity throughout much of the north-central section of the country, was created by flooding lands taken from the Cheyenne River Sioux Reservation and the Standing Rock Reservation. Between 1948 and 1962, the Army Corps of Engineers used eminent domain to seize and then flood nearly 56,000 acres of Standing Rock land with water from the Missouri River. The flooded land was the most fertile portion of the reservation (Erdrich 2016).

5. Less than a week after taking the oath of office, President Trump signed an executive order to speed up approval of the Dakota Access Pipeline project by ordering the Army Corps of Engineers to issue the easement allowing construction to start (Henry and Cama 2017).

6. There were only several hundred people at Wounded Knee as opposed to the thousands who have come to Standing Rock.

7. In December's bitter cold, more than eleven thousand protesters were still at Standing Rock (Taliman 2016).

8. The Pyramid Lake Paiutes were the first Native Nation to pass and send a letter of support to the Standing Rock Sioux engaged in protesting the Dakota Access Pipeline (Hawley interview 2017).

9. In 2012 the Nevada Indian Commission recognized Flora Greene's contributions to preserving Paiute traditions by giving her the Contributor Supporter of the Year Award and in 2017 she was given a Nevada Heritage Award (Walker 2018).

10. Voting by mail is problematic, given that there is very limited access to mail services on the reservation.

11. The Pyramid Lake Paiutes had been engaged in a thirty-year struggle with Nevada politicians over water rights and protecting their access to the Truckee River system that feeds Pyramid Lake (Davis interview 2017; Hawley interview 2017).

12. One of their attorneys told me that he could only handle a voting rights case every couple of years because it is hard to get legal fees covered in these cases. He is a solo practice attorney who uses the money obtained from other legal work to fund voting rights litigation.

13. In early 2017, a North Dakota state legislator introduced a bill that would exempt a driver from penalties if he or she hit a protester standing on a road. Representative Keith Kempenich (39th District), who is a leading Republican member of the North Dakota House, having served his "oil patch" district since 1994, sponsored HB 1203. When asked about the reasons for introducing the bill, Kempenich stated, "There's a line between protests and terrorism," and when a protester "comes up on the roadway and challenges a motorist that's an intentional act of intimidation—the definition of terrorism" (Agrawal 2017).

14. While the Black Lives Matter Movement raised public awareness of police use of force against African Americans, there has been little media attention to cases involving American Indians (Schroedel and Chen 2017).

15. James Watt, the interior secretary under President Reagan, was even more derogatory in his comments, describing American Indians as "incompetent wards of the government" (Landry 2016). What makes this comment even more troubling is that the Bureau of Indian Affairs is part of the Department of the Interior.

16. Although most Americans do not think about the fact that they have dual citizenship (e.g., national and state citizenship), there are important Supreme Court decisions establishing which rights are accorded people due to their national citizenship and which are a function of state-designated rights. See, for example, *Slaughterhouse Cases* (1873) and *Minor v. Happersett* (1875). The difference is that enrolled members of federally recognized Native Nations have a third citizenship, which has been accorded legal recognition for more than 180 years and gives them specific rights based on that citizenship. See *Worcester v. Georgia* (1832).

17. Terms such as "American Indian" and "Native American" that are used to describe indigenous peoples create a false sense that they are a single homogeneous group. Rollins (2004: 127–128) pointed out this fallacy when he stated that these terms "[disguise] the incredible cultural diversity" of the different Native Nations and suggests that it might be more appropriate to think of these terms as akin to using "European" to describe the people living on that continent. Whenever possible it is preferable to use the name of a specific Native Nation or linguistic/social group (e.g., Gros Ventre or Oglala). There are many instances where a reference must be made to all indigenous peoples and I use "American

Indian," "Native American," and "Native" interchangeably because there is no single agreed-upon term.

18. Huntington's basic thesis is that in the post–Cold War world, the main source of international conflict would pit civilizations with different cultural understandings against one another. Most notably, Huntington argued there would be conflict between Western democracies and Islamic peoples. Not surprisingly, this thesis has been criticized by many scholars for ignoring both the diversity within these groupings and the interdependence among them. See, for example, Cox 2000; Russett, Oneal, and Cox 2000; Sen 1999; Welch 1997.

19. As Woodard (2018: 9) notes, "Paternalistic federal policies target Native people with heavy-handed precision. . . . If a tribe wants to build a housing development or protect a sacred site, if a tribal member wants to start a business or plant a field, a federal agency can modify or scuttle the plans. Conversely, if a corporation or other outside interest covets reservation lands or resources, the federal government becomes an obsequious bondservant, helping the non-Native entity get what it wants at bargain-basement prices."

20. Forsyth is named after the general who commanded the 7th Cavalry during the Wounded Knee Massacre, where roughly three hundred nonbelligerent and largely unarmed Lakota were killed.

21. The "stickiness" is most obvious on reservations and the "border towns" located just off-reservation. This point was brought home to me while I was in Montana doing field research related to the *Wandering Medicine v. McCulloch* case (2014). People explained to me that there were some cafés and restaurants that were "Indian friendly," which meant a mixed-race party could get served there, and others were not, so we needed to avoid the latter. But I remember seeing posters advertising a reenactment of "Custer's heroic last stand" in even an "Indian friendly" café.

22. Although there are a number of important histories that cover different periods of Native activism (Reinhardt 2007; Smith and Warrior 1996), less attention has been paid to the ways that individual actors understand how their actions fit within both a broader movement and their often complicated lives. A notable exception is Kent Blansett's (2018) recent history of Richard Oakes's life.

CHAPTER 2

1. Although Huntington (1993, 1996) was not describing encounters between Euro-Americans and Natives when he coined the phrase "clash of civilizations," the framework provides a useful starting point for analyzing the interactions.

2. The Hopi living on the summits of mesas in Arizona were unusual in that land was viewed as attached to particular homes in villages (Barnes 2015: 33).

3. This different sense of humans' relationship with land was expressed by the Shawnee leader Tecumseh, who stated, "Why not sell the air, the clouds, the Great Sea, as well as the Earth?" (McMaster and Trafzer 2004: 125).

4. Although a number of language groups used hieroglyphics marked on birch bark to record important events, the first fully fleshed-out written Native language was developed around 1815 by Sequoyah, who created a system for translating spoken Cherokee into a written form using eighty-five characters, each of which stands for a sound (Cherokee Nation 2017a).

5. Puritans used the analogy of King David's slaughtering the "wicked" in the Old Testament to justify war against the Pequot. The reservation system as a means of segregating indigenous people originated in the aftermath of the Pequot War of 1637. Pequot survivors were forced to live in a prescribed area, become Christian, and take on European ways of life (McMaster and Trafzer 2004: 122–123). See Vaughn (1995) for a summary of the scholarship on Puritan-Pequot relations and causes of the Pequot War.

6. The relatively strong position of Native Nations can be seen in the nature of the treaties signed during the colonial era. More than three-quarters of the treaties were designed to secure military alliances or friendship. Less than 20 percent involved agreements where the Native Nation gave up land (DeJong 2015: 4).

7. Having different Native Nations meet to discuss issues and reach agreements was a well-established practice that predated treaty councils with the U.S. government. However, a major difference between the two types is that all-Native councils reached common understandings that relied on the parties giving their word rather than agreements embodied in written documents. One's word was considered sacred, with its meaning established through oral tradition, and created a relationship among parties that was based on trust—not words on a document (Nuttall 2014: 112–113).

8. Treaties were negotiated and signed by U.S. commissioners and leaders of Native Nations but did not become binding until ratified by the Senate. During the California gold rush period (1851–1852), commissioners negotiated and signed eighteen treaties with Native Nations in the state, but none were ratified because the state legislature asked the Senate to not act. Native people, who thought they were living on treaty-protected lands, were either driven out or killed by non-Indians wanting access to lands that might have gold (Harjo 2014: 3).

9. Congress has ratified 388 treaties with Native Nations. Another 219 treaties were negotiated but never ratified by Congress (DeJong 2015: 25–45). Most early treaties were friendship compacts, but nearly all after the War of 1812 were focused on the acquisition of land (Deloria 2004: 146).

10. Both the British and Americans sought support from Native Nations during the Revolutionary War. While most Native Nations supported the British, the Oneida and Delaware (Lenape) supported the revolutionaries. In a 1778 treaty, the Delaware gave the Americans permission to cross through their territory and attack British forts. In exchange the Continental Congress promised them the right to become a state after the end of hostilities. This commitment was only made twice to Native Nations; the Cherokee were the other recipients of such a promise (Deloria 2004: 145–146).

11. See Deloria and DeMallie (1999) for an in-depth examination of how negotiations between the U.S. government and Native Nations developed over time.

12. The 1787 Northwest Ordinance established policies to be followed in territories under U.S. governance. It stated, "The utmost good faith shall always be observed toward the Indians; their lands and property shall never be taken from them without their consent; and, in their property, rights, and liberty, they never shall be invaded or disturbed, unless in just and lawful wars authorized by Congress; but laws founded in justice and humanity shall, from time to time be made for preventing wrongs being done to them, and for preserving peace and friendship with them" (Journals of the Continental Congress 1787: 340–341).

13. The language in Article 1, Section 8, along with Trade and Intercourse Acts, established federal government primacy in interactions with Native Nations (Prucha 1984).

14. In 1800, Congress appropriated funds for the Indian Office in the War Department to use for "civilizing" Native peoples. Conversion to Christianity was viewed as central to the civilizing effort, so the Indian Office passed on the appropriated funds to Christian denominations for proselytizing among different Native Nations (Harjo 2014: 4).

15. Among Cherokee, the removal from their homes and forced walk to what is now Oklahoma is known as the "trail where they cried." Non-Cherokee often call it the Trail of Tears (Cherokee Nation 2017b).

16. The Navajo and Mescalero Apache had a similar experience (the Long Walk) in 1863 and 1864, when more than 8,000 people were marched 350 miles through the desert to Bosque Redondo, an internment camp near Fort Sumner, New Mexico (Mankiller 2004: 255).

17. The "discovery doctrine" originated with two papal bulls; the first was issued in 1452 by Pope Nicholas V and the second in 1493 by Pope Alexander VI. In the 1452 Bull Romanus Pontifex, Pope Nicholas V sanctioned the conquest, colonization, and confiscation of property from non-Christian nations. King Alfonso of Portugal used this bull as a mandate for making "discoveries" along the western coast of Africa and enslaving their peoples. Pope Alexander VI's papal bull *Inter Caetera* issued over four decades later sought to resolve disputes between Spain and Portugal about which country could claim specific non-Christian territories. In the *Inter Caetera*, Pope Alexander VI encouraged Christian nations to "discover" and claim lands, converting the inhabitants to the Christianity (Newcomb 1992).

18. *Johnson v. McIntosh* (1823) involved a dispute over whether a white man legally could purchase land from an Indian. Based on the "discovery doctrine," the Court ruled it was not possible to purchase land because the Indian had no legal title to the land. There is some evidence that Marshall was using the case to establish a precedent about the conditions under which the vesting of land titles could be passed on to successors in order to resolve an unrelated dispute about land titles that the state of Virginia wanted to pass on to Revolutionary War veterans but that in 1792 were now part of Kentucky, which wanted to reserve that land for its citizens (Robertson 2014: 69–73).

19. After Georgia passed a series of anti-Indian laws in the late 1820s, the Cherokee Nation asked the Supreme Court to overturn those laws and reaffirm the rights of the Cherokee Nation, but the Court in *Cherokee Nation v. Georgia* (1831) declined to rule on the merits of the case, instead holding that the Cherokee were not a "foreign" nation and lacked standing to sue.

20. The constitutional issue in *Worcester v. Georgia* (1832) was whether Georgia could have a criminal statute that prohibited non-Indians from going on Indian lands unless they had obtained a license from the state. The Court vacated the criminal conviction of Samuel Worcester on the grounds that only the federal government had the authority to pass laws dealing with Indians.

21. Forty years later, the meaning of the Marshall Trilogy was still unclear. In his 1873 congressional testimony, Indian commissioner Edward Smith stated he was confused about what was meant by the "double condition of sovereignty and wardship" (United States House of Representatives 1873). The meaning of the Marshall Trilogy is still in dispute, as Fletcher (2006: 696) notes: "There is a lot of great language in the Trilogy that supports tribal advocates and a lot of language that supports those who oppose tribal interests for whatever reason. . . . In other words, read the Trilogy closely, but don't bring the Trilogy with you when you're facing Chief Justice Roberts."

22. Unless a treaty involved war or peace, state governments during the Articles of Confederation period were allowed to sign treaties with Native Nations. Nothing in the Constitution explicitly altered that status, although Article 1, Section 8 gave Congress the authority to "regulate commerce with tribes" and Article 2, Section 2 gave the president the power to "make Treaties, provided two-thirds of the Senate present concur." Political leaders in Georgia and New York argued that nothing in the Constitution altered the practices of states with respect to making treaties with Native Nations and vociferously opposed the Marshall Court's rulings that gave power exclusively to the federal government (Deloria 2004: 146).

23. There were whites, known as "friends of the Indians," who pushed for citizenship and suffrage as a means of furthering assimilation. These generally well-meaning individuals believed that assimilation was the only way Native peoples could survive. Many Native individuals had no desire to give up their identities and saw these efforts as simply another Euro-American attempt to take more from them (Rollins 2004: 129).

24. The Treaty of Guadalupe Hidalgo gave Mexican citizens living in the newly gained U.S. territory a choice between becoming U.S. citizens and retaining Mexican citizenship (Barnes 2015: 180–181).

25. Neither the Emancipation Proclamation nor the Thirteenth Amendment applied in Indian Territory. The Cherokee, Creek, and Seminole gave up slavery at the end of the Civil War, but the Choctaw and Chickasaw only abolished slavery as part of an 1866 treaty with the U.S. government (Krauthamer 2013: 10).

26. Interestingly, a couple of years later Congress refused to investigate Colonel George Armstrong Custer's slaughter of peaceful Cheyenne women and children at Washita River.

27. The "excluding Indians not taxed" phrase appears in Section 2 of the Fourteenth Amendment that covers the apportionment of representation in the House of Representatives, but it was not included in Section 1 that defines "All persons born or naturalized in the United States" as citizens.

28. There was no guarantee that, if a Native American severed relations with his or her Nation and lived among whites, he or she would be considered a U.S. citizen. See, for example, *MacKay v. Campbell* (1871), where the court ruled that a man of mixed white and Chinook blood who had lived for many years as a white still could not be considered a citizen because of his Chinook blood.

29. The Board of Indian Commissioners in its annual report for 1869 stated that "the treaty system should be abandoned and . . . existing treaties should be abrogated" (Board of Indian Commissioners 1869: 10).

30. See An Act Making Appropriations for the Current and Continuing Expenses of the Indian Department, and for Fulfilling Treaty Stipulations with Various Indian Tribes, 16 Stat. 544 (March 3, 1871).

31. The Supreme Court in *Lone Wolf v. Hitchcock* (1903) stated that Congress can change or abrogate treaty rights without any input from the affected Native Nation. The legal rationale for this is called the plenary power doctrine and was first articulated by the Supreme Court in *U. S. v. Kagama* (1886). For alternative and less absolutist interpretations of the plenary power doctrine, see Wilkins and Lomawaima (2001).

32. Native Americans who accepted the offer of U.S. citizenship in exchange for taking land allotments were not allowed to rent, lease, or sell their lands for twenty-five years. The Burke Act postponed the granting of citizenship until the twenty-five-year trust period ended, but the president was given authority to shorten that period (Rollins 2004: 134).

33. There also was support for U.S. citizenship from some prominent Native Americans, including Dr. Carlos Montezuma from the Yavapai. In 1911, the Society of American Indians was formed with the goal of gaining full civil rights for American Indians (Dunbar-Ortiz and Gilio-Whitaker 2016: 173). Mostly white Progressive reformers, associated with the Women's National Indian Association, the Indian Rights Association, and the Lake Mohonk conference, lobbied aggressively for the passage of the Dawes Act (Hanson 1997: 196). They joined forces with western whites who wanted to break up reservations to gain access to the lands and resources held by the Native Nations (Rollins 2004: 133).

34. The most aggressive attempt to force assimilation, the mandatory removal of Native children from their homes and sending them to residential boarding schools, was developed during this period (Child 2004: 161). The first federal boarding school, the Carlisle Indian Industrial School, was established in 1878 in western Pennsylvania. The school's first superintendent had fought in the Indian Wars under General Philip Sheridan and Colonel George Armstrong Custer. The initial classes of students were chosen from the families of Native leaders who had fought against him, a strategy that gave them a great deal of leverage over influential families (Harjo 2014: 5–6).

35. For more on the impact of World War I military service on American Indians, see Britten (1997).

36. See Nackenoff (2006) for a discussion of reformers who supported American Indian citizenship.

37. In 1912 when Arizona gained statehood, American Indians comprised 14.3 percent of the population, so it is not surprising that state officials tried to find ways to exclude them from citizenship and voting. In two counties (Apache County and Navajo County), they comprised a majority of the population and in two additional counties they made up more than one-third of the population (Ferguson-Bohnee 2015: 1104).

38. Secretary of the Interior Hubert Work provided funding for an investigation and report titled *The Problem of Indian Administration* that found high levels of poverty, low life expectancy, poor education, high infant mortality rates, and a pervasive lack of medical care among American Indians. The report concluded that the forced assimilation policy had "resulted in much loss of land and an enormous increase in the details of administration without a compensating advance in the economic ability of the Indians" (Meriam 1928: 41).

39. In the late nineteenth and early twentieth centuries, reservation agents exercised an extraordinary amount of control over the lives of people living on reservations. On many reservations, Native people had to obtain permission to travel off-reservation (Reinhardt 2007: 21).

40. The most significant parts of the Indian Reorganization Act involved the creation of new governing structures, with an elected tribal council responsible for governing reservations, albeit still under the jurisdiction of the Office of Indian Affairs. The reservation agent would still have veto power over council decisions. Native Nations that adopted constitutions that conformed to the IRA model were provided access to economic development programs. A majority of all eligible voters (not those who actually cast ballots) had to vote "no" in a referendum for the model to be rejected. In the end, 174 reservations out of a total of 252 accepted the reorganized form of governance (Reinhardt 2007: 26–30).

41. The Indian Claims Commission was in existence until 1978.

42. The first code talkers were Choctaw, Cheyenne, Comanche, Osage, and Sioux, who sent military messages in their languages during World War I. This effort was expanded greatly

in World War II, when code talkers were used in the Pacific and European theaters. Although Navajo code talkers got most of the media attention, Hopi, Kiowa, Winnebago, Chippewa, Creek, Seminole, Lakota, Dakota, Menominee, Oneida, Pawnee, Sac Fox, and Choctaw were code talkers in World War II (United States Army 2017).

43. As veterans, Harrison and Austin felt they had earned the right to vote. Harrison was particularly affected by the widespread poverty among the elderly in his community. Under the "guardianship" rationale, they could not obtain Old Age Assistance and other federal benefits even though payroll taxes are deducted from the paychecks of Native Americans (Inter Tribal Council of Arizona 2004).

44. Harrison and Austin's lawsuit gained widespread support. Democratic congressman Richard Harless was one of the plaintiffs' attorneys. The American Civil Liberties Union, the National Congress of American Indians, and the U.S. Attorney's Office submitted briefs on Harrison and Austin's behalf (Inter Tribal Council of Arizona 2004).

45. According to Trujillo's daughter, her father's experience seeing large numbers of Native men volunteering to serve and then many dying in combat strengthened his commitment to voting rights (Abeita 2008).

46. As passed in 1953, House Concurrent Resolution No. 108 in Public Law 280 gave full criminal and some civil jurisdiction over the covered reservations to state governments. Senator Arthur Watkins (R-UT) and Representative E. Y. Berry (R-SD) played leading roles in the passage of House Concurrent Resolution No. 108 (Schroedel and Hart 2015: 10).

47. Some smaller Nations are referred to as bands. In California, the Spanish term *rancheria* is used to refer to a very small reservation.

48. While the relocation policies were one factor in the migration of American Indians from rural reservations to cities, many moved to take advantage of the greater economic opportunities available in urban areas. Although the migration of African Americans from the South to urban areas in the North is well known, the rate of movement among Native Americans for most of the twentieth century far exceeded that of African Americans (Blansett 2018: 78).

49. As part of the St. Lawrence Seaway project, New York used eminent domain to claim Barnhart Island even though the Iroquois had treaties from the late eighteenth and mid-nineteenth centuries giving them the island. The Iroquois tried to get compensation via a lawsuit, but the case was dismissed by the New York Court of Appeals (*St. Regis Tribe v. New York* 1958).

50. The Oahe Dam is 242 feet high and 9,300 feet long. Its reservoir extends for 250 miles (Schneiders 1997: 237). The others are the Fort Randall, Garrison, Big Bend, and Gavin Point dams.

51. Legislation, establishing and funding the Pick-Sloan Plan, was passed by Congress in 1944, but it was developed by business and government leaders from Montana, North Dakota, South Dakota, Wyoming, Kansas, Missouri, and Iowa who wanted to find ways to foster economic development, generate hydroelectric power, and ensure water availability for farmers during drought periods. Political and economic considerations influenced the decision to locate the dams on reservation lands. Locating dams near white cities or taking agricultural land from white ranchers and farmers would have generated costs that would have made the project unfeasible, but these concerns did not apply to the Sioux, whose lands were labeled "inferior" (Schneiders 1997).

52. According to Blansett (2018: 3), Native Nationalism encompasses the "long history of efforts to promote and protect the explicit rights of an Indigenous nation's governance,

lifeway, language, community, land, law, and peoples. It is based firmly on a foundation of indigenous sovereignty."

53. The National Indian Youth Council consciously modeled many actions on those undertaken by Black civil rights activists (Chrisman 2006). The difference, however, according to Blansett (2018: 4), is that "Red Power was never about civil rights or equal integration into the colonial nation-state; rather, it was about protecting indigenous human rights, especially as part of independent and sovereign nations." In 1967, Vine Deloria Jr., the executive director of NCAI, endorsed the use of the term "Red Power" (Blansett 2018: 72–73).

54. The American Indian Movement (AIM) originally was an urban movement aimed at protecting Chippewa who traveled back and forth between the Twin Cities and reservations from police brutality. Within a couple of years it had become an intertribal movement that "exploded across reservations and cities from North Carolina to the Pacific Northwest" (Smith and Warrior 1996: 138). There are several fine historical accounts that cover different aspects of the Wounded Knee standoff. Reinhardt (2007), Smith and Warrior (1996), and Sayer (1997), respectively, provide accounts of the history and politics of the Pine Ridge Reservation, the growth of the Red Power movement, and the Wounded Knee trials.

55. The fish-in protests led to litigation that forced states to recognize treaties that promised Native Nations the right to fish spawned in rivers and streams. This right was affirmed in the *U.S. v. Washington* (1974) ruling, which stated that Native Americans were entitled to catch up to 50 percent of fish spawned in the state.

56. See Pierson (2004) and Erdrich (2016).

CHAPTER 3

1. As part of Freedom Summer, more than 900 largely white students went to Mississippi to register voters and were still in Mississippi when the bodies of the slain civil rights workers were found. The administration was well aware of the fact that these volunteers also were at risk. They had experienced 1,000 arrests, as well as 35 shootings and 80 beatings, while doing the work (Graham 1992: 87–88).

2. The language in Section 2 was amended in 1982 in response to the Supreme Court's ruling in *City of Mobile v. Bolton* (1980). This is discussed in Chapter 4.

3. There were other permanent provisions, the most significant of which was the provision authorizing criminal and civil actions against people who interfered with the right to vote.

4. Many members of Congress thought the nonpermanent provisions, sometimes labeled the "special" provisions, might not need to be renewed after the initial five-year period. They hoped the five-year-long "cooling off" period after the Act's adoption would be enough to change discriminatory practices (United States House Judiciary Committee, HR Report 439: 15).

5. The formula initially used to determine whether a jurisdiction was subject to Section 5 pre-clearance was specified in Section 4(b) and had two parts: (1) whether the jurisdiction had a "test or device" that restricted registration and voting, and (2) whether less than 50 percent of the voting-age population was registered to vote on November 1, 1964, or less than 50 percent of that voting-age population voted in the 1964 presidential election. The date was later changed to November 1968 and finally moved to November 1972 during the 1975 reauthorization.

6. The fact that Congress chose to keep the 1972 date in its subsequent renewals opened the way for the Supreme Court in *Shelby County v. Holder* (2013) to argue that Section 4(b) was unconstitutional in that it violated the "equal sovereignty of the states" by treating them differently based on "40 year old facts that have no relationship to present day."

7. While it is possible for political jurisdictions to be subjected to pre-clearance through Section 2 with the mechanism established in Section 3(c), it is much more difficult because the plaintiffs often are required to prove intentional discrimination.

8. For more on the high levels of illiteracy in the affected counties and the impact of the ruling, see Ferguson-Bohnee (2015: 1112–1115).

9. For more on the data examined by Congress, see United States Commission on Civil Rights (1968).

10. There is a large body of academic research showing that media attention influences public perceptions of a problem's importance (Iyengar and Kinder 1987; Jamieson and Cappella 2008; McCombs 2004; Zaller 1992), as well as recent research (Arceneaux et al. 2016) suggesting that media attention also may affect the priorities of elected officials.

11. The United States Commission on Civil Rights, which was established by the 1957 Civil Rights Act, is an advisory body with a mandate to investigate and report on alleged violations of voting rights, other alleged forms of discrimination based on race, color, religion, sex, age, disability, and national origin, and in the "administration of justice" (United States Commission on Civil Rights 2016).

12. Apache County used literacy tests until 1972 (Ferguson-Bohnee 2015: 1114). The 1975 renewal of the Voting Rights Act made the ban on literacy tests a permanent part of the Act.

13. Yurth (2009), in a *Navajo Times* article commemorating the thirty-fifth anniversary of the case, wrote, "He [Tom Shirley] had lived in Apache County long enough to know the white Mormons had a stranglehold on the government, and they would not give it up."

14. In reaching its decision, the Supreme Court of Arizona, in banc, cited the following words from another Arizona case, *State ex rel. Nelson v. Jordan* (1969): "In this a democratic society, we are irretrievably wedded to the principle that, subject to constitutional limitations, the will of the majority as expressed in free elections must prevail."

15. The numbers and racial makeup of the districts are included in the court's ruling (*Goodluck v. Apache County* 1975) overturning the redistricting.

16. Nellie Shirley said that her husband's actions opened up not only county supervisory positions to Navajo but also the possibility of Navajo being elected to the state legislature (Ruelas 2014).

17. In South Dakota, property tax assessors were required to register people to vote when they assessed property values for tax purposes. The only reservation lands subject to state property taxes are those that were parceled out under the Dawes Act and its successors. These are referred to as "deeded" properties, but most reservation lands are held in common and not subject to state property taxes, as agreed to in the treaties establishing the reservation (McDonald, Pease, and Guest 2007: 202).

18. Washabaugh County, which included the eastern portion of the Pine Ridge Reservation, was merged in the early 1980s into Jackson County, directly to its north. In 2015, Shannon County, which is the western portion of the Pine Ridge Reservation, was renamed Oglala Lakota County.

19. From 1973 to 1980, the DOJ had an Office of Indian Rights within the Civil Rights Division (Landsberg 1997), which ensured that Native voting rights issues were not ignored (McCool, Olson, and Robinson 2007: 37).

20. According to the Leadership Conference (2017), the U.S. Commission on Civil Rights was an "integral player in key civil rights legislation" in the 1960s and 1970s, but its effectiveness declined dramatically under Reagan. The commission was supposed to be a nonpartisan independent body, but Reagan fired four of the six members and replaced them with "hard-line conservatives." Congress responded by passing legislation expanding the commission's membership to eight; each member now had a six-year term. Four members, including the chair, are appointed by the president. Two are appointed by the Senate Majority Leader and the final two are appointed by the Speaker of the House, but no more than four can belong to a single party, although independents can be appointed so it is not necessarily a straight split between Democrats and Republicans (see also Laney 2008).

21. Judicial rulings that the failure to provide Spanish-language election materials constituted a banned test or device that prevented Puerto Ricans from fully participating in elections in Chicago and New York City raised awareness of the need for minority language provisions. See *Puerto Rican Organization for Political Action v. Kusper* (1973) and *Torres v. Sachs* (1974). Mexican Americans such as Modesto Rodriguez also testified before the Subcommittee on Civil and Constitutional Rights of the House Judiciary Committee (Berman 2015).

22. See Campbell (1997) for information about the hundreds of indigenous language groupings that existed at the time of European contact.

23. Limited English proficiency is defined as not understanding or speaking English well enough to participate in elections (Tucker et al. 2008: 289).

24. The need for language assistance is particularly great among elderly Native Americans (Tucker et al. 2008: 291).

25. During the George W. Bush administration, much of the power and responsibility for the enforcement of litigation was taken away from attorneys in the Civil Rights Division and given over to political appointees with no background in civil rights but with ties to conservative legal groups, such as the Federalist Society (Rich 2007: 13–17).

26. The first ACLU voting rights case involving American Indian plaintiffs was in North Carolina, where the plaintiffs included both African Americans and members of the Lumbee Nation (*Canady v. Lumberton City Board of Education* 1981). Its first non-southern case involving Native Americans was *Windy Boy v. Big Horn County* (1986).

27. Thirty years ago, a University of South Dakota law professor pointed out that civil rights attorneys faced significant challenges in getting adequate recompense for their work (Davis 1989).

28. There are a number of early important vote denial cases. See, for example, *Shirley v. Superior Court for Apache County* (1973); *Goodluck v. Apache County*, later consolidated into *U.S. v. Arizona* (1976); *Little Thunder v. South Dakota* (1975); *U.S. v. South Dakota* (1979); *South Dakota v. U.S.* (1980).

29. *Independent School District of Tulsa v. Bell* (1976).

30. See *U.S. v. Town of Bartelme* (1978); *Shakopee Mdewakanton Sioux Community and the U.S. v. City of Prior Lake* (1985); and *U.S. v. Day County, Enemy Swim Sanitary District* (1999).

31. *American Horse v. Kunder* (1984) and *Fiddler v. Sieker* (1986) are examples of cases involving abuses related to the registration of people living on reservations.

32. See, for example, *Apache County High School No. 90 v. U.S.* (1980); *Black Bull v. Dupree School District* (1986); and *U.S. v. McKinley County* (1986).

33. Minority language issues were a factor in the *Apache County High School No. 90 v. U.S.* (1980) case, as well as in *U.S. v. San Juan County* (1983b), *U.S. v. New Mexico* (1988), *U.S. v. Cibola County* (1993), *U.S. v. Socorro County* (1993), and *U.S. v. Bernalillo County* (1998). There also were early cases involving Kere and Lakota speakers and, more recently, Yu'pik speakers.

34. There are dozens of cases where political jurisdictions either used at-large districts or adopted redistricting plans that resulted in vote dilution. See *Windy Boy v. Big Horn County* (1986) for an example of this form of vote dilution. Evidence presented in another Montana case, *Old Person v. Cooney* (2000), revealed that members of the redistricting commission expressed derision about the need for a redistricting plan that provided opportunities for Indians to gain representation in the state legislature.

CHAPTER 4

1. While *Allen v. State Board of Elections* (1969) was important, the effectiveness of Section 5 was still limited because it only applied to changes in laws and procedures, leaving intact existing ones that diluted minority electoral clout. Moreover, the Supreme Court in *Beer v. United States* (1976) held that only changes that were "retrogressive" (i.e., lessened existing minority voting strength) had to be pre-cleared.

2. Prior to *City of Mobile v. Bolden* (1980), the judicial standard was that electoral practices were prohibited if they denied minority populations an equal opportunity to "participate in the political processes and to elect legislators of their choice." See *White v. Regester* (1973).

3. Given that the 1901 Alabama constitution statutorily disenfranchised African Americans, it would be hard to argue that the 1911 adoption of at-large elections was motivated by a desire to disenfranchise them—a point that the district court made (Boyd and Markman 1983: 1353–1354).

4. According to McDonald (1992: 67), *City of Mobile v. Bolden* imposed an "onerous, new burden of proof, [and] litigation challenging discriminatory voting practices under the Constitution and Section 2 dried up. Some plaintiffs (both the Department of Justice and private parties) with pending cases dropped them, and virtually no new cases were filed. Defendants suddenly became intransigent and refused to discuss settlement."

5. The revised Section 2 language is as follows: "(a) No voting qualification or prerequisite to voting or standard, practice, or procedure shall be imposed or applied by any State or political subdivision in a manner which results in a denial or abridgement of the right of any citizen of the United States to vote on account of race or color, or in contravention of the guarantees set forth in section 10303(f)(2) of this title, as provided in subsection (b). (b) A violation of subsection (a) is established if, based on the totality of circumstances, it is shown that the political processes leading to nomination or election in the State or political subdivision are not equally open to participation by members of a class of citizens protected by subsection (a) in that its members have less opportunity than other members of the electorate to participate in the political process and to elect representatives of their choice. The extent to which members of a protected class have been elected to office in the State or political subdivision is one circumstance which may be considered: *Provided*, That nothing in this section establishes a right to have members of a protected class elected in numbers equal to their proportion in the population."

6. Within days of Congress's amending language in Section 2, the Supreme Court issued a ruling in *Rogers v. Lodge* (1982) that moved away from *City of Mobile v. Bolden*. While affirming the judicial standard of discriminatory intent, the Justices said it could be inferred from circumstantial evidence (McDonald 1992: 68).

7. The Senate factors are: (1) history of official voting-related discrimination; (2) extent to which voting is racially polarized; (3) use of voting practices or procedures that tend to enhance the opportunity for discrimination against the minority group, such as unusually large election districts and prohibitions on bullet voting; (4) exclusion of members of the minority group from candidate slating processes; (5) extent to which minority group members bear the effects of discrimination in areas such as education, employment, and health, which hinder their ability to participate effectively in political processes; (6) whether overt or subtle racial appeals are used in political campaigns; (7) extent to which minority candidates have won elections; (8) degree to which elected officials are unresponsive to the concerns of the minority group; and (9) whether the policy justification for the challenged law is tenuous (United States Senate Report 1982).

8. The only non-southern states covered under Section 5 prior to *Shelby v. Holder* (2013) were Alaska and Arizona. While there are Native populations in some southern states, most notably Mississippi and Texas, the main affected populations are African Americans and Latinos. Two South Dakota counties were covered (Department of Justice 2013). The remainder of Indian Country had to rely on Section 2 to fight second-generation voting rights abuses, unless the issue involved minority language issues.

9. See Thernstrom (1987).

10. See also *Miller v. Johnson* (1995); *Bush v. Vera* (1996); *Reno v. Bossier Parish School Board* (2000); and *Georgia v. Ashcroft* (2003).

11. See McCool, Olson, and Robinson (2007), as updated by Schroedel and Hart (2015), for a compendium of American Indian and Alaska Native voting rights cases.

12. Buffalo County commissioner Donita Loudner complained about West Bend voters having to vote in a chicken coop at a meeting of the Hyde County commissioners but faced pushback from the sheriff, who was worried about enforcement issues. The commissioners moved the location to a garage and erected a porta potty for the next election (Loudner interview 2017).

13. See, for example, *Windy Boy v. Big Horn County* (1986).

14. The Fort Belknap Reservation is only a small portion of the ancestral lands occupied by the Gros Ventre and Assiniboine Nations and promised in the 1851 and 1855 Fort Laramie Treaties (Fort Belknap Indian Community 2014a; Main interview 2017).

15. Mountain States Legal Foundation (MSLF) is a nonprofit supported by foundations funded by the Coors brewing family and Philip Anschutz, a billionaire known for funding conservative Republican candidates. The MSLF has a long history of supporting legal actions that are viewed as anti-Indian (Neary 2010).

16. The Gros Ventre and Assiniboine have a long history of functioning as a single community. In keeping with the requirements of the 1934 Indian Reorganization Act, they incorporated as a single governing body in 1937 (Fort Belknap Indian Community 2014b).

17. See also *Large v. Fremont County* (2010).

18. Plumage has been reelected several times and will complete her most recent term in 2020.

19. *Baker v. Carr* (1962) established the principle that the malapportionment of district lines was subject to judicial scrutiny.

20. *Brown v. Thomson* (1983) established the 10 percent deviation standard for state legislative and local electoral districts.

21. See *Viete v. Jubelvier* (2004).

22. The Crow Creek Sioux are descendants of Dakota and Winnebago, who were part of the 1862 Great Sioux Uprising, which started after some whites told starving Dakota to "eat grass" when annuity payments were late. After their surrender, President Lincoln approved the largest mass execution in the country's history. Thirty-eight Dakota warriors were hung and the surviving members were confined to the Crow Creek Reservation (Chomsky 1990).

23. One dam project resulted in more than 9,000 acres of fertile bottom land being taken from the Crow Creek and caused one-third of the families to be relocated. Another project took 6,417 acres and forced 11 percent of the population to move (Lawson 1996).

24. During the high-intensity 2002 Senate race, Republicans accused Natives engaged in get-out-the-vote activities on the reservation of buying votes because they were giving people chili and cornbread (Loudner interview 2017).

25. Similar issues were raised in *Blackmoon v. Charles Mix County* (2007), a case involving the Yankton Sioux.

26. The 2018 primary was held on June 6 and Isburg defeated Wulff. Since no one was running in the Republican primary and the state-mandated filing period for candidates had passed, everyone thought Isburg was about to become the county auditor. However, on June 14, an independent candidate, Dulcie Sinkie, announced that she was in the race (Oliver J. Semans, email communication with the author, July 14, 2018). Because it was a couple of months past the filing date, people questioned the legitimacy of the new candidate. South Dakota law requires candidates for county offices to turn their paperwork in to the county auditor by 5:00 p.m.on the final filing date (South Dakota Secretary of State 2018a). While it is possible that Sinkie gave the required paperwork to Wulff prior to the deadline and was inadvertently left off the primary ballot, the timing of her appearance as a candidate is striking. The secretary of state's office approved Sinkie's candidacy (South Dakota Secretary of State 2018b), but she lost in the general election.

27. The three main ways that redistricting can diminish minority voting power are: (1) cracking, where the minority population is fragmented and spread across majority white districts; (2) stacking, which involves combining different concentrations of minority populations (e.g., mixing Native Americans and Mexican Americans) into heavily white districts; and (3) packing, where the minority population is packed into as few districts as possible to ensure that the governing body is represented by majority white districts.

28. This was not the first attempt by South Dakota to "pack" Native American voters. Even though the South Dakota state constitution states that redistricting is to occur following the decennial census, the state in 1996 consolidated two majority Native American legislative districts whose voters primarily came from the Cheyenne River and Standing Rock reservations into a single district. Cheyenne River Sioux with attorneys from the ACLU successfully challenged the plan (*Emery v. Hunt* 2001; Sells 2012: 195).

29. Throughout the 1990s, the redistricting plan limited the ability of Native Americans to be elected to the state legislature. Most of the sessions included two members, but one session (1995–1996) only had one Native member (Montana Legislature 2017).

30. Since HB 309 was found unconstitutional, the number of Native Americans in the state legislature has ranged from eight to eleven, roughly on par with their percentage in the state's population (Montana Legislature 2017; Ragar 2019).

31. See, for example, *U.S. v. San Juan County* (1983b).

32. As part of a settlement, the state agreed to establish high schools in the 126 villages that were covered by the lawsuit (Cotton 1984).

33. The livelihood of people living in Native villages is based on subsistence: hunting, fishing, and gathering plants. Global warming, pollution, and bottom trawlers traveling in the Bering Sea are endangering the people's ability to provide for themselves, and they have great need for a political voice (Degnan interview 2017; Lincoln interview 2017; Oxereok interview 2017).

34. David Solomon (interview 2017) explained that in his village, located 140 miles north of Fairbanks, elders with limited English are tricked into voting the wrong way. He thought the wording on the ballot was designed to trick people with limited or no English. Fred Phillip (interview 2017) from Bethel also said that polling workers often are not able to explain things to these voters.

35. In November 2016, the Alaska Federation of Natives gave the Citizen of the Year Award to Toyukak for his courage in pursuing equal rights for Native voters (Demer 2016).

36. Minnesota did not have a state voter identification law. The federal Help America Vote Act, however, establishes what identification people who register by mail can be asked to show when they vote for the first time, but Kiffmeyer's directive was more restrictive than the federal law (*ACLU v. Kiffmeyer* 2004).

37. See *ACLU v. Kiffmeyer* (2004).

38. In 2012, Apache County in Nevada placed five hundred Navajo who attempted to register to vote on a list that could result in their being permanently removed from the rolls of potential voters. The affected people did not have identification with residential street addresses but instead had post office box addresses on their identification cards (Bogado 2012).

39. People living on the North Dakota part of the Standing Rock Reservation have to travel 120 miles round trip to reach a DMV (Woodard 2016).

40. The Supreme Court's decision to allow North Dakota to implement the new voter identification law generated substantial media coverage. The *Rachel Maddow Show* on MSNBC aired several prime-time segments about the voting law, Senator Heidi Heitkamp's reelection bid, and the potential impact on whether the Democrats could regain control of the Senate.

41. In summer 2016, I was part of a team doing survey research on reservations in South Dakota and Nevada. We found that only one-quarter of respondents indicated they had complete trust that voting by mail would result in the ballots being counted (Native American Voting Rights Coalition 2018). There is a growing body of academic research showing that voting by mail results in the loss of a substantial portion of votes. As Stewart (2010: 575) notes, "the pipeline that moves mail ballots between voters and election officials is very leaky."

42. See OJ Semans's recollection of how he and others decided to push for equal access to registration and early in-person absentee voting in Chapter 8.

43. *Brooks v. Gant* (2012) was the last important Native American voting rights case prior to the Supreme Court's 2013 decision in *Shelby County v. Holder* that rendered Section 5 pre-clearance unenforceable. Aside from cases involving the minority language and limited English proficiency provisions of the VRA, nearly all post-*Shelby* cases are litigated as violations of Section 2.

44. Chapter 5 is an in-depth case study of Jackson County.

45. See behind-the-scenes descriptions of this dispute in the stories by William Main Sr. in Chapter 7 and Donovan Archambault in Chapter 9.

46. The legal standard for fees to be awarded was established in *Buckhannon Board and Care Home, Inc. v. West Virginia Department of Health and Human Services* (2001).

47. See Adams (2014) for a story tracing the developments in *Wandering Medicine v. McCulloch* and the settlement.

48. See also the story by Johnnie Williams Jr. in Chapter 9.

49. See Roberts (2017) and Oliviero (2017).

50. For example, the ACLU's website about felony disenfranchisement in Arizona states that its impact "falls disproportionately on communities of color" but only provides data about African Americans (ACLU n.d.).

51. John Dossett, email communication with the author, July 5, 2018.

52. Berinsky, Burns, and Traugott (2001) labeled the two groups as the "resource rich" and the "resource poor."

53. One study found that even a slight change in the instructions provided with VBM ballots can trigger declines in voting (Michaelson et al. 2012).

54. John Dossett, email communication with the author, July 5, 2018.

55. Interestingly, data from King County in Washington show that voting in VBM systems increases when voters can place ballots in a twenty-four-hour drop box rather than simply relying on the mail system (Collingwood et al. 2018).

56. The importance of ongoing civic education was stressed by Gerald Stiffarm, who said parties need to be active throughout the year, not simply at election time. For many years, people from the Fort Belknap Reservation have tried, without success, to institute mock political campaigns and elections within the public schools as a form of civic education (Stiffarm interview 2017).

57. In 2016, an estimated 2.5 percent of the voting-age population was disenfranchised due to a felony conviction. The rate of disenfranchisement among voting-age African Americans is estimated to be 7.4 percent and there are suggestions, albeit with no data provided, that other minority communities are adversely impacted (Uggen, Larson, and Shannon 2016).

58. According to Woodard's (2018: 150–151) analysis of Department of Justice statistics, American Indians and Alaska Natives were 38 percent more likely than other populations to be under correctional supervision (incarceration, probation, or parole) in 2015 and generally received longer prison sentences for similar offenses, despite typically having minimal criminal histories.

59. See the National Conference of State Legislatures (2017) for a summary of the different categories of state laws on disenfranchisement.

60. The following is a listing of the five states, showing how much more likely an American Indian/Alaska Native is to be incarcerated compared to a white: Arizona 3.58, Nebraska 6.31, Nevada 2.20, Wisconsin 6.34, and Wyoming 4.17 (Wagner 2014).

61. Wyoming Statute 7–13–105 2016. For the statute text, see JUSTIA US Law: https://law.justia.com/codes/wyoming/2011/title7/chapter13/section7-13-105/, accessed 5/1/2019.

62. A.R.S. 13–912. For the text of the statute, see Arizona State Legislature: https://www.azleg.gov/ars/13/00912.htm, accessed 5/1/2019.

63. A.R.S. 13–905. For the text of the statute, see Arizona State Legislature: https://www.azleg.gov/ars/13/00905.htm, accessed 5/2/2019.

64. For a history of legal challenges to felony disenfranchisement, see Liles (2007).

65. South Dakota Codified Law 12–4-18 2012. For the text of the law, see South Dakota Legislature: https://sdlegislature.gov/Statutes/Codified_Laws/DisplayStatute.aspx?Type=Statute&Statute=12-4-18, accessed 5/2/2019.

66. Racial threat played a role in adopting felony disenfranchisement laws and their continued expansion (Behrens, Uggen, and Manza 2003; Fletcher 1999; Harvey 1994; Hench 1998).

67. Counterfactual models show that at least seven Senate races between 1970 and 1998 would have had different results if there had not been widespread felony disenfranchisement (Uggen and Manza 2002).

CHAPTER 5

1. See White (1978) for a discussion of how the Great Sioux Nation in the late seventeenth and early eighteenth centuries moved into prairies east of the Missouri River and then continued expanding westward until they had become the dominant power in the Plains region.

2. The Great Sioux Uprising lasted only 37 days but resulted in the death of 358 settlers, 29 militia members, 77 U.S. soldiers, and an estimated 29 Dakota (Chomsky 1990: 21). Another 38 Dakota were hung, following military tribunals (Chomsky 1990: 13).

3. The Bozeman Trail was the most direct route to gold fields in Montana. The government was deeply in debt, needing to pay off loans used to fund the Civil War and Reconstruction; as a result, it had a large stake in the gold being mined (Drury and Clavin 2013: 5–6).

4. The Sioux creation story holds that deities created the Siouan people in a netherworld, but they were then brought to the surface through a portal, the Wind Cave in the Black Hills (Drury and Clavin 2013: 50).

5. Although few non-Indians have ever heard of Red Cloud, his legacy is kept alive on the Pine Ridge Reservation, which has the Red Cloud High School and Heritage Center run by Jesuits.

6. Custer had a reputation for brutality, including the attack on a peaceful band of Cheyenne at Washita River just outside of present-day Cheyenne, Oklahoma.

7. Custer's memory is kept alive through the attachment of his name to the county that includes much of the Black Hills. The county seat, also named Custer, holds the annual Gold Discovery Days, an event focused on Custer and the 7th Calvary's discovery of gold in the Black Hills in 1874.

8. The siege at Wounded Knee ended with the arrest of 562 protesters and 185 federal indictments, but only a handful of protesters were convicted (Sayer 1997: 3).

9. On December 28, 1890, a starving band of Lakota traveled to the Pine Ridge Indian agency in order to participate in Ghost Dance ceremonies. The group, mostly comprised of women and children, camped overnight at the Wounded Knee Creek, where they were surrounded by a detachment of more than 500 soldiers from the 7th Cavalry under the command of Colonel James Forsyth and armed with Hotchkiss guns (an early type of machine gun). Early the next morning, troopers entered the encampment and started disarming the Lakota. A rifle held by an elderly deaf man went off accidentally, and the Cavalry opened fire with the Hotchkiss guns and hundreds of mostly unarmed Lakota were killed. General Nelson Miles, the commanding general for the region, toured the site on the following day. He believed that Forsyth had purposely engineered a massacre and relieved him of his command. The military

later reversed that decision, exonerating Forsyth and promoting him to major general (Hill 2013).

10. See Brave Heart (1998) for a discussion of the series of "cataclysmic events," including Wounded Knee, which have induced historical trauma and unresolved historical grief among the Lakota.

11. The merger occurred shortly after South Dakota lost voting rights cases involving the "unorganized" counties (Todd, Shannon, and Washabaugh).

12. Many of the white-owned farms and ranches passed into non-Indian control more than a half century ago when government policies encouraged the deeding of Indian land to whites (Massey 2015a: 10).

13. The most influential study on social contact theory is Allport's 1954 study, *The Nature of Prejudice*, which found that intergroup contact reduces social prejudice. This finding has been replicated more than five hundred times (Pettigrew and Tropp 2008).

14. According to Massey (2015a: 11) many whites said they almost never went on the Rez and many Oglala refused to go to Kadoka because they said the prejudice there is palpable.

15. Until the latter part of the twentieth century, South Dakota law included several provisions that made it difficult for Native Americans to register. Registration was done in the county auditor's office, but people in "unorganized counties" had to travel to another county to register. State law, however, required that tax assessors automatically register property owners as voters whenever they were conducting assessments. Since most reservation lands are not taxed, very few Native Americans were automatically registered, but large numbers of whites were registered without going to the county auditor's office. County auditors were prohibited from appointing Native Americans as deputy auditors (McDonald, Pease, and Guest 2007).

16. Information about absentee voting procedures in Jackson County was posted on the county courthouse's door.

17. Tom Poor Bear, letter of May 6, 2013, was shared with the author.

18. During the VRA's 1982 reauthorization, Section 2 was amended such that voting rights litigation must take into account the "totality of circumstance of the local electoral process." The Senate Judiciary Committee issued a 1982 report that listed factors that may be relevant when deciding whether the "totality of circumstance" resulted in the minority population being denied an equal opportunity to vote. With respect to this book's research, the most relevant factors are: a history of voting discrimination, voting practices that "enhance the opportunity for discrimination against the minority population," and whether discrimination in education, employment, and health care make it harder for the minority group to participate.

19. The eight students were Robert Saporito, Joey Torres, Andrea Walters, Peter Abkarian, Carlin Crisanti, Gary Hawk, Anna Phillips, and Ashley Shue.

20. This study was approved by the Claremont Graduate University's Institutional Review Board and by the Oglala Sioux Tribal Research Review Board.

21. The following statement was read to people who were approached about taking the survey: "Hello, my name is ——— and I am a graduate student from Claremont Graduate University in California, researching the relationship between travel distance, shopping, and voting patterns. Would you be willing to take four or five minutes to answer some questions about where you go to shop and the method you use to vote in state and national elections? I know your time is valuable, so you are invited to enter a drawing for a $100 gift card to Walmart/Target. The chance of winning in the drawing is roughly one in fifty."

22. Native Americans found it hard to answer a standard Census Bureau question that asked how many people lived in their household because so many people lacked stable living situations and were moving from place to place. After struggling, a man from Potato Creek finally said his household included somewhere between eleven and seventeen people.

23. United States Census Bureau, "DP02—Selected Social Characteristics in the United States, Jackson County, South Dakota," *2006–2010 American Community Survey Selected Population Tables* (Washington, DC: U.S. Census Bureau), https://factfinder.census.gov/bkmk/table/1.0/en/ACS/10_SF4/DP02/0500000US46071/popgroup~002|006, accessed 12/2/2019.

24. United States Census Bureau, "DP03–Selected Economic Characteristics, Jackson County, South Dakota." *2006–2010 American Community Survey Selected Population Tables* (Washington, DC: U.S. Census Bureau, 2010), https://factfinder.census.gov/bkmk/table/1.0/en/ACS/10_SF4/DP03/0500000US46071/popgroup~002|006, accessed 12/2/2019.

25. United States Census Bureau, "B19013—Median Household Income in the Past 12 Months (In 2010 Inflation-Adjusted Dollars), Jackson County, South Dakota," *2006–2010 American Community Survey Selected Population Tables* (Washington, DC: U.S. Census Bureau). https://factfinder.census.gov/bkmk/table/1.0/en/ACS/10_SF4/B19013/0500000US46071/popgroup~002|006|115, accessed 12/2/2019.

26. United States Census Bureau, "DP03—Selected Economic Characteristics, Jackson County, South Dakota," *2006–2010 American Community Survey Selected Population Tables*, (Washington, DC: U.S. Census Bureau, 2010), https://factfinder.census.gov/bkmk/table/1.0/en/ACS/10_SF4/DP03/0500000US46071/popgroup~002|006. accessed 12/2/2019.

27. United States Census Bureau, "B19301—Per Capita Income in the Past 12 Months (In 2010 Inflation-Adjusted Dollars), Jackson County, South Dakota," *2006–2010 American Community Survey Selected Population Tables* (Washington, DC: U.S. Census Bureau), https://factfinder.census.gov/bkmk/table/1.0/en/ACS/10_SF4/B19301/0500000US46071/popgroup~002|006|115, Accessed 12/2/2019.

28. United States Census Bureau, "DP03—Selected Economic Characteristics, Jackson County, South Dakota," *2006–2010 American Community Survey Selected Population Tables*, (Washington, DC: U.S. Census Bureau, 2010), https://factfinder.census.gov/bkmk/table/1.0/en/ACS/10_SF4/DP03/0500000US46071/popgroup~002|006, accessed 12/2/2019.

29. United States Census Bureau, "DP02—Selected Social Characteristics: Jackson County by Race."

30. United States Senate (1982).

31. See also *Buckanaga v. Sisseton Independent School District* (1986); *Stabler v. County of Thurston* (1997); *Old Person v. Cooney* (2000). For a more in-depth discussion of these factors and their impact, see McDonald, Pease, and Guest (2007: 203–205).

32. Individuals on the Pine Ridge Reservation talked about occasionally spending weeks stranded when roads are blocked by heavy snowfalls and flooding. While we could not verify this information because we visited during the summer, the heavy snow followed by flooding in the late winter and early spring of 2019 resulted in people being stranded for extended periods, as noted by the *New York Times* (Smith 2019).

33. Academics have found that even small travel distances have a measurable impact in reducing voting (Gimpel and Schuknecht 2003; Dyck and Gimpel 2005; Haspel and Knotts 2005; McNulty, Dowling, and Ariotti 2009; Brady and McNulty 2011).

34. Opportunity cost is a concept derived from microeconomic theory. When resources are limited, opportunity cost is the value of what is given up by making a different choice.

35. See https://poboxes.usps.com/poboxonline/search/landingPageValidation.do.

36. There also is the problem of lost votes when people vote by mail. According to Stewart (2010: 575), "the pipeline that moves mail ballots between voters and election officials is very leaky."

37. Even though Jackson County is one of the most rural counties in South Dakota, it has a very low rate of absentee voters, 8 percent in 2012, compared to the rate for the state as a whole of over 30 percent. The data come from the secretary of state's website.

38. See http://www.census/gov/rdo/pdf/CVAP_10to_14_Documentation.pdf.

39. Precinct-level turnout data can be obtained from the secretary of state's official website. http://electionresults.sd.gov/VoterTurnoutDetails.aspx?map = TURN.

40. Even though we asked no questions about voting choices and partisanship, many white respondents made racist statements about President Obama. There also were a lot of anti–Hillary Clinton comments among white respondents. Interestingly, very few Lakota made comments about political figures.

41. United States Census Bureau (2012).

42. http://electionresults.sd.gov/VoterTurnoutDetails.aspx?map = TURN.

43. It is impossible to ascertain from the data whether some portion of the voting-age population is ineligible to vote. South Dakota has one of the nation's harshest felony disenfranchisement statutes.

44. We want to acknowledge the assistance provided by Jackson County auditor Vicki Wilson, who graciously explained local procedures and provided data used in this chapter.

45. The Potato Creek polling location was moved to a private home after the previous polling place, the Green Valley Fire Hall, burned down.

46. According to the Census Bureau, 74 percent of the people living in the Long Valley zip code area are white. Census 2010 and 2000 Data Comparison for ZIP Code 57547, Long Valley, SD, http://www.zip-codes.com/zip-code/57547/zip-code-57547-census-comparison.asp, accessed 9/24/2014.

47. The 2016 turnout figures for the two heavily Native American precincts are comparable to their rates in the 2014 off-year election when Precinct 7 had a turnout rate of 36.6 percent and Precinct 8 was at 42.3 percent.

48. The turnout rates in the heavily white counties of South Dakota are roughly comparable to the turnout rate in white Jackson County precincts, but the turnout rate in predominantly Native American counties is very low. For example, in 2016, the turnout in Oglala Lakota County that encompasses most of the western portion of the Pine Ridge Reservation was the lowest in the state at 36.73 percent. http://electionresults.sd.gov/ResultsList.aspx?type = CTYALL.

49. https://sdsos.gov/elections-voting/election-resources/election-history/2010/2010_general_election_turnout_state_county_precinct.aspx.

50. This failure among white residents to consider working together with residents from the reservation to solve common problems was widespread. People in Kadoka discussed economic development initiatives, particularly efforts designed to attract tourists, but none mentioned collaborating with the Lakota. This was striking, given that many tourists in towns such as Wall go to exhibits of Native history and want to buy American Indian crafts.

CHAPTER 6

1. In many ways the narratives included in this chapter, as well as those in the next few chapters, fit within the context of "public narratives" where individual stories serve as a link

to broader ones that build a sense of community and then inspire action to achieve a common goal (Ganz 2009, 2011; Simpson 2017). But this narrative trajectory was an organic outgrowth of the interview process rather than something I imposed upon it. The first time I heard about "public narratives" was in May 2019, long after completing the interviews and transcribing individual stories. It was the interview subjects, not me, who made the connections between their lives and broader social justice narratives.

2. Alessandro Portelli (2005) uses the term "co-created" to describe the oral history process. Others use either "shared authority" or "sharing authority" to emphasize the collaborative nature of oral history (Frisch 2003; Shopes 2003).

CHAPTER 7

1. Of particular concern is the need to respect and honor the social and cultural practices of Native Nations. For more on this, see Trimble, Sommer, and Quinlan (2008).

2. Wilson (2000: 1) says that her earliest memories of the stories told by her grandmother are those about the Great Sioux Uprising of 1862.

3. This phrase is also the title of a booklet about building health partnerships with Native Nations (National Congress of American Indians Policy Research Center and Montana State University Center for Native Health Partnerships 2012).

CHAPTER 10

1. For more on the Purcell Principle and the Supreme Court's recent shifts away from halting changes just prior to elections, see Hasen (2016a, 2016b).

2. Turtle Mountain Reservation is located in Rolette County. Initially there were some issues in obtaining county-approved addresses—one individual had to return to county offices three times before getting assistance and then was told that the county had two different mapping systems, each which gave him different addresses (Stern 2018) —but this was better than what people faced in Sioux County, which includes the Standing Rock Reservation. The official responsible for coordinating the provision of 911 address, the ones the county suggested that should be used for voter IDs, is the sheriff. Not only might that be a deterrent, particularly given the actions of non-Native law enforcement during the Standing Rock protests, the sheriff also has many other responsibilities and cannot be easily reached. As recounted in a *New York Times* article, the sheriff was unreachable on a number of occasions when voters without addresses tried to reach him over a period of several days following the Court's decision. Another individual, a tribal elder and teetotaler, was deeply offended when the sheriff assigned him an address that was of a local bar (Astor 2018a).

3. A couple days after the Supreme Court's October 9 decision to allow North Dakota to implement the strict voter ID law, Bret Healy from Four Directions asked Claremont Graduate University (CGU) faculty (Jean Schroedel and Brian Hilton) whether there was a way to create addresses using GIS. A team from CGU overlaid precinct maps on satellite images showing all streets and roads on the different reservations. Then each precinct was divided into quadrants with assigned addresses. Voters could point to their houses on those precinct maps and then be given a unique identifier (an address created for their precinct followed by a number—001, 002, etc.). Tribal voting letters using these addresses were tested during the early voting period and were accepted, albeit with some reluctance (Four Directions 2019).

4. Following the 2018 elections, North Dakota's Republican governor, Doug Bergum, announced that he would display the flags of the state's five Native Nations in the state's

Memorial Hall and called for "mutual respect and understanding" among all North Dakotans (Folley 2019). South Dakota's newly elected governor, Kristi Noem, proposed bringing flags of the state's nine Native Nations into the capitol rotunda (Rickert 2019), but the gesture was viewed as a hollow one. She has refused to oppose the Keystone XL pipeline and bills that would label protests as "riot boosting." The Oglala Sioux Tribal Council has banned her from entering the Pine Ridge Reservation (Daugherty 2019; Fugleberg 2019).

5. Only one-fifth of reservation roads are paved and most are just dirt. The flooding of roads makes it impossible at times for ambulances to reach people (Vock 2017: 50–51).

6. For an in-depth history of white-Native relations in San Juan County, see McCool's expert witness report (2015).

7. According to Massey (2015b), white elected officials also are church leaders. He estimates roughly 20 percent of Navajo are Mormon.

8. See, for example, *Meyers v. Board of Education* (1995) and *Sinajini v. Bd. of Educ.* (1997), which addressed the quality of education provided to Navajo students, and *Utah v. Pharris* (1993) and *Crank, Loren v. Utah Judicial Council* (1996), which involved discriminatory practices in jury selection. Early voting rights cases include *Yanito v. Barber* (1972) and *United States v. San Juan County* (1983a), dealing with Section 2, and *U.S. v. San Juan County* (1983b), dealing with Section 203.

9. In the past, Navajos were elected from two of the five school board districts. The switch to district elections for the county commission made it possible for Mark Maryboy to be elected as a county commissioner, but whites still maintained a majority (Langlois 2016).

10. Data compiled by McCool (2015: 157) show that from 1976 through 2014 whites have had substantially higher turnout rates than Native Americans in every election except for one.

11. In 2014, the San Juan County Commission decided to move to an all vote-by-mail system, which the Navajo Human Rights Commission said violated the minority language provisions of the VRA. Moreover, the mail service is unreliable, so it is not even clear that many would receive the ballots (*Navajo Nation Human Rights Commission v. San Juan County* 2016).

12. There are 100,000 sites within the monument that contain Native American artifacts (Vock 2017: 52).

13. Mormon Navajos, like Commissioner Benally, often politically align with white Mormons (Groat Notes 2017).

14. In Navajo chapter house meetings, 98 percent voted in favor of keeping protections for Bears Ears, which suggests that Benally's position is at odds with that of most Navajo.

15. The District 3 Democratic primary race pitted the incumbent, Rebecca Benally, an outspoken Navajo advocate of removing Bears Ears from federal government control, against another Navajo, Kenneth Maryboy, who had been deeply involved in creating the monument. Maryboy's victory (626–574) undermined the claim that Navajo support dismantling Bears Ears National Monument (Trahant 2018a).

16. When Grayeyes ran in 2012, a similar accusation was made but the previous county clerk rejected it (Tanner 2018c). The Republican candidate and his supporters ran several ads that warned voters about the dangers of getting a second Navajo on the commission (McCool 2015: 129).

17. According to Massey (2015b: 28), there are no Native deputies within the San Juan County Sheriff's Department.

18. Little Elk, an enrolled member of the Rosebud Sioux Tribe, coordinated Obama's 2008 Native outreach and served on the transition team and in the Department of the Interior before returning home to work on local economic development.

19. The following is a small sampling of the range of organizations. The largest organization is the National Congress of American Indians (NCAI), which was formed in 1944. Many of the intertribal councils date to the 1950s, as does the Affiliated Tribes of the Northwest. The Native American Rights Fund (NARF) was created in 1971, as was the National Tribal Chairmen's Association. The Alliance of Sovereign Indian Nations (TASIN), established in 1995, is a coalition of nine small California Native Nations. The Coalition of Large Tribes (COLT), which was formed in 2011, includes twelve Native Nations with large land reservations. The First America Project, which was started in 2018, is possibly the newest. Its focus is on climate change issues in Washington state.

20. Although increasing numbers of Native Americans are active in nontribal politics, some still feel that culturally it is not appropriate because they belong to sovereign Nations (Melendez interview 2017).

21. The quote was included in material from Thomas Main's funeral and provided by his grandson.

22. Democratic candidates included Debra Haaland, a Laguna Pueblo, who won in a safe New Mexico district (Trahant 2018b). Another Democratic woman, Sharice Davids, from the Ho-Chunk Nation, won in a Kansas district that usually elects Republicans. Davids's candidacy gained credibility when Emily's List endorsed her (Emily's List 2018). The other Democrats are two Cherokees (Jason Nichols and Amanda Douglas) who ran and lost against strong Republican candidates in Oklahoma. Nichols lost to incumbent Republican Markwayne Mullin, also from the Cherokee Nation. Tom Cole, from the Chickasaw Nation, also was easily reelected. Other Republican candidates included Dino Rossi, a Tlingit who lost in Washington state, and the pro-Trump former Department of the Interior bureaucrat Gavin Clarkson from the Choctaw Nation, who lost in New Mexico.

23. Not only were crowds of people present to watch the Capitol Hill swearing-in ceremony of Davids and Haaland, but many more watched online and on television (Agoyo 2019).

24. One of the big surprises of the 2018 election cycle was Ruth Buffalo's victory that flipped a safe Republican North Dakota assembly seat to the Democrats for the first time ever. One of the great ironies is that the defeated candidate, Randy Boehning (R-Fargo), had been the lead sponsor of strict voter ID laws, including the one that threatened to disenfranchise Native voters in 2018. While Buffalo emphasized health-care issues in her campaign (Astor 2018c), Boehning had been damaged by his history of soliciting sex via the gay sex app Grindr (Johnson 2018).

BIBLIOGRAPHY

Abeita, Jes. 2008. "One Man, Many Votes: Native Americans' Struggle with the First Freedom." *Alibi* 17(27). July 3–9. http://alibi.com/feature/23805/One-Man-Many-Votes.html. Accessed 6/16/2018.

ACLU. N.d. *Felony Disenfranchisement in Arizona.* https://aclu.org/felony-disenfranchsiment-arizona. Accessed 7/18/2018.

Adams, John S. 2014. "Montana Indian Voting Lawsuit Settled." *Great Falls Tribune*, June 12. https://www.greatfallstribune.com/story/news/politics/2014/06/12/montana-indian-voting-lawsuit-settled/10389781/. Accessed 6/21/2018.

Agoyo, Acee. 2019. "Native Women Make History with Seats in New Congress." *Indian County Today*, January 14. https://www.indianz.com/News/2019/01/04/native-women-make-history-congress.asp. Accessed 4/20/2019.

Agrawal, Nina. 2017. "In North Dakota, It Could Become Legal to Hit a Protester with Your Car." *Los Angeles Times*, February 3. http://www.latimes.com/nation/la-na-bills-protest-criminal-20170201-story.html. Accessed 2/5/2017.

Allport, Gordon. 1954. *The Nature of Prejudice.* New York: Addison Wesley.

Alvarez, R. Michael, Dustin Beckett, and Charles Stewart III. 2011. "Voting Technology, Vote-by-Mail, and Residual Votes in California." *Political Research Quarterly* 66(3): 658–670.

American Horse, Denver. 2016. "Veteran Warrior Wakte'Glipi to Come Home in Triumph & Victory." *Lakota Country Times*, March 17. http://www.lakotacountrytimes.com/news/2016-11-03/Voices/VETERAN_WARRIOR_WAKTE_GLIPITO_COME_HOME_IN_TRIUMPH.html. Accessed 2/27/2017.

Arceneaux, Kevin, Martin Johnson, Rene Lindstadt, and Ryan J. Vander Wielen. 2016. "The Influence of News Media on Political Elites: Investigating Strategic Responsiveness in Congress." *American Journal of Political Science* 60(1): 5–29.

Astor, Maggie. 2018a. "In North Dakota, Native Americans Try to Turn an ID Law to Their Advantage." *New York Times*, October 30. https://www.nytimes.com/2018/10/30/us/politics/north-dakota-voter-id.html. Accessed 11/3/2018.

Astor, Maggie. 2018b. "In North Dakota, Native Americans Try to Turn ID Law into a Gain." *New York Times*, October 31: A11.

Astor, Maggie. 2018c. "Meet the Native Woman Who Beat the Sponsor of North Dakota's ID Law." *New York Times*, November 13. https://www.nytimes.com/2018/1/13/politics/north-dakota-ruth-buffalo.html. Accessed 12/1/2018.

Barnes, Ian. 2015. *The Historical Atlas of Native Americans.* New York: Chartwell Books.

Behrens, Angela, Christopher Uggen, and Jeff Manza. 2003. "Ballot Manipulation and the 'Menace of Negro Domination': Racial threat and Felon Disenfranchisement in the United States, 1850–2002." *American Journal of Sociology* 109(3): 559–605.

Bergman, Elizabeth, and Philip A. Yates. 2011. "Changing Election Methods: How Does Mandated Vote-by-Mail Affect Individual Registrants." *Election Law Journal* 10(2): 115–127.

Berinsky, Adam J. 2005. "The Perverse Consequences of Electoral Reform in the United States." *American Political Research* 33(4): 471–491.

Berinsky, Adam J., Nancy Burns, and Michael W. Traugott. 2001. "Who Votes by Mail? A Dynamic Model of the Individual-Level Consequences of Voting-by-Mail Systems." *Public Opinion Quarterly* 65(2): 178–197.

Berman, Ari. 2015. "The Lost Promise of the Voting Rights Act." *Atlantic*, August 5. https://www.theatlantic.com/politics/archive/2015/08/give-us-the-ballot-expanding-the-voting-rights-act/399128/. Accessed 7/12/2018.

Bernstein, Robert, Anita Chadha, and Robert Montjoy. 2001. "Overreporting Voting: Why It Happens and Why It Matters." *Public Opinion Quarterly* 65: 22–44.

Blansett, Kent. 2018. *A Journey to Freedom: Richard Oakes, Alcatraz, and the Red Power Movement.* New Haven, CT: Yale University Press.

Board of Indian Commissioners. 1869. *Annual Report of the Board of Indian Commissioners.* Washington, DC: Government Printing Office.

Bogado, Aura. 2012. "How Native Voters Are Routinely Disenfranchised in Arizona." *Color Lines: News for Action*, October 18. http://colorlines.com/archives/2012/10/democracy_in_suspense. Accessed 12/10/2012.

Boyd, Thomas M., and Stephen J. Markman. 1983. "The 1982 Amendments to the Voting Rights Act: A Legislative History." *Washington and Lee Law Review* 40(4): 1347–1428.

Brady, Henry E., and John E. McNulty. 2011. "Turning Out to Vote: The Costs of Finding and Getting to the Polling Place." *American Political Science Review* 105(1): 115–134.

Brave Heart, Maria Yellow Horse. 1998. "The Return to the Sacred Path: Healing the Historical Trauma Response Among the Lakota." *Smith College Studies in Social Work* 68(3): 287–305.

Brennan Center for Justice. 2012. *Voting Rights & Elections.* New York: New York University School of Law. https://www.brennancenter.org/issues/voting-rights-elections. Accessed 5/31/2014.

Britten, Thomas A. 1997. *American Indians in World War I: At Home and at War.* Albuquerque: University of New Mexico Press.

Brown, Dee. 1971. *Bury My Heart at Wounded Knee.* New York: Holt, Rinehart & Winston.

Bruyneel, Kevin. 2004. "Challenging American Boundaries: Indigenous Peoples and the 'Gift' of U.S. Citizenship." *Studies in American Political Development* 18 (Spring): 30–43.

Buckley, Elena Saaveda. 2018. "Standing Rock's Countdown to Election Day." *High Country News,* October 26. https://www.hcn.org/articles/tribal-affairs-standing-rock-countdown-to-election-day. Accessed 4/29/2019.

Cahalan, Donald. 1968. "Correlates of Respondent Accuracy in the Denver Validity Study." *Public Opinion Quarterly* 32: 607–621.

Campbell, Lyle. 1997. *The Historical Linguistics of Native America.* Oxford: Oxford University Press.

Campbell, Matthew L., and Natalie A. Landreth. 2018. "Brakebill, et al. v. Jaeger (ND Voter ID Law)." *Native American Rights Fund*, April 3. http://www.narf.org/cases/nd-voter-id. Accessed 6/19/2018.

Cassell, Carol A. 2003. "Overreporting and Electoral Participation Research." *American Politics Research* 31(1): 81–92.

Champagne, Duane. 2015. "Indigeneity or Ethnicity? A Choice That Could Harm Tribal Identities." *Indian Country Today*, March 22. https://newsmaven.io/indiancountrytoday/archive/indigeneity-or-ethnicity-a-choice-that-could-harm-tribal-identities-X8YqCVmCak-UlUK4RsLb_A/. Accessed 11/18/2016.

Cherokee Nation. 2017a. *Sequoyah and the Cherokee Syllabary*. http://www.cherokee.org/AboutTheNation/History/Facts/SequoyahandtheCherokeeSyllabry.aspx. Accessed 2/1/2017.

Cherokee Nation. 2017b. *A Brief History of the Trail of Tears*. http://www.cherokee.org/AboutTheNation/History/TrailofTears/ABriefHistoryoftheTrailofTears.aspx. Accessed 2/1/2017.

Child, Brenda. 2004. "Indian Education, American Education." In *Native Universe: Voices of Indian America*, ed. Gerald McMaster and Clifford E. Trafzer. Washington, DC: National Geographic Society.

Chomsky, Carol. 1990. "The United States-Dakota War Trials: A Study in Military Injustice." *Stanford Law Journal* 43(1): 13–98.

Chrisman, Gabriel. 2006. "The Fish-in Protests at Franks Landing." *Seattle Civil Rights & Labor History Project*. Seattle: University of Washington. http://depts.washington.edu/civilr/fish-ins.htm. Accessed 2/6/2017.

Clinton, Robert N. 2014. "Treaties with Native Nations: Iconic Historical Relics or Modern Necessity?" In *Nation to Nation: Treaties Between the United States & American Indian Nations*, ed. Suzan Shown Harjo. Washington, DC: Smithsonian Institution.

Cohen, Felix. 1942. *Handbook of Federal Indian Law*. Washington, DC: Government Printing Office.

Collingwood, Loren, William McGuire, Benjamin Gonzalez O'Brien, Katherine Baird, and Sarah Hampson. 2018. "Do Drop Boxes Improve Voter Turnout? Evidence from King County, Washington." *Election Law Journal* 17(1), published online March 1. https://www.liebertpub.com/doi/10.1089/elj.2017.0450?utm_source + sfmc&utm_medium = email&utm_campaign = ELJ%20F. Accessed 7/19/2018.

Connell, Evan. 1985. *Son of the Morning Star: Custer and the Little Big Horn*. New York: Harper Perennial.

Coriz, Garon. 2018. "Commentary: Trump Used Native Americans as Window Dressing for His Utah Monument Announcement." *Salt Lake Tribune*, January 6. https://www.sltrib.com/opinion/commentary/2018/01/06/commentary-trump-used-native-americans-as-window-dressing-for-his-utah-monument-announcement. Accessed 7/14/2018.

Cornell University Law School. 2017. "Voting Rights Act." *Wex Legal Dictionary*. https://www.law.cornell.edu/wex/voting_rights_act. Accessed 3/28/2017.

Cotton, Stephen E. 1984. "Alaska's 'Molly Hootch Case': High Schools and the Village Voice." *Education Research Quarterly* 8(4): 30–43.

Cox, Robert W. 2000. "Thinking About Civilizations." *Review of International Studies* 26(5): 217–234.

Creswell, John W., and Dana L. Miller. 2000. "Determining Validity in Qualitative Data." *Theory and Practice* 39(3): 124–130.

Data USA. 2016. *San Juan County, Utah*. http://datausa.io/profile/geo/san-juan-county-ut. Accessed 7/12/2018.

Daugherty, Owen. 2019. "American Indian Tribe Bans GOP Governor from Reservation over Opposition to Keystone Protestors." *The Hill*, May 2. https://thehill.com/homenews/

state-watch/441921-american-indian-tribe-bans-gop-governor-over-her. Accessed 5/3/2019.

Davidson, Chandler. 1992. "The Voting Rights Act: A Brief History." In *Controversies in Minority Voting*, ed. Chandler Davidson and Bernard Grofman. Washington, DC: Brookings Institution.

Davidson, Chandler. 1994. "The Recent Evolution of Voting Rights Law Affecting Racial and Language Minorities." In *Quiet Revolution in the South: The Impact of the Voting Rights Act, 1965–1990*, ed. Chandler Davidson and Bernard Grofman. Princeton, NJ: Princeton University Press.

Davis, Martha S. 1989. "Attorney Fee Awards in Voting Rights Litigation." *South Dakota Law Review* 34: 303–336.

De Tocqueville, Alexis. 2005. *Democracy in America and Two Essays on America*. New York: Penguin Classics.

DeJong, David H. 2015. *American Indian Treaties: A Guide to Ratified and Unratified Colonial, United States, Foreign, and Intertribal Treaties and Agreements, 1607–1911*. Salt Lake City: University of Utah Press.

Deloria, Vine, Jr. 1969. *Custer Died for Your Sins: An Indian Manifesto*. New York: Macmillan.

Deloria, Vine, Jr. 2004. "Promises Made, Promises Broken." In *Native Universe: Voices of Indian America*, ed. Gerald McMaster and Clifford E. Trafzer. Washington, DC: National Geographic Society.

Deloria, Vine, Jr., and Raymond J. DeMallie. 1999. *Documents of American Indian Diplomacy: Treaties, Agreements, and Conventions, 1775–1979*. Vols. 1 and 2. Norman: University of Oklahoma Press.

DeMarban, Alex. 2017. "Bering Sea Tribal Groups Slam Alaska Delegation for 'Standing by' as Trump Struck Order Giving Them a Voice." *Anchorage Daily News*, April 29. https://www.adn.com/arctic/2017/04/29/bering-sea-tribal-groups-slam-alaska-delegation-for-standing-by-as-trump-struck-order-giving-them-voice/. Accessed 11/7/2017.

Demer, Lisa. 2016. "AFN Board Recognizes Those Who Did Exceptional Work for Native People." *Alaska Dispatch News*, October 20. https://www.adn.com/alaska-news/rural-alaska/2016/10/20/afn-board-recognizes-those-who-did-exceptional-work-for-native-people/. Accessed 7/27/2017.

Department of Justice. 2013. *Jurisdictions Previously Covered by Section 5*. http://www.justice.gov/crt/jurisdictions-previously-covered-section-5. Accessed 5/25/2016.

Department of Justice. 2016. *Sanchez v. Cegavske: Statement of Interest of the United States of America*. October 3. https://www.justice.gov/crt/case-document/sanchez-v-cegavske. Accessed 1/24/2017.

Department of Justice, Civil Rights Division. 2016. *Sanchez v. Cegavske: Statement of Interest of the United States of America*. October 3. http://www.justice.gov/crt/case-document/sanchez-v-cegavske. Accessed 1/24/2017.

Drury, Bob, and Tom Clavin. 2013. *The Heart of Everything That Is: The Untold Story of Red Cloud, an American Legend*. New York: Simon and Schuster.

Dunbar-Ortiz, Roxanne. 2014. *An Indigenous Peoples' History of the United States*. Boston: Beacon Press.

Dunbar-Ortiz, Roxanne, and Dina Gilio-Whitaker. 2016. *"All the Real Indians Died Off" and Other Myths About Native Americans*. Boston: Beacon Press.

Dyck, Joshua J., and James G. Gimpel. 2005. "Distance, Turnout and the Convenience of Voting." *Social Science Quarterly* 86(3): 531–548.

Elul, Gabrielle, Sean Freeder, and Jacob M. Grumbach. 2017. "The Effect of Mandatory Mail Ballot Elections in California." *Election Law Journal: Rules, Politics, and Policy* 16(3): 397–415.

Emily's List. 2018. *Sharice Davids: U.S. House, Kansas.* https://www.emilyslist.org/candidates/sharice-davids. Accessed 7/25/2018.

Erdrich, Louise. 2016. "Holy Rage: Lessons from Standing Rock." *New Yorker*, December 22. http://www.newyorker.com/news/news-desk/holy-rage-lessons-from-standing-rock. Accessed 1/18/2017.

Executive Order 13754. 2016. *Northern Bering Sea Climate Resilience.* December 9. https://obamawhitehouse.archives.gov/the-press-office/2016/12/09/executive-order-northern-bering-sea-reilience. Accessed 7/25/2018.

Farmer, Paul. 2005. "Never Again? Reflections on Human Values and Human Rights." *Tanner Lectures on Human Values.* March. https://tannerlectures.utah.edu/-documents/a-to-z/f/Farmer-2006.pdf. Accessed 5/3/2019.

Ferguson-Bohnee, Patty. 2015. "The History of Indian Voting Rights in Arizona: Overcoming Decades of Voter Suppression." *Arizona State Law Journal* 47: 1099–1144.

Fletcher, George. 1999. "Disenfranchisement as Punishment: Reflections on the Racial Uses of *Infamia.*" *UCLA Law Review* 46: 1895–1908.

Fletcher, Matthew L. M. 2006. "The Iron Cold of the Marshall Trilogy." *North Dakota Law Review* 82: 627–696.

Folley, Aris. 2019. "North Dakota Governor Tearfully Announces Native American Tribal Flags to Now Be on Display in Memorial Hall." *The Hill*, January 4. https://thehill.com/homenews/state-watch/42348/north-dakota-governor-tearully-announces-native-american-tribal-flags. Accessed 1/5/2019.

Fort Belknap Indian Community. 2014a. *Fort Belknap History.* https://ftbelknap.org/history. Accessed 5/29/2017.

Fort Belknap Indian Community. 2014b. *About the Fort Belknap Indian Reservation.* https://ftbelknap.org/. Accessed 5/29/2017.

Four Directions. 2016. *Four Directions: Advancing Equality at the Ballot Box Across Indian Country.* http://www.fourdirectionsvote.com. Accessed 1/24/2017.

Four Directions. 2019. *2018 General Election Reports.* April.

Frisch, Michel. 2003. "Sharing Authority: Oral History and the Collaborative Process." *Oral History Review* 30(1): 111–113.

Fugleberg, Jeremy. 2019. "Can Oglala Sioux Tribe Ban Gov. Kristi Noem from Reservation? Here's What the Law Says." *Argus Leader*, May 7. https://www.argusleader.com/story/news/business-journal/2019/05/07/oglala-sioux-tribe-bans-gov-noem-pine-ridge-reservation/3661748002. Accessed 5/14/2019.

Galligan, Thomas C., Jr., and Michael T. Reyvaan. 1981. "Pacific Northwest Indian Treaty Fishing Rights." *University of Puget Sound Law Review* 5: 99–129.

Ganz, Marshall. 2009. "What Is Public Narrative: Self, Us & Now." Harvard Working Paper, Office of Scholarly Communication. https://nrs.harvard.edu/urn-3:HUL.InstRepos:30760283. Accessed 5/13/2019.

Ganz, Marshall. 2011. "Public Narrative, Collective Action, and Power." Harvard Working Paper, Office of Scholarly Communication. https://dash.harvard.edu/bitstream/handle/1/29314925/Public_Narrative_Collective_Action_and-Power.pdf?sequence=1. Accessed 5/13/2019.

Gehrke, Robert. 2018. "Ouster of Anti–Bears Ears Commissioner One Important and Overlooked Primary Election Result." *Salt Lake Tribune*, June 28. https://www.sltrib.com/news/politics/2018/06/28/gehrke-anti-bears. Accessed 6/29/2018.

Gerber, Alan S., Gregory Huber, and Seth J. Hill. 2013. "Identifying the Effect of All-Mail Elections on Turnout: Staggered Reform in the Evergreen States." *Political Science Research and Methods* 1(1): 91–116.

Gimpel, James G., and Jason E. Schuknecht. 2003. "Political Participation and the Accessibility of the Ballot Box." *Political Geography* 22: 471–488.

Golafshani, Nahid. 2003. "Understanding Reliability and Validity in Qualitative Research." *Qualitative Report* 8(4): 597–606.

Gover, Kevin. 2014. Foreword to *Nation to Nation: Treaties Between the United States & American Indian Nations*, ed. Suzan Shown Harjo. Washington, DC: Smithsonian Books.

Graham, Hugh Davis. 1992. *Civil Rights and the Presidency: Race and Gender in American Politics, 1960–1972*. New York: Oxford University Press.

Groat Notes. 2017. "San Juan County Leaders Want to Remind Native Americans 'Who Conquered Who.'" December 8. https://medium.com/@groatnotes/san-juan-county-leaders-want-to-remind-native-americans-who-conquered-who-74ecb6723f47. Accessed 7/14/2018.

Grofman, Bernard, and Chandler Davidson. 1992. *Controversies in Minority Voting: The Voting Rights Act in Perspective*. Washington, DC: Brookings Institution.

Gronke, Paul, and Peter Miller. 2012. "Voting by Mail and Turnout in Oregon: Revisiting Southwell and Burchett." *American Politics Quarterly* 40(6): 976–997.

Gross, Lawrence W. 2014. *Anishinaabe Ways of Knowing and Being*. Burlington, VT: Ashgate Publishing Company.

Hamilton, Alexander, James Madison, and John Jay. 2003. *The Federalist Papers*, ed. Clinton Rossiter and Charles R. Kesler. New York: Signet Classics.

Hanson, Jeffrey R. 1997. "Ethnicity and the Looking Glass: The Dialectics of National Indian Identity." *American Indian Quarterly* 21(Spring): 195–208.

Harjo, Suzan Shown. 2014. Introduction to *Nation to Nation: Treaties Between the United States & American Indian Nations*, ed. Suzan Shown Harjo. Washington, DC: Smithsonian Books.

Harvey, Alice. 1994. "Ex-Felon Disenfranchisement and Its Influence on the Black Vote: The Need for a Second Look." *University of Pennsylvania Law Review* 142: 1145–1189.

Hasen, Rick. 2016a. "Did the Supreme Court Kill the 'Purcell Principle' for Election Litigation? Maybe, Maybe Not." *Election Law Blog*, February 20. https://electionlawblog.org/?p=80165. Accessed 4/26/2019.

Hasen, Richard L. 2016b. "Reining in the Purcell Principle." *Florida State University Law Review* 43: 427–464.

Haspel, Moshe, and H. Gibbs Knotts. 2005. "Location, Location: Precinct Placement and the Costs of Voting." *Journal of Politics* 76(2): 560–573.

Hattam, Victoria. 2007. *In the Shadow of Race: Jews, Latinos and Immigrant Politics in the United States*. Chicago: University of Chicago Press.

Hayoun, Massoud. 2019. "There's a Growing Push to Rescind the Medals of Honor Awarded to the U.S. Soldiers at Wounded Knee." *Pacific Standard Magazine*, February 22. https://psmag.com/social-justice/theres-a-growing-push-to-rescind-the-medals-of-honor-awarded-to-the-us-soldiers-at-wounded-knee. Accessed 3/22/2019.

Hench, Virginia E. 1998. "The Death of Voting Rights: The Legal Disenfranchisement of Minority Voters." *Case Western Law Review* 48: 727–798.

Henry, Devin, and Timothy Cama. 2017. "Trump Takes Action to Move Forward with Keystone, Dakota Access Pipelines." *The Hill*, January 24. http://thehill.com/policy/energy-environment/315852-trump-orders-keystone-dakota-access-pipeline-applications-to-move. Accessed 1/25/2017.

Hernandez, Raymond. 2006. "After Challenges, House Approves Renewal of Voting Act." *New York Times*, July 14. http://www.nytimes.com/2006/07/14/washington/14rights.html?mcubz = 0. Accessed 7/28/2017.

Hill, Dana Lone. 2013. "The Wounded Knee Medals of Honor Should Be Rescinded." *Guardian*, February 18. https://www.theguardina.com/commentisfree/2013/feb/18/massacre-wounded-knee-medals-honor-rescinded. Accessed 3/22/2019.

Hooghe, Marc. 2018. "Trust and Elections." In *The Oxford Handbook of Social and Political Trust*, ed. Eric Uslander. New York: Oxford University Press.

Horsman, Reginald .1981. *Race and Manifest Destiny*. Cambridge, MA: Harvard University Press.

Horwitz, Tony. 2014. "The Horrific Sand Creek Massacre Will Be Forgotten No More." *Smithsonian Magazine* 45(8).

Hunter, David H. 1976. "The 1975 Voting Rights Act and Language Minorities." *Catholic University Law Review* 25(2): 250–270.

Huntington, Samuel P. 1993. "The Clash of Civilizations?" *Foreign Affairs* 72(3): 22–49.

Huntington, Samuel P. 1996. *The Clash of Civilizations and the Remaking of World Order*. New York: Simon and Schuster.

Hyman, Colette A. 2008. "Survival at Crow Creek, 1863–1866." *Minnesota History* 9(Winter): 148–161.

Inter Tribal Council of Arizona. 2004. *The History of Indian Voting in Arizona*. http://itcaonline.com/?page_id = 910. Accessed 6/16/2018.

Iverson, Peter. 1985. "Building Toward Self-Determination: Plains and Southwestern Indians in the 1940s and 1950s." *Western Historical Quarterly* 16: 163–173.

Iyengar, Shanto, and Donald R. Kinder. 1987. *News That Matters: Television and American Opinion*. Chicago: University of Chicago Press.

Jamieson, Kathleen Hall, and Joseph N. Cappella. 2008. *Echo Chamber: Rush Limbaugh and the Conservative Media Establishment*. Oxford: Oxford University Press.

Jardine, Lilias Jones. 2004. "Tribal-State Relations Involving Land and Resources in the Self-Determination Era." *Political Research Quarterly* 57(2): 295–303.

Jasso-Aguilar, Rebeca. 1999. "Sources, Methods and Triangulation in Needs Analysis: A Critical Perspective in a Case Study of Waikiki Hotel Maids." *English for Specific Purposes* 18(1): 27–46.

Jefferson, Thomas. 2000. "In Congress, July 4, 1776: The Unanimous Declaration of the Thirteen United States of America." In *The Declaration of Independence and Other Great Documents of American History, 1775–1865*, ed. John Grafton. Mineola, NY: Dover Publications.

Johnson, Tamra. 2012. "AAA Monthly Gas Price Report: August 2012 Trends and September Outlook." *AAA News Room*. https://newsroom.aaa.com/2012/08/aaa-monthly-gas-price-report-august-2012-trends-and-september-outlook/. Accessed 8/1/2018.

Johnson, Ryan. 2018. "Fargo Lawmaker Involved in Gay Dating App Controversy to Seek Re-election." *West Fargo Pioneer*, March 19. https://www.westfargopioneer.com/news/

4419844-fargo-lawmaker-involved-gay-dating-app-controversy-seek-re. Accessed 12/1/2018.

Journals of the Continental Congress. 1787. *National Archives Microfilm Publication M332, Roll 9, Miscellaneous Papers of the Continental Congress, 1774–1789: Records of the Continental Congress and the Constitutional Convention, 1774–1789*. Record Group 360, National Archives.

Karp, Jeffrey A., and Susan A. Banducci. 2000. "Going Postal: How All-Mail Elections Influence Turnout." *Political Behavior* 22(3): 223–239.

King, Desmond S., and Rogers M. Smith. 2008. "Strange Bedfellows? Polarized Politics? The Quest for Racial Equity in Contemporary America." *Political Research Quarterly* 61(4): 686–703.

Krauthamer, Barbara. 2013. *Black Slaves, Indian Masters: Slavery, Emancipation, and Citizenship in the Native American South*. Chapel Hill: University of North Carolina Press.

Landry, Alysa. 2016. "Ronald Reagan: 'Maybe We Should Not Have Humored [Natives].'" *Indian Country Today Digital Indigenous News*, October 4. https://newsmaven.io/indiancountrytoday/archive/ronald-reagan-maybe-we-should-not-have-humored-natives-63OPG1c5AEeWld8XWLQq4Q/. Accessed 1/25/2017.

Landsberg, Brian K. 1997. *Enforcing Civil Rights: Race Discrimination and the Department of Justice*. Lawrence: University of Kansas Press.

Laney, Garrine P. 2008. "The U.S. Commission on Civil Rights: History, Funding, and Current Issues." CRS Report for Congress. Order Code: RL34699.

Langlois, Krista. 2016. "How a Utah County Silenced Native American Voters and How Navajos Are Fighting Back." *High Country News*, June 13. http://www.hcn.org/issues/48.10/how-a-utah-county-silenced-native-american-voters-and-how-navajos-are-fighting-back. Accessed 3/26/2017.

Langlois, Krista. 2018. "An Historic Win in Utah Is Good News for Bears Ears." *Patagonia*, November 19. https://www.patagonia.com/blog/search/krita%20langlois/?. Accessed 4/30/2019.

Lawson, Michael L. 1996. Testimony Before the Joint Hearing of the Senate Committee on Indian Affairs and the House Subcommittee on Native American Affairs on S. 1264, A Bill to Provide for Certain Benefits of the Missouri River Pick-Sloan Project to the Crow Creek Sioux Tribe and for Other Purposes. September 9, Ordered to be printed. ftp://ftp.loc.gov/pub/thomas/cp104/sr362.txt. Accessed 7/18/2018.

Lawyers' Committee on Civil Rights Under Law. 2018. *Settlement Announced in Navajo Nation Human Rights Commission v. San Juan County*. February 22. https://lawyerscommittee.org/press-release/settlement-announced-navajo-nation-human-rights-commission-v-san-juan-county. Accessed 7/12/2018.

Leadership Conference. 2017. *U.S. Commission on Civil Rights*. http://www.civilrights.org/enforcement/commission. Accessed 3/27/2017.

Leonard, Devin. 2019. "Life Is Good for a Pipeline Billionaire. Most of the Time." *Bloomberg Businessweek*, March 29. https://www.scribd.com/article/403562111/life-is-good-for-a-pipeline-billionaire-most-of-the-time. Accessed 11/20/2019.

Liles, William Walton. 2007. "Challenges to Felony Disenfranchisement Laws: Past, Present and Future." *Alabama Law Review* 58(3): 615–629.

Loftus, Elizabeth F. 1975. "Leading Questions and the Eyewitness Report." *Cognitive Psychology* 7: 560–572.

Maffly, Brian. 2018. "The San Juan Clerk May Be Investigated After a Federal Judge Says He Crossed the Line in Illegally Dumping Navajo Willie Grayeyes from the Ballot." *Salt Lake Tribune*, August 10. https://www.sltrib.com/news/2018/08/judge-says-utah-clerk. Accessed 8/27/2018.

Mankiller, Wilma. 2004. "A New Path for the People." In *Native Universe: Voices of Indian America*, ed. Gerald McMaster and Clifford E. Trafzer. Washington, DC: National Geographic Society.

Martin, Jill. 2002. "Neither Fish, Flesh, Fowl, nor Good Red Herring: The Citizenship Status of American Indians, 1830–1924. " In *American Indians and U.S. Politics: A Companion Reader*, ed. John Meyer. Westport, CT: Praeger.

Mask, Deirdre. 2018. "Where the Streets Have No Names, the People Have No Vote." *New York Times*, October 19. https://www.nytimes.com/2081/10/19/opinion/sunday/north-dakota. Accessed 4/1/2019.

Massey, Garth. 2015a. "Expert Report: *Thomas Poor Bear et al. v. Jackson County, South Dakota.*" Case No. 5:14-CV-5059-KES.

Massey, Garth. 2015b. *Expert Witness Report, Navajo Nation et al. v. San Juan County, et al.* August 25. https://turtletalk.files.wordpress.com/2015/12/183-massey-expert-report.pdf. Accessed 7/13/2018.

Mauer, Richard. 2012. "Alaska Lawmaker Plans Renewed Push for Voter Photo ID Law Here." *Anchorage Daily News*, December 8. https://bit.ly/2usnlAr. Accessed 1/18/2013.

May, Gary. 2013. "Scalia's Understanding of the Voting Rights Act Is Shortsighted." *Washington Post*, April 26. https://www.washingtonpost.com/opinions/scalias-understanding-of-the-voting-rights-act-is-shortsighted/2013/04/26/2b63179e-ad07-11e2-b6fd-ba6f5f26d70e_sto ry.html?utm_term=.2e729bce618b. Accessed 8/9/2017.

McCombs, Maxwell E. 2004. *Setting the Agenda: The Mass Media and Public Opinion*. Cambridge, MA: Polity Press.

McCool, Daniel. 2015. *Expert Witness Report in the Case of Navajo Nation v. San Juan County, UT, Case No. 2:12-cv-00039-RS*. August 15. https://Utahdinebikeyah.org/wp-content/uploads/2016/05/Discrimination-Report-McCool-8-15.pdf. Accessed 7/13/2018.

McCool, Daniel, Susan M. Olson, and Jennifer L. Robinson. 2007. *Native Vote: American Indians, the Voting Rights Act, and the Right to Vote*. New York: Cambridge University Press.

McDonald, Laughlin. 1992. "The 1982 Amendments of Section 2 and Minority Representation." In *Controversies in Minority Voting: The Voting Rights Act in Perspective*, ed. Bernard Grofman and Chandler Davidson. Washington, DC: Brookings Institution.

McDonald, Laughlin. 2010. *American Indians and the Fight for Equal Voting Rights*. Norman: University of Oklahoma Press.

McDonald, Laughlin, Janine Pease, and Richard Guest. 2007. "Voting Rights in South Dakota: 1982–2006." *Review of Law and Social Justice* 17(1): 195–247.

McMaster, Gerald, and Clifford E. Trafzer. 2004. "Our People: Giving Voice to Our Histories." In *Native Universe: Voices of Indian America*, ed. Gerald McMaster and Clifford E. Trafzer. Washington, DC: National Geographic Society.

McNulty, John E., Conor M. Dowling, and Margaret H. Ariotti. 2009. "Driving Saints to Sin: How Increasing the Difficulty of Voting Dissuades Even the Most Motivated Voters." *Political Analysis* 17(9): 435–455.

Melillo, Amanda. 2012. "How Minnesota's Voter ID Amendment Was Defeated." *Brennan Center for Justice*, November 8. https://www.brennancenter.org/blog/how-minnesota%E2%80%99s-voter-id-amendment-was-defeated. Accessed 1/28/2016.

Meriam, Lewis. 1928. *The Problem of Indian Administration*. Baltimore: Johns Hopkins University Press.

Michaelson, Melissa R., Neil Malhtra, Andrew Healy, Donald P. Green, Allison Carnegie, and Ali Adam Valenzuela. 2012. "The Effect of Prepaid Postage on Turnout: A Cautionary Tale for Election Administrators." *Election Law Journal* 11(3): 279–290.

Monet, Jenni. 2016. "After a Month of Conflict, Mass Media Arrives in Force at Standing Rock." *Indian Country Today Digital Indigenous News*, November 27. http://indiancountrytodaymedianetwor.com/2016/11/27/after-month-conflict-mass-media-arrives-in-force-at-standing-rock. Accessed 12/7/2016.

Monroe, Nathan W., and Dari E. Sylvester. 2011. "Who Converts to Vote-by-Mail? Evidence from a Field Experiment." *Election Law Journal* 10(1): 15–35.

Montana Legislature. 2017. *American Indians in the Montana Legislature, 1989–Present*. http://web.archive.org/web/20170528230216/http://leg.mt.gov/css/About-the-Legislature/Facts-and-Statistics/indian-legislators.asp. Accessed 5/30/2017.

Montero, David. 2016. "In Nevada, Some Native Americans Have to Travel 270 Miles to Vote." *Los Angeles Times*, November 8. http://www.latimes.com/nation/la-na-pol-nevada-ballot-journey-20161028-story.html. Accessed 1/24/2017.

Moyer, Judith. 1999. *Step-by-Step Guide to Oral History*. http://dohistory.org/on_your_own/toolkit/oralHistory.html. Accessed 7/8/2018.

Nackenoff, Carol. 2006. "Constitutionalizing Terms of Inclusion: Friends of the Indian and Citizenship for Native Americans 1880s–1920s." In *The Supreme Court and American Political Development*, ed. Ronald Kahn and Ken I. Kersch. Lawrence: University Press of Kansas.

National Conference of State Legislatures. 2017. *Felony Voting Rights*, April 30. https://www.ncsl.org/research/elections-and-campaigns/felon-voting-rights.aspx. Accessed 7/18/2018.

National Conference of State Legislatures. 2019. *Voter Identification Requirements/Voter ID Laws*. http://www.ncsl.org/research/elections-and-campaigns/voter-id.aspx. Accessed 3/21/2019.

National Congress of American Indians. 2012. "Access to Elections and Voter Registration a 'Civic Emergency' Says NCAI President." June 18. http://www.ncai.org/news/articles/2012/06/18/access-to-elections-and-voter-registration-a-civic-emergency-for-native-americans-says-ncai-president. Accessed 2/14/2014.

National Congress of American Indians Policy Research Center and Montana State University Center for Native Health Partnerships. 2012. "Walk Softly and Listen Carefully: Building Research Relationships with Tribal Communities." http://www.ncai.org/resources/ncai_publications/walk-softly-and-listen-carefully-building-research-relationships-with-tribal-communities. Accessed 8/5/2018.

Native American Rights Fund. 2017. *North Dakota Again Passes Discriminatory Voter ID Law*. May 9. https://www.narf.org/north-dakota-voter-id-law/. Accessed 7/27/2017.

Native American Rights Fund. 2018. *Court Protects North Dakota Voters in Upcoming Primary*. June 8. http://www.narf.org/nd-voting-rights. Accessed 6/19/2018.

Native American Voting Rights Coalition. 2018. *Voting Barriers Encountered by Native Americans in Arizona, New Mexico, Nevada and South Dakota*. January. https://www.narf.org/wordpress/wp-content/uploads/2018/01/2017NAVRCsurvey-summary.pdf.

Naylor, Celia E. 2008. *African Cherokees in Indian Territory: From Chattel to Citizens.* Chapel Hill: University of North Carolina Press.

Neary, Ben. 2010. "Indians Question Colorado Firm's Motives." *Native Times*, December 6. http://www.nativetimes.com/index.php/news/politics/4707-indians-question-colorado-firms-motives-in-vote-case. Accessed 1/5/2014.

Neff, John. 2013. "These Are Your Top 10 Best-selling Vehicles of 2012." Autoblog. https://www.autoblog.com/2013/01/04/these-are-your-top-10-best-selling-vehicles-of-2012/. Accessed 8/1/2018.

Newcomb, Steve. 1992. "Five Hundred Years of Injustice." *Shaman's Drum* (Fall): 18–20. http://ili.nativeweb.org/sdrm_art.html. Accessed 2/2/2017.

North Dakota Department of Transportation. 2017. *Drivers' License Sites.* https://www.dot.nd.gov/divisions/driverslicense/docs/drivers%20lic%20sites.pdf. Accessed 7/28/2017.

Nuttall, Arwen. 2014. "Language and World View at the Horse Creek Treaty." In *Nation to Nation: Treaties Between the United States & American Indian Nations*, ed. Suzan Shawn Harjo. Washington, DC: Smithsonian Institution.

O'Brien, Sharon. 1989. *American Indian Tribal Governments.* The Civilization of the American Indian Series. Vol. 192. Norman: University of Oklahoma Press.

Oliviero, Pierluigi. 2017. "Opinion: Voting by Mail in Santa Clara County Can Save Money, Increase Turnout and Speed Up Results." *Mercury News*, May 3. https://www.mercurynews.com/2017/05/03/opinion-voting-by-mail-in-santa-clara-county-can-save-money-increase-turnout-and-speed-up-results/. Accessed 7/20/2018.

Opinion of the Attorney General of Utah. 1956. March 23. Referenced in Daniel McCool, Susan M. Olson, and Jennifer L. Robinson, *Native Vote: American Indians and the Voting Rights Act and the Right to Vote,* 96.

Oral History Association. 2009. "Principles and Best Practices." http://www.oralhistory.org/about/principles-and-practices/. Accessed 8/2/2018.

Ostler, Jeffrey. 2004. *The Plains Sioux and U.S. Colonialism from Lewis and Clark to Wounded Knee.* Cambridge: Cambridge University Press.

Otstot, Roger S. N. *Reclamation Managing Water in the West: An Overview of the Pick-Sloan Missouri Basin Program.* Washington, DC: U.S. Department of the Interior. https://www.usbr.gov/gp/multimedia/publications/pick_sloan_overview.pdf. Accessed 3/18/2019.

Pember, Mary Annette. 2012. "Minnesota's Proposed Voter ID Constitutional Amendment Could Jeopardize Use of Tribal Identification." *Indian Country Today Media Network*, October 12. https://www.nativevote-mn.org/news/2012-news/Minnesota%E2%80%99s-Proposed-Voter-ID-Constitutional-Amendment.pdf. Accessed 2/17/2013.

Pettigrew, Thomas F., and Linda R. Tropp. 2008. "How Does Intergroup Contact Reduce Prejudice? Meta-analytic Tests of Three Mediators." *European Journal of Social Psychology* 38(6): 922–934.

Pierson, Paul. 2004. *Politics in Time: History, Institutions, and Social Analysis.* Princeton, NJ: Princeton University Press.

Portelli, Alessandro. 2005. *A Dialogical Relationship: An Approach to Oral History.* http://www.swaraj.org/shikshantar/expressions_portelli.pdf. Accessed 7/7/2018.

Prakash, Nidhi. 2016. "This 99-Year-Old Native American Woman Just Voted on Her Reservation for the First Time Ever." *Splinter*, November 8. https://splinternews.com/this-99-year-old-native-american-woman-just-voted-on-he-1793863543. Accessed 6/22/2018.

President's Committee on Civil Rights. 1947. *To Secure These Rights: The Report of the President's Committee on Civil Rights*. Washington, DC: Government Printing Office.

Prucha, Francis Paul. 1984. *The Great Father: The United States Government and the American Indians*. Lincoln: University of Nebraska Press.

Public News Service. 2018. *Native American Candidates Rising in 2018 Elections*. May 21. https://www.publicnewsservice.org/2018-05-21/civic-engagement/native-american-candidates-rising-in-2018-elections/a62568-1. Accessed 7/25/2018.

Ragar, Shaylee. 2019. "Record Number of Native American Legislators in Montana Are Making Their Presence Felt." *Missoulian*, January 19. https://missoulian.com/news/state-and-region/govt-and-politics/record-number-of-native-american-legislators-in-montana-are/article_ef2f232f-7adf-5cd8-b0dd-cab62a25368c.html. Accessed 3/21/2019.

Reilly, Katie. 2018. "A New North Dakota Law Threatened Native American Votes. They Responded by Turning Out in Historic Numbers." *Time*, November 7. http://time.com/5446971/norht-dakota-native-american-turnout/. Accessed 11/10/2018.

Reinhardt, Akim D. 2007. *Ruling Pine Ridge: Oglala Lakota Politics from the IRA to Wounded Knee*. Lubbock: Texas Tech University Press.

Report of the Attorney General, State of South Dakota. 1932. Vol. 1931–1932, letter of June 2. Referenced in Daniel McCool, Susan M. Olson, and Jennifer L. Robinson, *Native Vote: American Indians and the Voting Rights Act and the Right to Vote*, 140.

Report of the Attorney General, State of South Dakota. 1963. Vol. 1963–1964, letter of July 5. Referenced in Daniel McCool, Susan M. Olson, and Jennifer L. Robinson, *Native Vote: American Indians and the Voting Rights Act and the Right to Vote*, 140.

Report of the Attorney General, State of South Dakota. 1977. Vol. 1977–1978, Opinion No. 77–73, August 25. Referenced in Daniel McCool, Susan M. Olson, and Jennifer L. Robinson, *Native Vote: American Indians and the Voting Rights Act and the Right to Vote*, 137.

Rich, Paul D. 2007. "The Attack on the Professionalism of the Civil Rights Division." In *Erosion of Rights: Declining Civil Rights Enforcement Under the Bush Administration*, ed. William L. Taylor, Dianne M. Piche, Crystal Rosario, and Joseph D. Rich. Washington, DC: Citizens' Commission on Civil Rights.

Richardson, Seth A. 2016a. "DOJ Will Monitor Polls in Washoe, Mineral Counties." *Reno Gazette Journal*, November 7. https://www.rgj.com/story/news/politics/2016/11/07/doj-monitor-polls-washoe-mineral-counties/93425008/. Accessed 6/15/2018.

Richardson, Seth A. 2016b. "Tribal Plaintiffs in Voting Rights Suit to Be Given Award from State." *Reno Gazette Journal*, November 18. http://www.rgj.com/story/news/politics/2016/11/18/tribal-plaintiffs-voting-rights-suit-given-award-state/94092738. Accessed 6/15/2018.

Rickert, Levi. 2019. "All Nine South Dakota Tribal Flags to Be on Permanent Display at State Capitol." *Native Knot*, March 5. https://www.nativeknot.com/newa/Native-American-Newa/All-Nine-South-Dakota-Tribal-Flags-to-be-on-Permanent-Display-at.html. Accessed 5/14/2019.

Roberts, David. 2017. "Voting by Mail Is Fair, Safe, and Easy. Why Don't More States Use It?" *Vox*, May 27. https://www.vox.com/policy-and-politics/2017/5/27/15701708/voting-by-mail. Accessed 7/20/2018.

Robertson, Lindsay G. 2014. "Unintended Consequences: *Johnson v. M'Intosh* and Indian Removal." In *Nation to Nation: Treaties Between the United States & American Indian Nations*, ed. Suzan Shown Harjo. Washington, DC: Smithsonian Institution.

Rogers, Kim Lacy. 1988. "Oral History and the History of the Civil Rights Movement." *Journal of American History* 75(2): 567–576.

Rollins, Willard Hughes. 2004. "Citizenship and Suffrage: The Native American Struggle for Civil Rights in the American West, 1830–1965." *Nevada Law Journal* 5(1): 126–140.

Ruelas, Richard. 2014. "Long Walk to Voting Rights for Navajos." *Arizona Republic*, January 19. https://www.pressreader.com/usa/the-arizona-republic/20140120/281492159178960. Accessed 2/26/2017.

Russett, Bruce M., John R. Oneal, and Michaelene Cox. 2000. "Clash of Civilization, or Realism and Liberalism Déjà Vu? Some Evidence." *Journal of Peace Research* 37(5): 583–608.

Satz, Ronald. 1996. *Chippewa Treaty Rights*. Madison: University of Wisconsin Press.

Sayer, John William. 1997. *Ghost Dancing the Law: The Wounded Knee Trials*. Cambridge, MA: Harvard University Press.

Schattschneider, E. E. 1975. *The Semisovereign People: A Realist's View of Democracy in America*. New York: Dryden Press.

Schneiders, Robert Kelley. 1997. "Flooding the Missouri Valley: The Politics of Dam Selection and Design." *Great Plains Quarterly* 17(3): 237–249.

Schroedel, Jean, and Artour Aslanian. 2015. "Native American Vote Suppression: The Case of South Dakota." *Race, Gender & Class* 22(1/2): 308–323.

Schroedel, Jean, and Artour Aslanian. 2017. "A Case Study of Descriptive Representation: The Experience of Native Elected Officials in South Dakota." *American Indian Quarterly* 41(3): 250–286.

Schroedel, Jean, and Roger Chen. 2017. "Whose Lives Matter: The Media's Failure to Cover Police Use of Lethal Force Against Native Americans." *Race and Justice: An International Journal*: 1–26. https://doi.org/10.1177/2153368717734614.

Schroedel, Jean, and Ryan Hart. 2015. "Vote Dilution and Suppression in Indian Country." *Studies in American Political Development* 29: 1–28.

Schroedel, Jean, and Robert Saporito. 2017. "Voting Rights in Indian Country." *Social Justice Forum* 2: 5–13.

Schroedel, Jean, Joey Torres, Andrea Walters, and Joseph Dietrich. 2017. "The Voting Rights Act's Pre-Clearance Provisions: The Experience of Native Americans in South Dakota." *American Indian Culture and Research Journal* 41(4): 1–21.

Sells, Bryan. 2012. "The Voting Rights Act in South Dakota." In *The Most Fundamental Right*, ed. Daniel McCool, 188–226. Bloomington: Indiana University Press.

Sen, Amartya. 1999. "Democracy as a Universal Value." *Journal of Democracy* 10(3): 3–17.

Sentencing Project. 2018. "Trends in U.S. Corrections." *Sentencing Project*. https://sentencingproject.org/wp-content/uploads/2016/01/Trends-in-US-Corrections.pdf. Accessed 8/13/2018.

Shopes, Linda. 2003. "Sharing Authority." *Oral History Review* 30(1): 102–110.

Silver, Brian D., Barbara A. Anderson, and Paul R. Abramson. 1986. "Who Over-reports Voting." *American Political Science Review* 80: 613–624.

Simpson, Joe. 2017. "The Power of 'Usness.'" *Social Business* 7(3–4): 293–312.

Slovic, Paul, David Zionts, Andrew K. Woods, Ryan Goodman, and Derek Jinks. 2013. In *The Behavioral Foundations of Policy*, ed. Eldar Shafir. New York: Russell Sage Foundation.

Smith, Mitch. 2019. "'A State of Emergency': Native Americans Stranded for Days by Flooding." *New York Times*, March 24. https://www.nytimes.com/2019/03/24/us/midwest-flooding-pine-ridge.html. Accessed 3/24/2019.

Smith, Paul Chaat, and Robert Allen Warrior. 1996. *Like a Hurricane: The Indian Movement from Alcatraz to Wounded Knee*. New York: New Press.

South Dakota Advisory Committee to the U.S. Commission on Civil Rights. 2000. *Native Americans in South Dakota: An Erosion of Confidence in the Justice System*. http://www.ucsccr.gov/pubs/sac/sd03000/main.htm. Accessed 5/16/ 2016.

South Dakota Secretary of State. 2016. *Elections and Voting*. http://electionresults.sd.gov.results VoterTurnout.aspx. Accessed 7/15/2018.

South Dakota Secretary of State. 2018a. *2018 Election Information*. https://sdsos.gov/elections-voting/upcoming-elections/general-information/2018-candidate-calendar.aspx. Accessed 7/16/2018.

South Dakota Secretary of State. 2018b. *2018 Candidate List*. https://sos.sd.gov/Elections/CandidateList.aspx? = eid = 2908&eid = 291. Accessed 7/16/2018.

Southwell, Priscilla L., and Justin I. Burchett. 2000. "The Effect of All-Mail Elections on Voter Turnout." *American Politics Quarterly* 28(1): 72–79.

Staff. 2003. "A Historic Moment in Blaine County." *Havre Daily News*, January 2. http://www.havredailynews.com/story/2003/01/02/local/a-historic-moment-in-blaine-county/400573.html. Accessed 5/29/2017.

Stern, Mark Joseph. 2018. "North Dakota Is Entering 'No Longer a Democracy' Territory with Its Latest Efforts to Disenfranchise Native Americans." *Slate*, October 31. Accessed 4/20/2019.

Stevens, Taylor. 2019. " 'I'm Sure It's a Culture Shock for Most of You': Navajos Take the Majority of the San Juan County Commission." *Salt Lake Tribune*, January 7. https://www.sltrib.com/news/politics/2019/01/07/san-jusan-county/. Accessed 4/30/2019.

Stewart, Charles, III. 2010. "Losing Votes by Mail." *New York University Journal of Legislation and Public Policy* 13(3): 573–602.

Stubben, Jerry D. 2006. *Native Americans and Political Participation: A Reference Handbook*. Santa Barbara, CA: ABC CLIO.

Sturgis, Patrick, Ian Brunton-Smith, Jouni Kuha, and Jonathan Jackson. 2014. "Ethnic Diversity, Segregation, and Social Cohesion of Neighborhoods in London." *Ethnic and Racial Studies* 37(8): 1286–1309.

Taliman, Valerie. 2016. "Thousands of Veterans Descend on Standing Rock to Protect and Serve." *Indian Country Today Digital Indigenous News*, December 4. https://newsmaven.io/indiancountrytoday/archive/thousands-of-veterans-descend-on-standing-rock-to-protect-and-serve-CsmzQI5XsEOz9ZyQf2WoZw/. Accessed 12/7/2016.

Tanner, Courtney. 2018a. " 'We've Been Disenfranchised': Republicans in San Juan County Say Redrawn Voter Districts Unfairly Favor Navajos." *Salt Lake Tribune*, April 10. https://www.sltrib.com/news/politics/2018/04/08/weve-been-disenfranchised-republicans-in-san-juan-county-say-redrawn-voter-districts-unfairly-favor-navajos/. Accessed 6/9/2018.

Tanner, Courtney. 2018b. " 'It's Hearsay': Navajo Democrat Responds After San Juan County Kicks Him off the Special Election Ballot." *Salt Lake Tribune*, May 13. https:// www.sltrib.com/news/politics/2018/05/11/its-hearsay-navajo-democrat-responds-after-san-juan-county-kicks-him-off. Accessed 7/14/2018.

Tanner, Courtney. 2018c. "Navajo Democrat Files Suit Against San Juan County After He Was Kicked off Special Election Ballot." *Salt Lake Tribune*, June 20. https://www.sltrib.com/news/politics/2018/06/20/navajo-democrat-files-suit-against-san-juan-county-after-he-was-kicked-off-the-special-election-ballot/. Accessed 7/14/2018.

Tchekmedyian, Alene, and Melissa Etehad. 2016. "2 Years of Opposition, 1,172 Miles of Pipe, 1.3 Million Facebook Check-ins: The Numbers to Know About the Standing Rock Protests." *Los Angeles Times*, November 1. http://www.latimes.com/nation/la-na-standing-rock-numbers-20161101-story.html. Accessed 12/28/2016.

Thernstrom, Abigail. 1987. *Whose Votes Count? Affirmative Action and Minority Voting Rights.* Cambridge, MA: Harvard University Press.

Trahant, Mark. 2018a. "Bears Ears Gains a Voice with #NativeVote18 Results." *Indian Country Today*, June 28. https://www.indianz.com/News/2018/06/28/mark-trahant-bears-ears-gains-a-voice-wi.asp. Accessed 4/30/2019.

Trahant, Mark. 2018b. "Ready for Change? 11 Native Candidates Are Running." *Trahant Reports*, March 15. https://www.indianz.com/News/2018/03/15/mark-trahant-ready-for-change-11-native.asp. Accessed 7/25/2018.

Trimble, Charles E., Barbara W. Sommer, and Mary Kay Quinlan. 2008. *The American Indian Oral History Manual: Making Many Voices Heard.* Walnut Creek, CA: Left Coast Press.

Truesdell, Barbara. 2017. *Oral History Techniques: How to Organize and Conduct Oral History Interviews.* www.indiana.edu/~cshm/oral_history_techniques.pdf. Accessed 7/3/2018.

Tucker, James Thomas, Rodolfo Espino, Tara Brite, Shannon Conley, Ben Horowitz, Zak Walter, and Shon Zelman. 2008. "Voting Rights in Arizona: 1982–2006." *Review of Law and Social Justice* 17(2): 283–365.

Uggen, Christopher, Ryan Larson, and Sarah Shannon. 2016. *6 Million Lost Voters: State-Level Estimates of Felony Disenfranchisement, 2016.* Sentencing Project. https://www.sentencingproject.org/publications/6-million-lost-voters-state-level-estimates-felony-disenfranchisement-2016/. Accessed 7/18/2018.

Uggen, Christopher, and Jeff Manza. 2002. "Democratic Contraction? Political Consequences of Felon Disenfranchisement in the United States." *American Sociological Review* 67(6): 777–803.

United States Army. 2017. *American Indians in the United States Army.* https://www.army.mil/americanindians/code_talkers.html. Accessed 3/29/2017.

United States Census Bureau. 2010a. "Census 2010 and 2000 Data Comparisons for Zip Code 57547, Long Valley, SD." http://www.zip-codes.com/zip-code/57547/zip-code-57547-census-comparison.asp. Accessed 9/24/2014.

United States Census Bureau. 2010b. "DP02—Selected Social Characteristics: Jackson County Totals." *American Community Survey, 2010.* Washington, DC: U.S. Census Bureau. http://factfinder.census.gov/bkmk/table/1.0/en/ACS/10_SF4/DP02/0500000US46071/popgroup~0021006. Accessed 12/2/2019.

United States Census Bureau. 2010c. "DP03—Selected Economic Characteristics: Jackson County Totals." *American Community Survey, 2010.* Washington, DC: U.S. Census Bureau. http://factfinder.census.gov/bkmk/table/1.0/en/ACS/10_SF4/DP03/0500000US46071/popgroup~0021006. Accessed 12/2/2019.

United States Census Bureau. 2010d. "B19013-Median Household Income in the Past 12 Months (In 2010 Inflation-Adjusted Dollars). Jackson County, South Dakota." *2006–2010 American Community Survey, Selected Population Tables.* Washington, DC: U.S. Census Bureau. http://factfinder.census.gov/bkmk/table/1.0/en/ACS/10_SF4/DP03/0500000US46071/popgroupup~00210061115. Accessed 12/2/2019.

United States Census Bureau. 2017. *Quick Facts: San Juan County, Utah.* http://www.census.gov/quickfacts/facts/table/sanjuancountyutah/PST0217. Accessed 7/12/2018.

United States Commission on Civil Rights. 1968. *Political Participation*. Washington, DC: Government Printing Office.

United States Commission on Civil Rights. 1975. *The Voting Rights Act: Ten Years After*. Washington, DC: United States Commission on Civil Rights.

United States Commission on Civil Rights. 2016. *Mission*. http://www.usccr.gov/about/index.php. Accessed 3/27/2017.

United States Department of Energy. 2012. "Fuel Economy of 2012 Ford F 150 Pickup." www.fueleconomy.gov. Accessed 2/24/2015.

United States House of Representatives. 1873. *Annual Report of the Commissioner of Indian Affairs*. 43rd Cong., 1st Sess., H. Ex. doc. 1, pt. 5, Serial 1601.

United States House of Representatives. HR Rep. 439, reprinted in 1965 USSCAN 2446.

United States Senate. 1982. *Voting Rights Extension Act*. Report of the Committee of the Judiciary, Senate Report 97–417, 97th Cong., 2nd Sess., GPO.

Vaughn, Alden T. 1995. *Roots of American Racism: Essays on the Colonial Experience*. New York: Oxford University Press.

Vock, Daniel C. 2017. "Lone Country." *Governing* (July): 48–54.

Vonnahme, Greg. 2012. "Registration Deadlines and Turnout in Context." *Political Behavior* 34: 765–779.

Wagner, Peter. 2014. "Tracking State Prison Growth in 50 States." *Prison Policy Initiative*, May 28. https://www.prisonpolicy.org/reports/overtime.html. Accessed 7/18/2018.

Walker, Cassandra. 2018. "Recent Deaths Of Native Matriarchs Leave Ripples of Respect, Honor and Gratefulness." *First Nation's Focus*, June 20. https://wwwfirstnationsfocus.com/features/recent-deaths-of-native-matriarchs/leave-ripples-of-respect-honor-and-gratefulness/June 20.

Wang, Ching-Hsing. 2016. "Political Trust, Civic Duty and Voter Turnout: The Mediation Argument." *Social Science Journal* 53(3): 291–330.

Welch, David A. 1997. "The 'Clash of Civilizations' Thesis as an Argument and as a Phenomenon." *Security Studies* 6(4): 197–216.

Westfargomusings. 2016. http://westfargomusings.wordpress.com/2016/05/31. Accessed 7/27/2017.

Whitaker, Morgan. 2013. "Scalia: Renewing Voting Rights Act a 'Perpetuation of Racial Entitlement.'" MSNBC, October 2. http://www.msnbc.com/politicsnation/scalia-renewing-voting-rights-act. Accessed 7/28/2017.

White, Richard. 1978. "The Winning of the West: The Expansion of the Western Sioux in the Eighteenth and Nineteenth Centuries." *Journal of American History* 65(2): 319–343.

Wilkins, David E., and K. Tsianina Lomawaima. 2001. *Uneven Ground: American Indian Sovereignty and Federal Law*. Norman: University of Oklahoma Press.

Wilkins, David E., and Heidi Kiiwetinepinesiik Stark. 2011. *American Indian Politics and the American Political System*. 3rd ed. Lanham, MD: Rowman & Littlefield.

Wilkinson, Charles, and Eric Briggs. 1977. "The Evolution of the Termination Policy." *American Indian Law Review* 5(1): 139–185.

Wilson, Angela Cavender. 1996. "Grandmother to Granddaughter: Generations of Oral History in a Dakota Family." *American Indian Quarterly* 20(1): 7–13.

Wilson, Angela Cavender. 2000. "Educating America: The Historian's Responsibility to Native Americans and the Public." *Perspectives on History* (May): 1–6.

Wolfley, Jeanette. 1991. "Jim Crow, Indian Style: The Disenfranchisement of Native Americans." *American Indian Law Review* 16: 167–202.

Woodard, Stephanie. 2014. "Oglala VP: 'Our Civil Rights Are Being Violated.'" *Indian Country Today Media Network*, September 25. http://indiancountrytodaymedianetwork.com/2014/09/25/oglala-vp-our-civil-rights-are-being-violated. Accessed 10/7/2014.

Woodard, Stephanie. 2016. "Native Voters Turned Away at Polls Sue North Dakota." *Impact Fund*, April 15. https://www.impactfund.org/social-justice-blog/native-voters-turned-away-at-polls-sue-north-dakota. Accessed 7/27/2017.

Woodard, Stephanie. 2018. *American Apartheid: The Native American Struggle for Self-determination and Inclusion.* New York: Ig Press.

Yurth, Cindy. 2009. "A Leader with Backbone: 35 Years Later, Apache County's First Elected Dine Supervisor Speaks Out." *Navajo Times*, September 3. http://navajotimes.com/politics/2009/0909/090309supe.php. Accessed 2/25/2017.

Zaller, John R. 1992. *The Nature and Origins of Mass Opinion*. New York: Cambridge University Press.

COURT CASES

ACLU v. Kiffmeyer. 2004. No. 04-CV-4653 (D. Minn.).

Allen v. Merrell. 1956. 6 Utah 2d 32, 305 P.2d 490.

Allen v. State Board of Elections. 1969. 393 U.S. 544.

American Horse v. Kunder. 1984. Civ. No. 84–5159 (D.S.D.).

Amicus Curiae Brief of the Alaska Federation of Natives, Native Voters and Tribes in Shelby County v. Holder. 2013.

Apache County v. United States. 1966. 256 F. Supp. 903, 906 (D.D.C.).

Apache County High School No. 90 v. U.S. 1977. Civ. No. 77–1815 (D.D.C.), Memorandum Opinion, June 12, 1980.

Avery v. Midland County. 1968. 390 U.S. 474.

Baker v. Carr. 1962. 369 U.S. 186.

Beer v. United States. 1976. 425 U.S. 130, 96 S. Ct. 1357.

Black Bull v. Dupree School District. 1986. Civ. No. 86–3012 (D.S.D.).

Blackmoon v. Charles Mix County. 2007. 505 F. Supp. 2nd 585 (D.S.D.).

Blaine County v. U.S. 2005. 544 U.S. 992.

Bone Shirt v. Hazeltine. 2006. U.S. App. LEXIS 21409 (8th Cir.).

Brakebill v. Jaeger. 2016. No. 1: 16-CV-008 DLH (D.N.D.).

Brakebill v. Jaeger. 2018. No. 18–1725 (8th Cir.).

Brooks v. Gant. 2012. No. 5: CV-05003-Doc. 66 (D.S.D.).

Brown v. Board of Education of Topeka. 1954. 347 U.S. 483.

Brown v. Montana Districting and Reapportionment Commission. 2003. No. ADV-2003–72 (Mont. 1st Jud. Dist. Ct. Lewis & Clark County).

Brown v. Thomson. 1983. 462 U.S. 835.

Buckanaga v. Sisseton Independent School District. 1986. 804 F.2d 469 (8th Cir.).

Buckhannon Board and Care Home, Inc. v. West Virginia Department of Health and Human Services. 2001. 532 U.S. 598, 121 S. Ct. 1835, 149 L. Ed. 2d 855.

Bush v. Vera. 1996. 517 U.S. 952.

Canady v. Lumberton City Board of Education. 1981. 454 U.S. 957.

Cherokee Nation v. Georgia. 1831. 30 U.S. 1.

City of Mobile v. Bolden. 1980. 446 U.S. 55.

Crank, Loren v. Utah Judicial Council. 1996. Order and Decree. Civ. No. 9307–26. October 27. (Seventh Jud. Dist. Court, San Juan County, UT.)
Dred Scott v. Sandford. 1857. 60 U.S. 393.
Earl Old Person v. Brown. 2002. 312 F.3d 1036 (9th Cir.).
Elk v. Wilkins. 1884. 112 U.S. 94.
Emery v. Hunt. 2001. 272 F.3d 1042 (8th Cir.).
Fiddler v. Sieker. 1986. Civ. No. 86–3050 (D.S.D.).
Georgia v. Ashcroft. 2003. 539 U.S. 461.
Goodluck v. Apache County. 1975. 417 F. Supp. 13, 14 (D. Ariz.); 1976, aff. 429 U.S. 876.
Harrison v. Laveen. 1948. 196 P.2d 456 (Ariz.).
Hootch v. Alaska State-Operated School System. 1975. 536 P.2d 793 (Alaska).
Independent School District of Tulsa v. Bell. 1976. Civ. No. 76-c (N.D. Okla.).
Janis v. Nelson. 2009. No. CR09–5019 KES. (D.S.D.).
Johnson v. McIntosh. 1823. 21 U.S. 543.
Kirkie v. Buffalo County. 2003. Civ. No. 03-CV-3011-CBK (D.S.D.).
Large v. Fremont. 2005. Civ. No. 05-CV-270-ABJ (D. Wyo.).
Large v. Fremont County. 2010. 709 F. Supp. 2d 1176 (D. Wyo.).
Little Thunder v. South Dakota. 1975. 518 F.2d 1253 (8th Cir.).
Lone Wolf v. Hitchcock. 1903. 187 U.S. 553.
MacKay v. Campbell. 1871. 16 F. Cas. 161 (D. Ore.).
Meyers v. Board of Education. 1995. 905 F. Supp. 1544 (D. Utah).
Miller v. Johnson. 1995. 515 U.S. 900.
Minor v. Happersett. 1875. 88 U.S. 162.
Montoya v. Bolack. 1962. NMSC-073, 70 N.M. 196, 372 P.2d 387.
Navajo Nation v. San Juan County. 2016. Case No. 2:12-cv-00039-RJS-DPB (D. Utah).
Navajo Nation Human Rights Commission v. San Juan County. 2016. Case No. 2:16-Cv-00154-JNP-BCW (D. Utah).
Nick v. Bethel Settlement. 2010. No. 3:07-CV-00098-TMB-MMM-JKS. Doc. 787–2.
Old Person v. Cooney. 2000. 230 F.3d 1113 (9th Cir.).
Opsahl v. Johnson. 1917. 163 N.W. 988 (Minn.).
Poor Bear v. County of Jackson. 2015. No. 5:14-CV-05059-KES.
Porter v. Hall. 1928. 34 Ariz. 308.
Puerto Rican Organization for Political Action v. Kusper. 1973. 490 F.2d 575 (7th Cir.).
Reno v. Bossier Parish School Board. 2000. 528 U.S. 320.
Richardson v. Ramirez. 1974. 418 U.S. 24.
Rogers v. Lodge. 1982. 458 U.S. 613.
Sanchez v. Cegavske. 2016. Case No. 3:16-CV-00523-MMD-WGC.
Shakopee Mdewakanton Sioux Community and the U.S. v. City of Prior Lake. 1986. 771 F.2d 1153 (8th Cir. 1985), cert. denied, 475 U.S. 1011.
Shaw v. Reno. 1993. 509 U.S. 630.
Shelby County v. Holder. 2013. 133 S. Ct. 2616.
Shirley v. Superior Court for Apache County. 1973. 513 P.2d 939, 941 (Ariz.).
Sinajini v. Bd. of Educ. 1997. 964 F. Supp. 319 (D. Utah).
Slaughterhouse Cases. 1873. 83 U.S. 36.
Smith v. Allwright. 1944. 321 U.S. 649.
South Dakota v. U.S. 1980. 1981. Civ. No. 80–1976 (D.D.C.) Consent Decree. December 2.

Stabler v. County of Thurston. 1997. 129 F.3d 1015 (8th Cir.).
State ex. rel Nelson v. Jordan. 450 P.2d 383 (Ariz. 1969).
St. Regis Tribe v. New York. 1958. 5 N.Y. 2d 24.
Swift v. Leach. 1920. 178 N.W. 437 (N.D.).
Thornburg v. Gingles. 1986. 478 U.S. 30.
Torres v. Sachs. 1974. 381 F. Supp. 309 (S.D.N.Y.).
Toyukak v. Treadwell. 2014. No. 3:13-CV-137-SLG (D. Alaska).
Trujillo v. Gurley. 1948. Civ. No. 1353 (D.N.M.).
U.S. v. Arizona. 1975. 417 F. Supp. 13 (D. Ariz.); aff. 429 U.S. 876 (1976).
U.S. v. Bernalillo County. 1998. Civ. No. 98–156BB (D.N.M.).
U.S. v. Blaine County. 2004a. 363 F.3d 897 (9th Cir.).
U.S. v. Blaine County. 2004b. Supp. 2d 1145 (D.S.D.).
U.S. v. Blaine County. 1999. Complaint. Civ. No. 99–122-GF (D. Mont). November 16.
U.S. v. Blaine County. 2000. Defendants' Answer to Complaint. January 3.
U.S. v. Cibola County. 1993. Civ. No. 93–1134-LH/LFG (D.N.M.).
U.S. v. Day County, Enemy Swim Sanitary District. 1999. Civ. No. 99–1024 (D.S.D.).
U.S. v. Kagama. 1886. 118 U.S. 375.
U.S. v. McKinley County. 1986. Civ. No. 86–0028M (D.N.M.).
U.S. v. New Mexico. 1988. Civ. No. 88–1457-SC (D.N.M.).
U.S. v. San Juan County. 1983a. C-83–1286W (D. Utah).
U.S. v. San Juan County. 1983b. Civ. No. 83–1287 (D. Utah). Agreed Settlement and Order, April 4, 1984.
U.S. v. Socorro County. 1993. Civ. No. 93–1244-JP (D.N.M.).
U.S. v. South Dakota. 1980. 636 F.2d 241 (8th Cir.).
U.S. v. Town of Bartelme. 1978. Civ. No. 78-C-101 (E.D. Wisc.).
U.S. v. Washington. 1974. 384 F. Supp. 312, 327–28 (W.D. Wash.).
Utah v. Pharris. 1993. 846 P.2d 454 (Court of Appeals Utah).
Viete v. Jubelvier. 2004. 541 U.S. 267.
Wandering Medicine v. McCulloch. 2014. 906 F. Supp. 2d 1083 (D.C. Mont.).
White v. Regester. 1973. 412 U.S. 755.
Windy Boy v. Big Horn County. 1986. 647 F. Supp. 1002 (D. Mont.).
Worcester v. Georgia. 1832. 31 U.S..
Yanito v. Barber. 1972. 348 F. Supp. 587 (D. Utah).

INTERVIEWS

Archambault, Donovan. 2017. Interview by author, Anchorage, AK.
Davis, Janet. 2017. Interview by author, Skype from Nixon, NV.
Degnan, Charles. 2017. Interview by author, Anchorage, AK.
Ferguson-Bohnee, Patty. 2017. Interview by author, Phoenix, AZ.
Hawley, Vincent. 2017. Interview by author, Skype from Nixon, NV.
Healy, Bret. 2018. Interview by author, telephone.
Landreth, Natalie. 2017. Interview by author, Anchorage, AK.
Ledesma, Bhie-Cie. 2017. Interview by author, Hungry Valley, NV.
Lewis, John. 2017. Interview by author, Tempe, AZ.
Lincoln, Harry. 2017. Interview by author, Anchorage, AK.
Little Elk, Wizipan Garriott. 2017. Interview by author, Mission, SD.

Loudner, Donita. 2017. Interview by author, Fort Thompson, SD.
Main, William T., Sr. 2017. Interview by author, Fort Belknap, MT.
Martinez, Elveda. 2017. Interview by author, Schurz, NV.
McDonald, Laughlin. 2017. Interview by author, Washington, DC.
Melendez, Arlan. 2017. Interview by author, Reno, NV.
Oxereok, Frank, Jr. 2017. Interview by author, Anchorage, AK.
Phillip, Fred. 2017. Interview by author, Anchorage, AK.
Sazue, Brandon J., Sr. 2017. Interview by author, Fort Thompson, SD.
Sells, Bryan. 2017. Interview by author, Washington, DC.
Semans, Barbara. 2017. Interview by author, Claremont, CA.
Semans, Oliver J., Sr. 2017. Interview by author, Claremont, CA.
Solomon, David. 2017. Interview by author. Anchorage, Alaska.
Stiffarm, Gerald. 2017. Interview by author, Fort Belknap, MT.
Williams, Johnnie, Jr. 2017. Interview by author, Schurz, NV.

INDEX

ACKNOWLEDGMENTS

More than any previous research that I've undertaken in my three decades as a university professor, this project could be completed only with the assistance of countless other people. I started this journey with little knowledge of Indian Country. As such, I've had to learn from the real experts, the people whose struggles are recounted here. Foremost among these are OJ Semans and Barb Semans, whose stories are included in Chapter 8. As founders of Four Directions, OJ and Barb have been an integral part of the recent upsurge in voting rights activism. They have graciously shared their knowledge with me, and this book would have been impossible without them. Thank you. In the same vein, I owe a debt of gratitude to Bret Healy, a white South Dakota rancher whose journey through Indian Country preceded mine. I also want to single out David Wilkins, who has provided academic guidance throughout.

My deepest debt is to the people whose stories are included in this volume: Donovan Archambault, Patty Ferguson-Bohnee, Natalie Landreth, John Lewis, William Main Sr., Laughlin McDonald, Bryan Sells, Barbara Semans, OJ Semans, and Johnnie Williams Jr. You have inspired me. Thank you. I also am appreciative of the help provided by Wassilie Andrews, Janet Davis, Charles Degnan, Larry Gross, Little Buck Harjo, Vinton Hawley, Travis Lane, Teri Larson, Bhie-Cie Ledesma, Harry Lincoln, Donita Loudner, Deron Marquez, Elveda Martinez, Garth Massey, Arlan Melendez, Dan McCool, Stacey Montooth, Michael Ondelay, Frank Oxereok Jr., Fred Phillip, Rob Rosenstein, Steven Sandven, Brandon Sazue Sr., David Solomon, Erich Steinman, Gerald Stiffarm, Jim Tucker, and Stephanie Woodard.

This project benefited from the community of scholars at Claremont Graduate University (CGU). Faculty colleagues, especially Heather Campbell, Debbie Freund, Brian Hilton, Tom Kniesner, Javier Rodriguez, Melissa Rogers, and Michael Uhlmann, have provided support when needed. But this project would not have reached fruition without the assistance of a wonderful group of CGU graduate students. I am especially appreciative of research assistants Joey Torres, Joseph Dietrich, and Aaron Berg, who spent countless hours doing much of the grunt work involved in preparing a manuscript for publication. The following graduate students also were involved in this project: Peter Abkarian, Kristen Almaraz, Artour Aslanian, Edward Berdan, Laura Brantley, Carlin Crisanti, David Edlefsen, Gary Hawk, Savannah Eccles Johnston, Alma Keshavarz, Joseph Lake, Kara Mazarias, Angus McClellan, Troy Mikanovich, Amy Nantkes, Anna Phillips, Robert Saporito, Ashely Shue, and Andrea Walters. Thank you.

Although I have long been a master at stretching research dollars, finding the resources necessary to complete this project was challenge. Special thanks to the Lear Family Foundation, which has provided funding for this and many other CGU projects. Thank you for your long support and commitment. I also want to thank Ken Ramirez and the San Manuel Band of Mission Indians for helping out when I desperately needed additional funding. Also thanks to the leaders of the Fort Belknap Indian Community for putting me up at the domestic violence shelter when I needed a place to stay in Montana, to Steven Sandven for providing housing for my students and me when we were doing surveys on the Pine Ridge Reservation, and to Donna Semans for doing the same in Nevada.

The last group to be acknowledged is made up of individuals who have been with me throughout the process as I grappled with, first, whether to write a book and, second, the shape that it would take. Thank you, Peter Agree, from the University of Pennsylvania Press, for pushing me to write this book. You are a marvel. But I would be remiss if I did not express my gratitude to entire Penn Press team, including but not limited to Gigi Lamm, Erica Ginsburg, and Robert Lockhart. I also must acknowledge the thoughtful suggestions provided by the outside readers, David Wilkins and Carol Nackenoff. Thank you, it is a better book because of you. Finally, I would be remiss if I ignored my family's patience. My son, John Peretz, has tolerated my continually reminding him of the importance of voting and political engagement. As always, I am indebted to Paul Peretz. From the beginning, Paul has been part of this journey, even tolerating a "vacation" spent traveling to Nevada reservations. After 35 years of marriage, he is still my greatest supporter and occasional critic.